MW00949413

LAS VEGAS

TRAVEL GUIDE

2019

SHOPS, *RESTAURANTS*, *CASINOS*, *ATTRACTIONS & NIGHTLIFE*

The Most Positively
Reviewed and Recommended
by Locals and Travelers

EGP
Editorial

LAS VEGAS

TRAVEL GUIDE

2019

SHOPS, RESTAURANTS, CASINOS, ATTRACTIONS & NIGHTLIFE

LAS VEGAS TRAVEL GUIDE 2019
Shops, Restaurants, Casinos, Attractions & Nightlife

© Jeffrey S. Millman, 2019
© E.G.P. Editorial, 2019

ISBN-13: 978-1720548935
ISBN-10: 1720548935

INDEX

LAS VEGAS TRAVEL GUIDE 2019

Shops, Restaurants, Casinos, Attractions & Nightlife

*This directory is dedicated to Las Vegas Business Owners and Managers
who provide the experience that the locals and tourists enjoy.
Thanks you very much for all that you do and thank for being the "People Choice".*

*Thanks to everyone that posts their reviews online and
the amazing reviews sites that make our life easier.*

*The places listed in this book are the most positively reviewed
and recommended by locals and travelers from around the world.*

*Thank you for your time and enjoy the directory that is
designed with locals and tourist in mind!*

TOP 500 SHOPS

The Most Recommended by Locals and Travelers
(From #1 to #500)

#1
D&R House Of Diamonds
Category: Jewelry, Watches, Bridal
Average price: Modest
Area: Westside
Address: 410 S Rampart Blvd
Las Vegas, NV 89145
Phone: (702) 758-3421

#2
Yosi Vapor Boutique
Category: Tobacco Shop, Vape Shop
Average price: Modest
Area: Chinatown
Address: 5115 Spring Mountain Rd
Las Vegas, NV 89146
Phone: (702) 463-6688

#3
iFocus Vision Center
Category: Optometrists,
Eyewear & Opticians
Average price: Modest
Area: Spring Valley
Address: 9484 W Flamingo Rd
Las Vegas, NV 89147
Phone: (702) 473-5660

#4
One 2 Vapor
Category: Vape Shop
Average price: Modest
Area: Southeast
Address: 8868 S Eastern Ave
Las Vegas, NV 89123
Phone: (702) 476-1488

#5
Alternate Reality Comics
Category: Comic Book, Booktore
Average price: Inexpensive
Area: University, Eastside
Address: 4110 S Maryland Pkwy
Las Vegas, NV 89119
Phone: (702) 736-3673

#6
English Garden Florist
Category: Florist
Average price: Modest
Area: University
Address: 4171 S Maryland Pkwy
Las Vegas, NV 89119
Phone: (702) 740-4770

#7
Silver Post
Category: Jewelry, Shoe Store,
Leather Goods
Average price: Modest
Area: Southeast
Address: 7680 Las Vegas Blvd S
Las Vegas, NV 89123
Phone: (702) 227-3005

#8
MaximuM Comics
Category: Comic Book
Average price: Inexpensive
Area: Spring Valley
Address: 5130 S Fort Apache Rd
Las Vegas, NV 89148
Phone: (702) 367-0755

#9
House of Smokes & Gifts
Category: Tobacco Shop
Average price: Inexpensive
Area: Southeast
Address: 1263 E Silverado Ranch Blvd
Las Vegas, NV 89123
Phone: (702) 896-0340

#10
The Dancing Dandelion
Flower Shop
Category: Florist
Average price: Modest
Area: Southwest
Address: 8520 W Warm Springs Rd
Las Vegas, NV 89113
Phone: (702) 260-4809

#11
Clearvision Eye
Center - Southwest
Category: Optometrists,
Eyewear & Opticians
Average price: Modest
Area: Spring Valley
Address: 6910 S Rainbow Blvd
Las Vegas, NV 89118
Phone: (702) 476-2323

#12
Fit For A Bride
Category: Bridal, Sewing & Alterations
Average price: Modest
Area: Chinatown
Address: 3305 West Spring
Mountain Rd, Las Vegas, NV 89102
Phone: (702) 260-6578

#13
Truvape
Category: Tobacco Shop, Vape Shop
Average price: Modest
Area: Chinatown
Address: 4059 Spring Mountain Rd
Las Vegas, NV 89102
Phone: (702) 463-3377

#14
Beauty To Beauty
Category: Hair Salon,
Cosmetics & Beauty
Average price: Modest
Area: Chinatown
Address: 4631 W Spring Mountain Rd
Las Vegas, NV 89102
Phone: (702) 873-8800

#15
Knyew
Category: Men's Clothing
Average price: Modest
Area: Chinatown
Address: 3999 Spring Mountain Rd
Las Vegas, NV 89102
Phone: (702) 252-5212

#16
Belly Bliss
Category: Massage, Baby Gear
& Furniture, Medical Spa
Average price: Modest
Area: Spring Valley
Address: 5761 South Fort Apache
Las Vegas, NV 89148
Phone: (702) 597-5158

#17
NAKED A Boutique For Skin
Category: Hair Removal, Skin Care,
Cosmetics & Beauty
Average price: Modest
Area: Westside
Address: 6655 W Sahara Ave
Las Vegas, NV 89146
Phone: (702) 544-9844

#18
Encore
Category: Hotel, Casino,
Resort, Home Decor
Average price: Expensive
Area: The Strip
Address: 3131 Las Vegas Blvd. South
Las Vegas, NV 89109
Phone: (702) 770-8000

#19
Strip Gun Club
Category: Guns & Ammo,
Gun/Rifle Ranges
Average price: Expensive
Area: The Strip
Address: 2235 Las Vegas Blvd S
Las Vegas, NV 89104
Phone: (702) 777-4867

#20
The Art of Shaving
Category: Barbers,
Cosmetics & Beauty
Average price: Expensive
Area: The Strip
Address: 3930 Las Vegas Blvd S
Las Vegas, NV 89119
Phone: (702) 632-9356

#21
The Forum Shop
Category: Fashion
Average price: Expensive
Area: The Strip
Address: 3570 Las Vegas Boulevard South,
Las Vegas, NV 89109
Phone: (702) 893-4800

#22
Town Square Las Vegas
Category: Shopping Center
Average price: Modest
Area: Southeast
Address: 6605 Las Vegas Blvd S
Las Vegas, NV 89119
Phone: (702) 269-5001

#23
Chanel
Category: Accessories
Average price: Exclusive
Area: Eastside
Address: 3131 Las Vegas Blvd S
Las Vegas, NV 89109
Phone: (702) 765-5055

#24
Lush
Category: Cosmetics & Beauty
Average price: Modest
Area: The Strip
Address: 3950 Las Vegas Blvd
Las Vegas, NV 89119
Phone: (702) 227-5874

#25
Barneys New York
Category: Department Store
Average price: Exclusive
Area: The Strip
Address: 3325 Las Vegas Blvd S
Las Vegas, NV 89109
Phone: (702) 629-4200

#26
Morgan Taylor Jewelers
Category: Jewelry
Average price: Expensive
Area: Westside
Address: 7995 W Sahara Ave
Las Vegas, NV 89117
Phone: (702) 259-8011

#27
Sephora
Category: Cosmetics & Beauty
Average price: Expensive
Area: Westside
Address: 3377 Las Vegas Blvd S
Las Vegas, NV 89109
Phone: (702) 735-3896

#28
Red Rock Running Company
Category: Sporting Goods
Average price: Modest
Area: Northwest
Address: 7350 W Cheyenne Ave
Las Vegas, NV 89129
Phone: (702) 870-4786

#29
Bass Pro Shop
Category: Outdoor Gear
Average price: Modest
Area: Southwest
Address: 8200 Dean Martin Dr
Las Vegas, NV 89139
Phone: (702) 730-5200

#30
Scarlett Vapors & Smoke Shop
Category: Tobacco Shop
Average price: Modest
Area: Southeast
Address: 1725 E Warm Springs Rd
Las Vegas, NV 89119
Phone: (702) 750-0553

#31
Walgreens
Category: Convenience Store, Drugstore, Cosmetics & Beauty
Average price: Modest
Area: The Strip
Address: 3339 Las Vegas Blvd S
Las Vegas, NV 89109
Phone: (702) 369-8166

#33
Bettie Page Boutique
Category: Accessories
Average price: Expensive
Area: Eastside
Address: 3500 Las Vegas Blvd S
Las Vegas, NV 89109
Phone: (702) 369-8277

#32
Patty's Closet
Category: Women's Clothing
Average price: Modest
Area: Southwest
Address: 7920 S Rainbow Blvd
Las Vegas, NV 89139
Phone: (702) 263-6452

#34
Vato Cigars
Category: Tobacco Shop, Lounge
Average price: Modest
Area: Downtown
Address: 128 Fremont St
Las Vegas, NV 89101
Phone: (323) 377-8286

#35
Blick Art Materials
Category: Art Supplies, Hobby Shop
Average price: Modest
Area: Westside
Address: 290 S Decatur Blvd
Las Vegas, NV 89107
Phone: (702) 368-0209

#36
B & L Shoe & Luggage Repair
Category: Shoe Repair, Leather Goods
Average price: Inexpensive
Area: Southeast
Address: 4912 S Eastern Ave
Las Vegas, NV 89119
Phone: (702) 454-9991

#37
John Fish Jewelers
Category: Jewelry
Average price: Modest
Area: Eastside
Address: 953 E Sahara Ave
Las Vegas, NV 89104
Phone: (702) 731-1323

#38
Montage Hair Studio
Category: Hair Salon, Cosmetics & Beauty,
Permanent Makeup
Average price: Modest
Area: Westside
Address: 7795 W Sahara 104/105
Las Vegas, NV 89117
Phone: (702) 367-1967

#39
Rod Works
Category: Home Decor
Average price: Modest
Area: Northwest, Summerlin
Address: 10470 W Cheyenne Ave
Las Vegas, NV 89129
Phone: (702) 433-8500

#40
Pro Cyclery
Category: Bikes, Bike Rentals
Average price: Modest
Area: Westside
Address: 7034 W Charleston Blvd
Las Vegas, NV 89117
Phone: (702) 228-9460

#41
Casa Fuente Cigars
Category: Tobacco Shop
Average price: Expensive
Area: The Strip
Address: 3500 Las Vegas Blvd S
Las Vegas, NV 89109
Phone: (702) 731-5051

#42
Peter Lik Gallery
Category: Art Gallery
Average price: Exclusive
Area: Eastside
Address: 3500 Las Vegas Blvd S
Las Vegas, NV 89109
Phone: (702) 836-3310

#43
Target
Category: Grocery, Discount Store
Average price: Modest
Area: Anthem
Address: 695 S Green Valley Pkwy
Henderson, NV 89052
Phone: (702) 216-7100

#44
Nordstrom
Category: Department Store
Average price: Expensive
Area: The Strip
Address: 3200 Las Vegas Blvd S
Las Vegas, NV 89109
Phone: (702) 862-2525

#45
Homegoods
Category: Department Store
Average price: Modest
Area: Centennial
Address: 6670 N Durango Drive
Las Vegas, NV 89149
Phone: (702) 656-1337

#46
Pacific Archery Sales
Category: Sporting Goods, Archery
Average price: Modest
Area: Chinatown
Address: 4084 Schiff Dr
Las Vegas, NV 89103
Phone: (702) 367-1505

#47
Manolo Blahnik
Category: Shoe Store
Average price: Exclusive
Area: The Strip
Address: 3131 Las Vegas Blvd
Las Vegas, NV 89109
Phone: (702) 770-3477

#48
American Shooters
Category: Gun/Rifle Ranges,
Guns & Ammo
Average price: Modest
Area: Chinatown
Address: 3440 Arville St
Las Vegas, NV 89102
Phone: (702) 719-5000

#49
Zia Records
Category: Music & DVDs,
Videos & Video Game Rental
Average price: Modest
Area: Eastside
Address: 4225 S Eastern Ave
Las Vegas, NV 89119
Phone: (702) 735-4942

#50
Vape2o
Category: Tobacco Shop
Average price: Modest
Area: Anthem
Address: 11041 S Eastern Ave
Henderson, NV 89052
Phone: (702) 685-8273

#51
Burberry
Category: Men's Clothing,
Women's Clothing
Average price: Expensive
Area: The Strip
Address: 3325 Las Vegas Blvd S
Las Vegas, NV 89109
Phone: (702) 382-1911

#52
Vapor Bombz Vegas
Category: Tobacco Shop
Average price: Modest
Area: Eastside
Address: 1370 E Flamingo Rd
Las Vegas, NV 89119
Phone: (702) 683-8273

#53
Herve Leger
Category: Women's Clothing, Accessories
Average price: Exclusive
Area: The Strip
Address: 3663 Las Vegas Blvd S
Las Vegas, NV 89109
Phone: (702) 732-4529

#54
World of Coca-Cola
Category: Hobby Shop
Average price: Modest
Area: The Strip
Address: 3785 Las Vegas Blvd S
Las Vegas, NV 89109
Phone: (702) 270-5952

#55
International CES
Consumer Electronics Show
Category: Electronics
Average price: Exclusive
Area: Eastside
Address: Las Vegas Convention Center
Las Vegas, NV 89109
Phone: (866) 858-1555

#56
Vegas Vapor Emporium
Category: Tobacco Shop
Average price: Modest
Area: Summerlin
Address: 1591 N Buffalo Dr
Las Vegas, NV 89128
Phone: (702) 778-9600

#57
Gucci
Category: Leather Goods,
Men's Clothing, Children's Clothing
Average price: Exclusive
Area: The Strip
Address: 3600 Las Vegas Blvd.
South, Las Vegas, NV 89109
Phone: (702) 732-9300

#58
Fashion Show
Category: Shopping Center
Average price: Modest
Area: The Strip
Address: 3200 Las Vegas Blvd S.
Ste. 600, Las Vegas, NV 89109
Phone: (702) 369-8382

#59
Bettie Page
Category: Women's Clothing
Average price: Expensive
Area: The Strip, Eastside
Address: 3667 Las Vegas Blvd S
Las Vegas, NV 89136
Phone: (702) 636-1100

#60
En Fuego Cigars & Lounge
Category: Tobacco Shop, Lounge
Average price: Modest
Area: The Strip
Address: 328 W Sahara Ave
Las Vegas, NV 89102
Phone: (702) 384-9262

#61
Bauman Rare Book
Category: Booktore
Average price: Exclusive
Area: Eastside
Address: 3327 Las Vegas Blvd S
Las Vegas, NV 89109
Phone: (702) 948-1617

#62
Puff Vapors
Category: Tobacco Shop
Average price: Inexpensive
Area: Southwest
Address: 7835 S Rainbow Blvd
Las Vegas, NV 89139
Phone: (702) 614-7833

#63
MAC Cosmetics
Category: Cosmetics & Beauty,
Makeup Artists
Average price: Modest
Area: Eastside
Address: 3500 Las Vegas Blvd.
South Las Vegas, NV 89109
Phone: (702) 699-9021

#64
Kiki De Montparnasse
Category: Lingerie, Women's Clothing
Average price: Exclusive
Area: The Strip
Address: 3720 Las Vegas Blvd S
Las Vegas, NV 89109
Phone: (702) 736-7883

#65
Fresh
Category: Cosmetics & Beauty
Average price: Expensive
Area: The Strip
Address: 3500 Las Vegas Blvd S, Ste 6
Las Vegas, NV 89109
Phone: (702) 631-5000

#66
Plant World Nursery
Category: Nurseries & Gardening
Average price: Modest
Area: Westside
Address: 5301 W Charleston Blvd
Las Vegas, NV 89146
Phone: (702) 878-9485

#67
Cycle Gear
Category: Motorcycle Dealer,
Motorcycle Repair, Sporting Goods
Average price: Modest
Area: Westside
Address: 344 S. Decatur Blvd
Las Vegas, NV 89107
Phone: (702) 877-4327

#68
HOV Las Vegas
Category: Tobacco Shop
Average price: Modest
Area: Westside
Address: 4601 W Sahara Ave
Las Vegas, NV 89102
Phone: (702) 410-5205

#69
Zia Records
Category: Music & DVDs,
Vinyl Records
Average price: Modest
Area: Westside
Address: 4503 W Sahara
Las Vegas, NV 89102
Phone: (702) 233-4942

#70
World Market
Category: Home Decor, Furniture Store,
Beer, Wine & Spirits
Average price: Modest
Area: Southwest
Address: 3890 Blue Diamond Rd
Las Vegas, NC 89139
Phone: (702) 269-4465

#71
Anthropologie
Category: Women's Clothing, Accessories
Average price: Expensive
Area: The Strip
Address: 3500 Las Vegas Blvd S
Las Vegas, NV 89109
Phone: (702) 650-0466

#72
Inglot Cosmetics
Category: Cosmetics & Beauty,
Makeup Artists
Average price: Modest
Area: Southeast
Address: 6671 Las Vegas Blvd
S Las Vegas, NV 89119
Phone: (702) 405-6300

#73
Costco
Category: Department Store,
Wholesale Store
Average price: Modest
Area: Summerlin
Address: 801 S Pavilion Center Dr
Las Vegas, NV 89144
Phone: (702) 352-2050

#74
Chrome Hearts
Category: Jewelry
Average price: Exclusive
Area: The Strip
Address: 3500 Las Vegas Blvd S
Las Vegas, NV 89109
Phone: (702) 893-9949

#75
**Las Vegas Premium
Outlets - North**
Category: Shopping Center,
Outlet Store
Average price: Modest
Area: Downtown
Address: 875 S Grand Central Pkwy
Las Vegas, NV 89106
Phone: (702) 474-7500

#76
Sephora
Category: Cosmetics & Beauty
Average price: Expensive
Area: The Strip
Address: 3500 Las Vegas Blvd S
Las Vegas, NV 89109
Phone: (702) 228-3535

#77
Kettlemuck's Toy Shoppe
Category: Toy Store
Average price: Modest
Area: Anthem
Address: 10895 Eastern Ave
Henderson, NV 89052
Phone: (702) 776-8349

#78
Discount Beads
Category: Jewelry, Art Supplies
Average price: Modest
Area: Spring Valley
Address: 4266 S Durango Dr
Las Vegas, NV 89147
Phone: (702) 360-4266

#79
The Vapery
Category: Tobacco Shop
Average price: Modest
Area: Southwest
Address: 8060 S Rainbow Blvd
Las Vegas, NV 89139
Phone: (702) 485-5888

#80
Sephora
Category: Cosmetics & Beauty
Average price: Modest
Area: Southeast
Address: 6671 Las Vegas Blvd S
Las Vegas, NV 89119
Phone: (702) 361-3727

#81
Lululemon Athletica
Category: Sport Wear,
Women's Clothing, Yoga
Average price: Expensive
Area: The Strip
Address: 3200 Las Vegas Blvd S
Las Vegas, NV 89109
Phone: (702) 696-1282

#82
Louis Vuitton
Category: Leather Goods,
Men's Clothing
Average price: Exclusive
Area: The Strip
Address: 3131 Las Vegas Blvd S
Las Vegas, NV 89109
Phone: (702) 650-9007

#83
Paper and Home
Category: Cards & Stationery,
Graphic Design
Average price: Modest
Area: Spring Valley
Address: 4555 S. Fort Apache Rd
Las Vegas, NV 89147
Phone: (702) 776-8243

#84
Lush Handmade Cosmetics
Category: Cosmetics & Beauty
Average price: Expensive
Area: The Strip
Address: 3200 Las Vegas Blvd Fashion
Show Dr, Las Vegas, NV 89109
Phone: (702) 792-0930

#85
Target
Category: Department Store
Average price: Modest
Area: Spring Valley
Address: 4155 S Grand Canyon Dr
Las Vegas, NV 89147
Phone: (702) 251-0330

#86
Undefeated
Category: Shoe Store, Men's Clothing
Average price: Expensive
Area: Eastside
Address: 4480 Paradise Rd
Las Vegas, NV 89108
Phone: (702) 732-0019

#87
REI
Category: Sport Wear,
Outdoor Gear, Bikes
Average price: Expensive
Area: Westside
Address: 710 S Rampart Blvd
Las Vegas, NV 89145
Phone: (702) 951-4488

#88
Gaia Flowers
Category: Flowers & Gifts
Average price: Inexpensive
Area: Downtown
Address: 6 E. Charleston Blvd.
Las Vegas, NV 89104
Phone: (702) 997-0222

#89
Optic Gallery
Category: Optometrists, Eyewear &
Opticians, Laser Eye Surgery/Lasik
Average price: Modest
Area: Southeast
Address: 5905 S Eastern Ave
Las Vegas, NV 89119
Phone: (702) 893-3937

#90
All Fired Up
Category: Arts & Crafts
Average price: Modest
Area: Southeast
Address: 1651 E Sunset Rd
Las Vegas, NV 89119
Phone: (702) 269-4444

#91
Sin City Knit Shop
Category: Knitting Supplies
Average price: Modest
Area: Southeast
Address: 2165 E Windmill Ln
Las Vegas, NV 89123
Phone: (702) 641-0210

#92
Quick Repair Jewelry
Category: Jewelry
Average price: Inexpensive
Area: Westside
Address: 7632 Westcliff Dr
Las Vegas, NV 89145
Phone: (702) 434-9333

#93
Gorilla Radio Smoke Shop
Category: Tobacco Shop
Average price: Modest
Area: Eastside
Address: 4225 S Eastern Ave
Las Vegas, NV 89119
Phone: (702) 818-4400

#94
Spinettis
Home Gaming Supplies
Category: Hobby Shop
Average price: Inexpensive
Area: Downtown
Address: 810 S Commerce St
Las Vegas, NV 89106
Phone: (702) 362-8767

#95
Charleston Antique Mall
Category: Antiques
Average price: Modest
Area: Westside
Address: 560 S Decatur Blvd
Las Vegas, NV 89107
Phone: (702) 228-4783

#96
Thimbleberry House
Category: Florist, Gift Shop
Average price: Modest
Area: Summerlin
Address: 1990 Village Center Cir
Las Vegas, NV 89134
Phone: (702) 979-6261

#97
Thomas Pink
Category: Men's Clothing
Average price: Expensive
Area: The Strip
Address: 3500 Las Vegas Blvd
S Las Vegas, NV 89109
Phone: (702) 731-0263

#98
Tobacco Town Cigars
Category: Tobacco Shop
Average price: Modest
Area: Westside
Address: 1000 S Rampart Blvd
Las Vegas, NV 89145
Phone: (702) 722-6600

#99
2nd Amendment Gun Shop
Category: Guns & Ammo
Average price: Modest
Area: Northwest
Address: 4570 N Rancho Dr
Las Vegas, NV 89130
Phone: (702) 272-2510

#100
ABC Store
Category: Department Store
Average price: Inexpensive
Area: The Strip
Address: 3200 Las Vegas Blvd
S Las Vegas, NV 89109
Phone: (702) 732-2358

#101
Tobacco Leaf
Category: Tobacco Shop
Average price: Modest
Area: Southeast
Address: 9400 S Eastern Ave
Las Vegas, NV 89123
Phone: (702) 897-5977

#102
Vavoom Girly Boutique
Category: Women's Clothing
Average price: Modest
Area: Eastside
Address: 4480 Paradise Rd
Las Vegas, NV 89169
Phone: (702) 413-0480

#103
The Container Store
Category: Home Decor, Kitchen & Bath
Average price: Modest
Area: Southeast
Address: 6521 Las Vegas Blvd
S Las Vegas, NV 89119
Phone: (702) 712-4801

#104
Costco
Category: Wholesale Store,
Eyewear & Opticians
Average price: Modest
Area: Centennial
Address: 6555 N Decatur Blvd
Las Vegas, NV 89131
Phone: (702) 415-2300

#105
Zombie Apocalypse Store
Category: Shopping
Average price: Modest
Area: Chinatown
Address: 3420 Spring Mountain Rd
Las Vegas, NV 89102
Phone: (866) 784-7882

#106
Gun Show Ammo
Category: Guns & Ammo
Average price: Modest
Area: Southeast
Address: 7291 S Eastern Ave
Las Vegas, NV 89119
Phone: (702) 722-2666

#107
Rouge Skin Hair & Makeup
Category: Makeup Artists,
Cosmetics & Beauty, Hair Salon
Average price: Modest
Area: Summerlin
Address: 2251 Rampart Blvd
Las Vegas, NV 89128
Phone: (702) 751-1681

#108
Original Penguin
Category: Fashion
Average price: Expensive
Area: Eastside
Address: 3663 Las Vegas Blvd
Las Vegas, NV 89109
Phone: (702) 734-0089

#109
Don Vicente Cigar Company
Category: Tobacco Shop
Average price: Inexpensive
Area: Downtown
Address: 624 Las Vegas Blvd
S Las Vegas, NV 89101
Phone: (702) 386-9117

#110
Fresh
Category: Cosmetics & Beauty
Supply, Skin Care
Average price: Modest
Area: The Strip
Address: 3327 Las Vegas Blvd
Las Vegas, NV 89109
Phone: (702) 699-9989

#111
Hermès Encore
Category: Shopping
Average price: Exclusive
Area: Eastside
Address: 3121 Las Vegas Blvd
S Las Vegas, NV 89109
Phone: (702) 650-3116

#112
Moondog Records
Category: Music & DVDs,
Vinyl Records
Average price: Modest
Area: University
Address: 4440 S Maryland Pkwy
Las Vegas, NV 89119
Phone: (702) 802-3333

#113
The Art of Shaving
Category: Cosmetics & Beauty
Supply, Barbers
Average price: Expensive
Area: The Strip
Address: 3200 Las Vegas Blvd
Las Vegas, NV 89109
Phone: (702) 733-9509

#114
The Arts Factory
Category: Art Gallery
Average price: Inexpensive
Area: Downtown
Address: 107 E Charleston Blvd
Las Vegas, NV 89104
Phone: (702) 676-1111

#115
REI
Category: Bikes, Outdoor Gear,
Sport Wear
Average price: Expensive
Area: Anthem
Address: 2220 Village Walk Dr
Henderson, NV 89052
Phone: (702) 896-7111

#116
Scoop NYC
Category: Fashion
Average price: Expensive
Area: Eastside
Address: 3500 Las Vegas Blvd
S Las Vegas, NV 89109
Phone: (702) 734-0026

#117
J.Glenn
Category: Home Decor, Jewelry
Average price: Modest
Area: Westside
Address: 750 S Rampart Blvd
Las Vegas, NV 89145
Phone: (702) 425-7636

#118
Coach Outlet Store
Category: Luggage, Accessories,
Outlet Store
Average price: Expensive
Area: Southeast
Address: 7400 Las Vegas Blvd
S Las Vegas, NV 89123
Phone: (702) 386-1067

#119
Powder and Sun
Category: Sporting Goods,
Men's Clothing, Surf Shop
Average price: Modest
Area: Spring Valley
Address: 4555 S Fort Apache Rd
Las Vegas, NV 89147
Phone: (702) 221-7669

#120
Jewelry City
Category: Jewelry
Average price: Exclusive
Area: Spring Valley
Address: 5060 S Fort Apache Rd
Las Vegas, NV 89147
Phone: (702) 331-2900

#121
Fruition
Category: Men's Clothing, Women's
Clothing, Accessories
Average price: Expensive
Area: University, Eastside
Address: 4139 S Maryland Pkwy
Las Vegas, NV 89119
Phone: (702) 796-4139

#122
Amber Unicorn Book
Category: Booktore
Average price: Inexpensive
Area: Westside
Address: 2101 S Decatur Blvd
Las Vegas, NV 89102
Phone: (702) 648-9303

#123
Red Rock Running Company
Category: Sporting Goods
Average price: Modest
Area: Anthem
Address: 120 S Green Valley Pkwy
Henderson, NV 89012
Phone: (702) 998-9054

#124
Davidson's Firearms
Category: Sporting Goods
Average price: Inexpensive
Area: Anthem
Address: 10890 S Eastern Ave
Henderson, NV 89052
Phone: (702) 456-6600

#125
Bad Attitude Boutique
The Corset Store
Category: Costume, Lingerie,
Women's Clothing
Average price: Expensive
Area: Eastside
Address: 953 E Sahara Ave
Las Vegas, NV 89104
Phone: (702) 646-9669

#126
Jewelry & Minerals of Las Vegas
Category: Jewelry
Average price: Modest
Area: Downtown
Address: 410 E Sahara Ave
Las Vegas, NV 89104
Phone: (702) 733-7166

#127
Las Vegas Market
Category: Furniture Store
Average price: Expensive
Area: Downtown
Address: 495 S Grand Central Pkwy
Las Vegas, NV 89106
Phone: (702) 599-9600

#128
Maximum Comics 3.0
Category: Comic Book
Average price: Inexpensive
Area: Centennial
Address: 7950 W Tropical Pkwy
Las Vegas, NV 89149
Phone: (702) 722-6642

#129
Cole Haan
Category: Shoe Store, Leather Goods
Average price: Expensive
Area: Downtown
Address: 875 S Grand Central Pkwy,
Ste 2119, Las Vegas, NV 89106
Phone: (702) 759-7812

#130
Las Vegas Gun Range
& Firearms Center
Category: Guns & Ammo
Average price: Expensive
Area: Southwest
Address: 4610 Blue Diamond Rd
Las Vegas, NV 89139
Phone: (702) 386-4867

#131
Saks Fifth Avenue
Category: Department Store
Average price: Exclusive
Area: The Strip
Address: 3200 Las Vegas Blvd
S Las Vegas, NV 89109
Phone: (702) 733-8300

#132
Target
Category: Department Store
Average price: Modest
Area: Southwest
Address: 4100 Blue Diamond Rd
Las Vegas, NV 89139
Phone: (702) 266-8049

#133
ABC Store
Category: Shopping Center
Average price: Inexpensive
Area: The Strip
Address: 3663 Las Vegas Blvd
S Las Vegas, NV 89109
Phone: (702) 733-7182

#134
Miracle Mile Shop
Category: Shopping Center
Average price: Modest
Area: The Strip
Address: 3663 Las Vegas Blvd
S Las Vegas, NV 89109
Phone: (702) 866-0703

#135
Little Shop of Magic
Category: Toy Store, Hobby Shop
Average price: Modest
Area: Spring Valley
Address: 4160 S Durango Dr
Las Vegas, NV 89147
Phone: (702) 307-6127

#136
Louis Vuitton
Category: Luggage
Average price: Exclusive
Area: The Strip
Address: 3720 Las Vegas Blvd
S Las Vegas, NV 89109
Phone: (702) 262-6189

#137
Charming Charlie - Las Vegas
Category: Accessories, Jewelry
Average price: Inexpensive
Area: Southeast
Address: 6521 Las Vegas Blvd
South Las Vegas, NV 89119
Phone: (702) 269-5342

#138
Tokyo Discount No 2
Category: Gift Shop
Average price: Modest
Area: Spring Valley
Address: 4960 S Fort Apache Rd
Las Vegas, NV 89148
Phone: (702) 227-3027

#139
Forever 21
Category: Women's Clothing, Accessories
Average price: Inexpensive
Area: The Strip
Address: 3200 S Las Vegas Blvd
S Las Vegas, NV 89109
Phone: (702) 735-0053

#140
Williams Costume Co
Category: Costume
Average price: Modest
Area: Downtown
Address: 1226 S 3rd St
Las Vegas, NV 89104
Phone: (702) 384-1384

#141
The Linq Las Vegas
Category: Fashion, Shopping Center
Average price: Modest
Area: The Strip
Address: 3545 Las Vegas Blvd
South Las Vegas, NV 89109
Phone: (800) 522-4700

#142
Optic Gallery
Category: Eyewear & Opticians,
Optometrists
Average price: Modest
Area: Spring Valley
Address: 7290 Arroyo Crossing Pkwy
Las Vegas, NV 89113
Phone: (702) 451-3937

#143
Las Vegas Fight Shop
Category: Sport Wear
Average price: Modest
Area: The Strip
Address: 3663 Las Vegas Blvd
S Las Vegas, NV 89109
Phone: (702) 366-0502

#144
Anthropologie
Category: Women's Clothing
Average price: Expensive
Area: Anthem
Address: 2275 Village Walk Dr
Henderson, NV 89052
Phone: (702) 617-2247

#145
Niketown Las Vegas
Category: Shoe Store
Average price: Modest
Area: The Strip
Address: 3500 Las Vegas Blvd
S Las Vegas, NV 89109
Phone: (702) 650-8888

#146
Vaping Aristocrats
Category: Tobacco Shop, Electronics
Average price: Modest
Area: Southeast
Address: 9775 S Maryland Pkwy
Las Vegas, NV 89183
Phone: (702) 724-8273

#147
Jeff White Custom Jewelry
Category: Jewelry
Average price: Modest
Area: Westside
Address: 410 S Rampart
Las Vegas, NV 89145
Phone: (702) 220-9099

#148
Mayer Eye Care
Category: Optometrists,
Eyewear & Opticians
Average price: Modest
Area: Southeast
Address: 1320 E Pebble Rd
Las Vegas, NV 89123
Phone: (702) 818-3100

#149
Jerry's Tux Shop
Category: Men's Clothing, Bridal
Average price: Modest
Area: Spring Valley
Address: 8650 W Tropicana Ave
Las Vegas, NV 89147
Phone: (702) 248-4777

#150
Computer Doctor BG
Category: IT Services & Computer Repair,
Electronics Repair, Computers
Average price: Modest
Area: Spring Valley
Address: 4075 S Durango Dr
Las Vegas, NV 89147
Phone: (702) 802-3300

#151
Galaxy Vapes
Category: Tobacco Shop
Average price: Inexpensive
Area: Spring Valley
Address: 3665 S Fort Apache Rd
Las Vegas, NV 89147
Phone: (702) 724-1570

#152
Desert Strings
Category: Musical Instruments
Average price: Modest
Area: Southeast
Address: 2121 E Tropicana Ave
Las Vegas, NV 89119
Phone: (702) 736-8934

#153
Pink Spot Vapors
Category: Tobacco Shop
Average price: Modest
Area: Centennial
Address: 6485 N Decatur Blvd
Las Vegas, NV 89131
Phone: (702) 655-8273

#154
Tokyo Discount
Category: Hobby Shop
Average price: Modest
Area: Southeast
Address: 9890 S Maryland Pkwy
Las Vegas, NV 89183
Phone: (702) 614-7916

#155
Burberry Ltd
Category: Men's Clothing,
Women's Clothing
Average price: Exclusive
Area: The Strip
Address: 3500 Las Vegas Blvd
S Las Vegas, NV 89109
Phone: (702) 731-0650

#156
Las Vegas Sock Market
Category: Accessories,
Women's Clothing
Average price: Modest
Area: The Strip
Address: 3950 Las Vegas Blvd
S Las Vegas, NV 89119
Phone: (702) 632-6990

#157
Trifecta Gallery
Category: Art Gallery
Average price: Modest
Area: Downtown
Address: 107 E Charleston Blvd
Las Vegas, NV 89104
Phone: (702) 366-7001

#158
Jeff Mitchum Gallery
Category: Art Gallery
Average price: Exclusive
Area: The Strip
Address: 3680 Las Vegas Blvd
Las Vegas, NV 89109
Phone: (800) 763-3074

#159
Bare Escentuals
Category: Cosmetics & Beauty
Average price: Modest
Area: The Strip
Address: 3200 S Las Vegas Blvd
Las Vegas, NV 89109
Phone: (702) 369-1556

#160
Edible Arrangements
Category: Florist
Average price: Expensive
Area: Southeast
Address: 8174 Las Vegas Blvd
S Las Vegas, NV 89123
Phone: (702) 263-1474

#161
Vapors Union
Category: Tobacco Shop
Average price: Modest
Area: Spring Valley
Address: 5479 S Rainbow Blvd
Las Vegas, NV 89118
Phone: (702) 816-3755

#162
Star Nursery
Category: Nurseries & Gardening
Average price: Modest
Area: Westside
Address: 8170 W Charleston Blvd
Las Vegas, NV 89117
Phone: (702) 360-7827

#163
Velvet Underground
Category: Comic Book
Average price: Inexpensive
Area: Westside
Address: 4241 W Charleston Blvd
Las Vegas, NV 89102
Phone: (702) 258-2689

#164
Emporium de Gondola
Category: Boating, Shopping
Average price: Modest
Area: The Strip
Address: 3355 Las Vegas Blvd
S Las Vegas, NV 89109
Phone: (702) 733-5000

#165
Vapor House LV
Category: Tobacco Shop
Average price: Modest
Area: University
Address: 4741 S Maryland Pkwy
Las Vegas, NV 89119
Phone: (702) 800-6462

#166
La Perla
Category: Lingerie
Average price: Exclusive
Area: The Strip
Address: 3500 Las Vegas Blvd S
Las Vegas, NV 89109
Phone: (702) 732-9820

#167
1 Hr Photo Shack
Category: Photography Store
Average price: Modest
Area: University
Address: 4632 S Maryland Prkwy
Las Vegas, NV 89101
Phone: (702) 798-7373

#168
Magnet Max
Category: Flowers & Gifts
Average price: Inexpensive
Area: The Strip
Address: 3663 Las Vegas Blvd
S Las Vegas, NV 89109
Phone: (702) 891-0477

#169
Elie Tahari
Category: Women's Clothing,
Shoe Store, Men's Clothing
Average price: Expensive
Area: Downtown
Address: 875 Grand Central Pkwy
Las Vegas, NV 89106
Phone: (702) 382-0663

#170
Skechers
Category: Shoe Store, Sporting Goods
Average price: Modest
Area: The Strip
Address: 3200 Las Vegas Blvd S
Las Vegas, NV 89109
Phone: (702) 696-9905

#171
Eyedentity Eye Care
Category: Optometrists,
Eyewear & Opticians
Average price: Inexpensive
Area: Spring Valley
Address: 10170 W Tropicana Ave
Las Vegas, NV 89147
Phone: (702) 873-2121

#172
Game Repair
Category: VIdeo Game Rental,
Electronics Repair
Average price: Modest
Area: Northwest
Address: 3250 N Tenaya Way
Las Vegas, NV 89129
Phone: (702) 655-1921

#173
Kiehl's Since 1851
Category: Cosmetics & Beauty,
Skin Care
Average price: Expensive
Area: The Strip
Address: 3500 South Las Vegas Blvd
Las Vegas, NV 89109
Phone: (702) 784-0025

#174
Tivoli Village
Category: Shopping Center
Average price: Expensive
Area: Westside
Address: 440 S Rampart
Las Vegas, NV 89144
Phone: (702) 570-7400

#175
Sephora
Category: Cosmetics & Beauty
Average price: Modest
Area: Eastside
Address: 3663 Las Vegas Blvd
S Las Vegas, NV 89109
Phone: (702) 737-0550

#176
CVS Pharmacy
Category: Drugstore
Average price: Inexpensive
Area: The Strip
Address: 3758 S Las Vegas Blvd
Las Vegas, NV 89109
Phone: (702) 262-9028

#177
Lock N Load Tactical
Category: Guns & Ammo
Average price: Modest
Area: Southeast
Address: 9340 S Eastern Ave
Henderson, NV 89123
Phone: (702) 360-4867

#178
Cosmic Comics
Category: Comic Book
Average price: Inexpensive
Area: Eastside
Address: 3830 E Flamingo Rd
Las Vegas, NV 89121
Phone: (702) 451-6611

#179
Walgreens
Category: Drugstore,
Convenience Store
Average price: Inexpensive
Area: The Strip
Address: 3717 Las Vegas Blvd
S Las Vegas, NV 89109
Phone: (702) 262-0635

#180
Neiman Marcus
Category: Men's Clothing, Women's
Clothing, Department Store
Average price: Exclusive
Area: The Strip
Address: 3200 Las Vegas Blvd S,
Ste 100, Las Vegas, NV 89109
Phone: (702) 731-3636

#181
LeSportac Outlet
Category: Accessories
Average price: Modest
Area: Downtown
Address: 875 South Grand Central Parkway,
Las Vegas, NV 89106
Phone: (702) 366-0698

#182
HomeGoods
Category: Home Decor
Average price: Modest
Area: Southwest
Address: 8435 W Warm Springs
Las Vegas, NV 89113
Phone: (702) 361-3692

#183
Sportman's Warehouse
Category: Outdoor Gear
Average price: Modest
Area: Centennial, Northwest
Address: 5647 Centennial Ctr Blvd
Las Vegas, NV 89149
Phone: (702) 474-1100

#184
Pure Foot & Spa
Category: Massage, Day Spa,
Cosmetics & Beauty
Average price: Inexpensive
Area: Spring Valley
Address: 6910 S Rainbow Blvd
Las Vegas, NV 89118
Phone: (702) 858-7873

#185
Toy Shack
Category: Toy Store
Average price: Expensive
Area: Downtown
Address: 450 Fremont St
Las Vegas, NV 89104
Phone: (702) 538-8600

#186
Coach
Category: Leather Goods
Average price: Modest
Area: Downtown
Address: 755 S Grand Central Pkwy,
Ste 1471, Las Vegas, NV 89106
Phone: (702) 386-9990

#187
ABC Store
Category: Flowers & Gifts
Average price: Inexpensive
Area: Downtown
Address: 23 Fremont St
Las Vegas, NV 89101
Phone: (702) 380-3098

#188
Juicy Couture
Category: Women's Clothing, Accessories
Average price: Expensive
Area: The Strip
Address: 3500 Las Vegas Blvd
S Las Vegas, NV 89109
Phone: (702) 365-5600

#189
Couture Bride
Category: Bridal
Average price: Expensive
Area: Westside
Address: 950 S Durango Dr
Las Vegas, NV 89145
Phone: (702) 647-7778

#190
Tokyo Discount
Category: Gift Shop
Average price: Modest
Area: Centennial
Address: 6475 N. Decatur Blvd
Las Vegas, NV 89131
Phone: (702) 431-8833

#191
The Lair Vapors
Category: Tobacco Shop
Average price: Modest
Area: Downtown
Address: 320 E Charleston Blvd
Las Vegas, NV 89104
Phone: (702) 858-5247

#192
Savers
Category: Thrift Store,
Vintage & Consignment
Average price: Inexpensive
Area: Summerlin
Address: 8530 W Lake Mead Blvd
Las Vegas, NV 89128
Phone: (702) 658-2880

#193
Lady C Leather
Category: Leather Goods, Lingerie
Average price: Modest
Area: Westside
Address: 4037 W Sahara Ave
Las Vegas, NV 89102
Phone: (702) 641-3834

#194
Man Cave
Category: Tobacco Shop
Average price: Modest
Area: Southeast, Anthem
Address: 855 Seven Hills Drive
Henderson, NV 89052
Phone: (702) 478-8008

#195
Apple Store
Category: Computers
Average price: Expensive
Area: The Strip
Address: 3200 Las Vegas Blvd
S Las Vegas, NV 89109
Phone: (702) 650-9550

#196
Apple Store
Category: Computers
Average price: Expensive
Area: The Strip
Address: 3500 Las Vegas Blvd
S Las Vegas, NV 89109
Phone: (702) 684-8800

#197
Bike World
Category: Bikes
Average price: Modest
Area: Eastside
Address: 2320 E Flamingo Rd
Las Vegas, NV 89119
Phone: (702) 735-7551

#198
Walgreens
Category: Drugstore, Cosmetics & Beauty,
Convenience Store
Average price: Modest
Area: Southeast
Address: 2389 E Windmill Ln
Las Vegas, NV 89123
Phone: (702) 837-9531

#199
Viva Salon
Category: Hair Salon, Makeup Artists,
Cosmetics & Beauty
Average price: Modest
Area: Summerlin
Address: 10870 W Charleston Blvd
Las Vegas, NV 89135
Phone: (702) 331-6000

#200
TJ Maxx
Category: Fashion
Average price: Modest
Area: Southwest
Address: 8435 W Warm Springs Rd
Las Vegas, NV 89113
Phone: (702) 361-3692

#201
Frame Fixer
Category: Eyewear & Opticians
Average price: Modest
Area: Westside
Address: 3961 W Charleston Blvd
Las Vegas, NV 89102
Phone: (702) 735-7879

#202
Tuxedo Junction
Category: Bespoke Clothing
Average price: Modest
Area: Westside
Address: 3540 W Sahara Ave
Las Vegas, NV 89102
Phone: (702) 873-8830

#203
Michael Kors
Category: Women's Clothing
Average price: Modest
Area: The Strip
Address: 3327 S Las Vegas Blvd,
Ste 2840, Las Vegas, NV 89109
Phone: (702) 731-2510

#204
Mcghie's Ski, Bike & Board
Category: Sporting Goods
Average price: Modest
Area: Spring Valley
Address: 4035 S Fort Apache Rd
Las Vegas, NV 89147
Phone: (702) 252-8077

#205
Frederick's of Hollywood
Category: Lingerie
Average price: Modest
Area: The Strip
Address: 3200 Las Vegas Blvd
S Space 2320, Las Vegas, NV 89109
Phone: (702) 893-9001

#206
AllSaints
Category: Accessories,
Men's Clothing, Women's Clothing
Average price: Expensive
Area: The Strip
Address: 3708 South Las Vegas Boulevard,
Las Vegas, NV 89109
Phone: (702) 722-5252

#207
Francesca's Collections
Category: Women's Clothing
Average price: Modest
Area: Southeast
Address: 6605 Las Vegas Blvd
S Las Vegas, NV 89119
Phone: (702) 263-4485

#208
Di Bella Flowers & Gifts
Category: Florist
Average price: Modest
Area: Downtown
Address: 2021 W Charleston Blvd
Las Vegas, NV 89102
Phone: (702) 384-1121

#209
Desert Rose Florist
Category: Florist
Average price: Modest
Area: Westside
Address: 1000 S Rampart Blvd
Las Vegas, NV 89145
Phone: (702) 898-6088

#210
Haute Chix Boutique
Southern Highlands
Category: Women's Clothing, Jewelry
Average price: Modest
Area: Southwest
Address: 10620 Southern Highlands Pkwy,
Las Vegas, NV 89141
Phone: (702) 269-5804

#211
Hair Plus Beauty Supply
Category: Cosmetics & Beauty,
Hair Extensions, Wigs
Average price: Modest
Area: Eastside
Address: 3810 Maryland Pkwy
Las Vegas, NV 89119
Phone: (702) 255-5510

#212
The Find
Category: Home Decor
Average price: Modest
Area: Southeast
Address: 3170 E Sunset Rd
Las Vegas, NV 89120
Phone: (702) 483-5550

#213
Big Lots
Category: Discount Store
Average price: Inexpensive
Area: Southwest
Address: 3940 Blue Diamond
Las Vegas, NV 89139
Phone: (702) 263-8760

#214
Costco
Category: Department Store
Average price: Modest
Area: Downtown
Address: 222 S Martin L King Blvd
Las Vegas, NV 89106
Phone: (702) 384-6247

#215
Spray Painting Artists
Category: Arts & Crafts
Average price: Modest
Area: Downtown
Address: 111 S 4th St
Las Vegas, NV 89101
Phone: (702) 385-0001

#216
Patina Decor
Category: Antiques,
Vintage & Consignment
Average price: Expensive
Area: Downtown
Address: 1211 S Main St
Las Vegas, NV 89104
Phone: (702) 776-6222

#217
David Yurman
Category: Jewelry
Average price: Exclusive
Area: The Strip
Address: 3500 S Las Vegas Blvd
Las Vegas, NV 89109
Phone: (702) 794-4545

#218
Cartier
Category: Jewelry, Accessories
Average price: Exclusive
Area: The Strip
Address: 3570 Las Vegas Blvd
S Las Vegas, NV 89109
Phone: (702) 733-6652

#219
First Time Vape
Category: Tobacco Shop
Average price: Modest
Area: Southeast
Address: 351 E Silverado Ranch Blvd
Las Vegas, NV 89183
Phone: (702) 483-5554

#220
A Garden Floral
Category: Florist
Average price: Modest
Area: Eastside
Address: 3801 Las Vegas Blvd
S Las Vegas, NV 89109
Phone: (702) 419-7525

#221
Giuseppe Zanotti Design
Category: Shoe Store
Average price: Exclusive
Area: The Strip
Address: 3500 Las Vegas Blvd
S Las Vegas, NV 89109
Phone: (702) 866-0055

#222
Milano's Fashion
Category: Sewing & Alterations,
Men's Clothing
Average price: Exclusive
Area: University
Address: 4155 S Maryland Pkwy
Las Vegas, NV 89119
Phone: (702) 735-6866

#223
Flowers by Michelle
Category: Florist
Average price: Modest
Area: Centennial
Address: 6510 N Buffalo Dr
Las Vegas, NV 89131
Phone: (702) 255-0209

#224
The Spirit Within U
Category: Gift Shop, Booktore
Average price: Modest
Area: Northwest
Address: 4780 West Ann Rd
North Las Vegas, NV 89031
Phone: (702) 658-2257

#225
ERA by Ciara
Category: Cosmetics & Beauty,
Makeup Artists
Average price: Modest
Area: Westside
Address: 420 S Rampart Blvd
Las Vegas, NV 89145
Phone: (702) 715-2013

#226
Ann Taylor Loft #1394
Category: Women's Clothing, Accessories
Average price: Modest
Area: Anthem
Address: 2235 Village Walk Drive
Henderson, NV 89052
Phone: (702) 207-6718

#227
iFly Mobile Repair
Category: Mobile Phone Repair,
Mobile Phones
Average price: Modest
Area: Westside
Address: 7776 W Sahara
Las Vegas, NV 89117
Phone: (702) 499-0171

#228
Lucky Brand Jeans
Category: Fashion
Average price: Modest
Area: The Strip
Address: 3667 S Las Vegas Blvd
Las Vegas, NV 89109
Phone: (702) 733-6613

#229
S S Audio
Category: Car Stereo Installation, Electronics
Average price: Modest
Area: Chinatown
Address: 5240 Spring Mountain Rd
Las Vegas, NV 89146
Phone: (702) 650-4444

#230
Vanity Body Sculpting
Category: Weight Loss Center,
Cosmetics & Beauty
Average price: Expensive
Area: Anthem
Address: 3019 Saint Rose Pkwy
Henderson, NV 89052
Phone: (702) 343-5435

#231
Neon Computers
Category: IT Services & Computer Repair,
Electronics Repair, Computers
Average price: Modest
Area: Spring Valley
Address: 6830 S Rainbow Blvd
Las Vegas, NV 89118
Phone: (702) 240-6366

#232
John Knopf Fine Art Photography Gallery
Category: Art Gallery
Average price: Exclusive
Area: The Strip
Address: 2000 S Las Vegas Blvd
Las Vegas, NV 89104
Phone: (702) 204-7905

#233
The Coach Store
Category: Leather Goods
Average price: Expensive
Area: The Strip
Address: 3500 Las Vegas Blvd
S Las Vegas, NV 89109
Phone: (702) 651-0363

#234
A Little White Wedding Chapel
Category: Bridal, Florist,
Wedding Planning
Average price: Inexpensive
Area: Downtown
Address: 1301 Las Vegas Blvd.
South Las Vegas, NV 89104
Phone: (702) 382-5943

#235
Marshalls
Category: Department Store,
Discount Store
Average price: Modest
Area: Anthem
Address: 9845 S Eastern Ave
Las Vegas, NV 89183
Phone: (702) 617-2910

#236
Dead Poet Book
Category: Booktore
Average price: Inexpensive
Area: Westside
Address: 937 S Rainbow Blvd
Las Vegas, NV 89145
Phone: (702) 227-4070

#237
Retro Vegas
Category: Antiques
Average price: Modest
Area: Downtown
Address: 1131 S Main St
Las Vegas, NV 89104
Phone: (702) 384-2700

#238
Roy's Liquor, Wine & Cigars
Category: Tobacco Shop, Beer,
Wine & Spirits
Average price: Modest
Area: Spring Valley, South Summerlin
Address: 3330 S Hualapai Way
Las Vegas, NV 89117
Phone: (702) 202-0111

#239
Simplicity Salon
Category: Cosmetics & Beauty,
Hair Salon, Nail Salon
Average price: Modest
Area: Spring Valley
Address: 6375 S Rainbow Blvd
Las Vegas, NV 89118
Phone: (702) 247-4247

#240
Tiffany & Co.
Category: Jewelry
Average price: Exclusive
Area: Eastside
Address: 3600 Las Vegas Blvd
S Las Vegas, NV 89109
Phone: (702) 697-5400

#241
Crystals at CityCenter
Category: Shopping Center
Average price: Exclusive
Area: The Strip
Address: 3720 Las Vegas Blvd
S Las Vegas, NV 89109
Phone: (702) 590-5570

#242
La Casa Cigars & Lounge
Category: Bar, Tobacco Shop,
Music Venues
Average price: Modest
Area: Westside
Address: 430 S Rampart Blvd
Las Vegas, NV 89145
Phone: (702) 407-1171

#243
The Home Depot
Category: Nurseries & Gardening,
Appliances, Hardware Store
Average price: Modest
Area: Spring Valley
Address: 7015 Arroyo Crossing Pky
Las Vegas, NV 89113
Phone: (702) 270-6446

#244
Oliver Peoples
Category: Eyewear & Opticians
Average price: Modest
Area: Downtown
Address: 875 S Grand Central Pkwy,
Ste 1605, Las Vegas, NV 89106
Phone: (702) 362-2000

#245
Hattitude
Category: Accessories
Average price: Expensive
Area: Eastside
Address: 3663 Las Vegas Blvd
S Las Vegas, NV 89109
Phone: (702) 732-1232

#246
Hobbytown USA
Category: Toy Store, Hobby Shop
Average price: Expensive
Area: Westside
Address: 4590 W Sahara
Las Vegas, NV 89102
Phone: (702) 889-9554

#247
Topshop
Category: Women's Clothing,
Men's Clothing, Accessories
Average price: Expensive
Area: Eastside
Address: 3200 Las Vegas Blvd
S Las Vegas, NV 89109
Phone: (702) 866-0646

#248
H&M
Category: Women's Clothing,
Men's Clothing, Accessories
Average price: Modest
Area: Southeast
Address: 6605 Las Vegas Blvd
Las Vegas, NV 89119
Phone: (702) 260-1481

#249
Prada
Category: Women's Clothing
Average price: Exclusive
Area: Eastside
Address: 3600 Las Vegas Blvd
S Las Vegas, NV 89109
Phone: (702) 866-6886

#250
Party City
Category: Party Supplies, Costume
Average price: Modest
Area: Eastside
Address: 4020 S Maryland Pkwy
Las Vegas, NV 89119
Phone: (702) 893-4600

#251
TaylorMade Golf Experience
Category: Golf, Outdoor Gear, Beer,
Wine & Spirits
Average price: Modest
Area: Southeast
Address: 6730 Las Vegas Blvd
S Las Vegas, NV 89119
Phone: (702) 896-4100

#252
Target Greatland
Category: Department Store
Average price: Modest
Area: Centennial
Address: 6480 Sky Pointe Dr
Las Vegas, NV 89131
Phone: (702) 839-1591

#253
Target
Category: Department Store, Grocery
Average price: Modest
Area: Centennial
Address: 6371 N Decatur Blvd
Las Vegas, NV 89130
Phone: (702) 515-8540

#254
Bed Bath & Beyond
Category: Home Decor, Kitchen & Bath
Average price: Modest
Area: Spring Valley
Address: 7175 Arroyo Crossing Pkwy
Las Vegas, NV 89113
Phone: (702) 617-4018

#255
Desert Rock Sport
Category: Sporting Goods
Average price: Modest
Area: Westside
Address: 8221 W Charleston Blvd
Las Vegas, NV 89117
Phone: (702) 254-1143

#256
Suite 160
Category: Shoe Store
Average price: Expensive
Area: The Strip
Address: 3930 S Las Vegas Blvd
Las Vegas, NV 89119
Phone: (702) 304-2513

#257
Henri Bendel
Category: Women's Clothing, Accessories
Average price: Expensive
Area: The Strip
Address: 3200 Las Vegas Blvd
S Las Vegas, NV 89109
Phone: (702) 836-9829

#258
Electric Lemonade Shop
Category: Vintage & Consignment,
Women's Clothing
Average price: Modest
Area: Downtown
Address: 220 E Charleston Blvd
Las Vegas, NV 89104
Phone: (702) 776-7766

#259
Hobby Lobby
Category: Arts & Crafts
Average price: Modest
Area: Spring Valley
Address: 4955 S Fort Apache Rd
Las Vegas, NV 89148
Phone: (702) 369-0064

#260
A Gamer's Paradise
Category: Electronics Repair,
Videos & Video Game Rental
Average price: Inexpensive
Area: University
Address: 1550 E Tropicana Ave
Las Vegas, NV 89119
Phone: (702) 478-3131

#261
The Gallery
Category: Art Gallery
Average price: Exclusive
Area: Eastside
Address: 3720 Las Vegas Blvd
S Las Vegas, NV 89109
Phone: (702) 590-8741

#262
Kohl's Department Store
Category: Shoe Store,
Men's Clothing, Women's Clothing
Average price: Modest
Area: Westside
Address: 8671 W Charleston Blvd
Las Vegas, NV 89117
Phone: (702) 387-3191

#263
Target
Category: Department Store
Average price: Inexpensive
Area: Southeast
Address: 9725 S Eastern Ave
Las Vegas, NV 89162
Phone: (702) 914-9555

#264
Nike Factory Store
Category: Sport Wear, Shoe Store
Average price: Modest
Area: Downtown
Address: 905 S Grand Central Pkwy
Las Vegas, NV 89106
Phone: (702) 382-8055

#265
Kenneth Cole
Category: Men's Clothing,
Women's Clothing, Shoe Store
Average price: Expensive
Area: The Strip
Address: 3377 South Las Vegas Boulevard
Las Vegas, NV 89109
Phone: (702) 836-1916

#266
Ted Baker Outlet
Category: Outlet Store
Average price: Expensive
Area: Downtown
Address: 875 S Grand Central Pkwy
Las Vegas, NV 89106
Phone: (702) 385-0090

#267
Gambler's General Store
Category: Hobby Shop
Average price: Modest
Area: Downtown
Address: 800 S Main St
Las Vegas, NV 89101
Phone: (702) 382-9903

#268
Vons
Category: Bakeries, Grocery, Florist
Average price: Modest
Area: Southeast
Address: 475 E Windmill Ln
Las Vegas, NV 89123
Phone: (702) 896-7544

#269
C-A-L Ranch Store
Category: Department Store
Average price: Modest
Area: Westside
Address: 232 N Jones
Las Vegas, NV 89107
Phone: (702) 430-7002

#270
The Black Room
Category: Lingerie, Adult
Average price: Modest
Area: Downtown
Address: 1000 E Sahara Ave
Las Vegas, NV 89104
Phone: (702) 685-8688

#271
Centennial Hills Family Eye Care
Category: Eyewear & Opticians,
Optometrists
Average price: Modest
Area: Centennial
Address: 7090 N Durango Blvd #110
Las Vegas, NV 89149
Phone: (702) 220-3937

#272
Ross Dress For Less
Category: Department Store
Average price: Inexpensive
Area: The Strip
Address: 3001 Las Vegas Blvd
S Las Vegas, NV 89109
Phone: (702) 731-3361

#273
Star Costume
& Theatrical Supply
Category: Costume, Accessories, Wigs
Average price: Modest
Area: Westside
Address: 3230 S Valley View Blvd
Las Vegas, NV 89102
Phone: (702) 731-5014

#274
Vapeco
Category: Tobacco Shop
Average price: Modest
Area: Westside
Address: 8380 W Sahara Ave
Las Vegas, NV 89117
Phone: (702) 979-6000

#275
Marshalls
Category: Department Store
Average price: Inexpensive
Area: Summerlin
Address: 10950 W Charleston Boulevard,
Las Vegas, NV 89135
Phone: (702) 838-7822

#276
Rhapsodille
Category: Women's Clothing
Average price: Inexpensive
Area: Southeast
Address: 2350 E Serene Ave
Las Vegas, NV 89123
Phone: (702) 227-5003

#277
Sam's Club
Category: Department Store
Average price: Modest
Area: Spring Valley
Address: 7100 Arroyo Crossing Pkwy
Las Vegas, NV 89113
Phone: (702) 260-9003

#278
Sam's Club
Category: Department Store
Average price: Modest
Area: Southeast
Address: 1910 E Serene Ave
Las Vegas, NV 89123
Phone: (702) 614-3372

#279
Zombie Zone
Category: Hobby Shop
Average price: Modest
Area: Westside
Address: 931 S Rainbow Blvd.
Las Vegas, NV 89145
Phone: (702) 362-1500

#280
Rhapsodielle
Category: Women's Clothing
Average price: Modest
Area: Southwest
Address: 8455 W Warm Springs Rd
Las Vegas, NV 89113
Phone: (702) 876-8922

#281
Intermix
Category: Fashion
Average price: Expensive
Area: Eastside
Address: 3500 Las Vegas Blvd, South
Las Vegas, NV 89109
Phone: (702) 731-1922

#282
Intermix
Category: Fashion
Average price: Expensive
Area: Eastside
Address: 3500 Las Vegas Blvd,
South, Las Vegas, NV 89109
Phone: (702) 731-1922

#283
Sweet Bubble Bath Confections
Category: Cosmetics & Beauty
Average price: Modest
Area: Southeast
Address: 6569 Las Vegas Blvd
S Las Vegas, NV 89119
Phone: (702) 778-5545

#284
The Vitacost Store
Category: Discount Store
Average price: Modest
Area: Southeast
Address: 840 Pilot Rd
Las Vegas, NV 89119
Phone: (702) 263-7193

#285
Louis Vuitton
Category: Luggage
Average price: Exclusive
Area: The Strip
Address: 3500 Las Vegas Blvd
S Las Vegas, NV 89109
Phone: (702) 732-1227

#286
Barnes & Noble
Category: Booktore
Average price: Modest
Area: Westside
Address: 8915 W Charleston Blvd
Las Vegas, NV 89117
Phone: (702) 242-1987

#287
Nike Factory Store
Category: Shoe Store
Average price: Modest
Area: Southeast
Address: 7400 Las Vegas Boulevard
S Las Vegas, NV 89123
Phone: (702) 896-7444

#288
Patty's Closet
Category: Women's Clothing
Average price: Modest
Area: Centennial
Address: 7010 N Durango Dr
Las Vegas, NV 89149
Phone: (702) 395-6455

#289
Lovebug Baby
Category: Baby Gear & Furniture
Average price: Modest
Area: Southeast, Anthem
Address: 9911 S Eastern Ave
Las Vegas, NV 89183
Phone: (702) 367-2229

#290
Marc By Marc Jacobs
Category: Men's Clothing,
Women's Clothing, Accessories
Average price: Expensive
Area: The Strip
Address: 3500 Las Vegas Blvd
Las Vegas, NV 89109
Phone: (702) 734-0220

#291
JCPenney
Category: Department Store, Baby Gear &
Furniture, Women's Clothing
Average price: Modest
Area: Spring Valley
Address: 4485 S Grand Canyon Dr
Las Vegas, NV 89147
Phone: (702) 876-3644

#292
The Shoppes at The Palazzo
Category: Shopping Center
Average price: Exclusive
Area: The Strip
Address: 3327 Las Vegas Blvd
S Las Vegas, NV 89109
Phone: (702) 414-4525

#293
Target
Category: Department Store, Grocery
Average price: Modest
Area: Westside
Address: 8750 W Charleston Blvd
Las Vegas, NV 89101
Phone: (702) 933-2300

#294
Walgreens
Category: Drugstore, Cosmetics & Beauty,
Convenience Store
Average price: Inexpensive
Area: The Strip
Address: 3765 Las Vegas Blvd
S Las Vegas, NV 89109
Phone: (702) 739-9645

#295
Nike Factory Store
Category: Shoe Store
Average price: Modest
Area: Anthem
Address: 9851 S Eastern Ave
Las Vegas, NV 89183
Phone: (702) 407-0165

#296
Express
Category: Fashion
Average price: Modest
Area: The Strip
Address: 3500 Las Vegas Blvd
S Las Vegas, NV 89109
Phone: (702) 892-0424

#297
Jimmy Choo
Category: Accessories
Average price: Exclusive
Area: Eastside
Address: 3500 Las Vegas Boulevard
S Las Vegas, NV 89109
Phone: (702) 691-2097

#298
**The District
At Green Valley Ranch**
Category: Shopping Center, Nightlife
Average price: Modest
Area: Anthem
Address: 2240 Village Walk Dr
Henderson, NV 89015
Phone: (702) 564-8595

#299
**Century 23 Computers
& Technology**
Category: IT Services & Computer Repair,
Computers
Average price: Expensive
Area: Westside
Address: 5000 W. Oakey Blvd.
Las Vegas, NV 89146
Phone: (702) 870-1534

#300
Lovo Cigars
Category: Tobacco Shop
Average price: Inexpensive
Area: Downtown
Address: 450 Fremont St
Las Vegas, NV 89101
Phone: (702) 384-4427

#301
Antiquities International
Category: Antiques
Average price: Exclusive
Area: The Strip
Address: 3500 S Las Vegas Blvd
Las Vegas, NV 89109
Phone: (702) 792-2274

#302
Marciano
Category: Women's Clothing, Accessories
Average price: Modest
Area: The Strip
Address: 3500 Las Vegas Blvd
S Las Vegas, NV 89109
Phone: (702) 369-0322

#303
Albertsons
Category: Grocery, Drugstore
Average price: Modest
Area: Centennial
Address: 8410 Farm Rd
Las Vegas, NV 89131
Phone: (702) 658-2030

#304
Boot Barn
Category: Shoe Store,
Men's Clothing, Women's Clothing
Average price: Expensive
Area: Southeast
Address: 7265 Las Vegas Blvd.
South Las Vegas, NV 89119
Phone: (702) 260-1888

#305
YESnick Vision Center
Category: Optometrists, Ophthalmologists,
Eyewear & Opticians
Average price: Modest
Area: Spring Valley, South Summerlin
Address: 10198 W Flamingo Rd
Las Vegas, NV 89147
Phone: (702) 966-2020

#306
**Performance Footwear
& Wide Shoes**
Category: Shoe Store
Average price: Modest
Area: The Lakes
Address: 9151 W Sahara Ave
Las Vegas, NV 89117
Phone: (702) 940-0150

#307
Sport Chalet
Category: Sporting Goods
Average price: Modest
Area: Westside
Address: 8825 W Charleston Blvd
Las Vegas, NV 89117
Phone: (702) 255-7570

#308
Smith's Food & Drug Center
Category: Grocery, Drugstore
Average price: Modest
Area: Centennial
Address: 7130 N Durango Dr
Las Vegas, NV 89149
Phone: (702) 647-2799

#309
Harry Winston
Category: Jewelry
Average price: Exclusive
Area: The Strip
Address: 3500 Las Vegas Blvd
S Las Vegas, NV 89109
Phone: (702) 933-7370

#310
Ancient Creations
Category: Jewelry
Average price: Expensive
Area: The Strip
Address: 3377 Las Vegas Blvd
S Las Vegas, NV 89109
Phone: (702) 414-3701

#311
Pink Spot Vapors
Category: Tobacco Shop
Average price: Modest
Area: Spring Valley
Address: 7290 Arroyo Crossing Pkwy
Spring Valley, NV 89113
Phone: (702) 655-8273

#312
Destination XL
Category: Men's Clothing
Average price: Modest
Area: Eastside
Address: 4211 Paradise Rd
Las Vegas, NV 89169
Phone: (702) 737-4855

#313
**Still Smoking Vapor
& Smoke Shop**
Category: Tobacco Shop
Average price: Expensive
Area: Westside
Address: 2605 S Decatur Blvd
Las Vegas, NV 89102
Phone: (702) 227-3021

#314
Eyesite of Anthem
Category: Optometrists,
Eyewear & Opticians
Average price: Modest
Area: Anthem
Address: 2505 Anthem Village Dr
Henderson, NV 89052
Phone: (702) 476-2225

#315
Oh My Godard Gallery
Category: Art Gallery
Average price: Expensive
Area: The Strip
Address: 3663 Las Vegas Boulevard
S Las Vegas, NV 89109
Phone: (702) 699-9099

#316
Winky Designs
Category: Watches, Jewelry, Accessories
Average price: Modest
Area: Downtown
Address: 707 Fremont St
Las Vegas, NV 89101
Phone: (858) 779-4659

#317
Glam Factory Vintage
Category: Thrift Store, Antiques
Average price: Modest
Area: Downtown
Address: 211 E Colorado St
Las Vegas, NV 89104
Phone: (702) 443-0131

#318
Roman Times
Category: Jewelry
Average price: Exclusive
Area: The Strip
Address: 3500 Las Vegas Boulevard
S Las Vegas, NV 89109
Phone: (702) 733-8687

#319
**See Right Now
with Timothy Perozek MD**
Category: Optometrists, Ophthalmologists,
Eyewear & Opticians
Average price: Modest
Area: Summerlin
Address: 653 N Town Center Dr
Las Vegas, NV 89144
Phone: (702) 982-1360

#320
CVS Pharmacy
Category: Drugstore
Average price: Inexpensive
Area: Eastside
Address: 4490 Paradise Rd
Las Vegas, NV 89109
Phone: (702) 696-7126

#321
GlamSquadShop
Category: Women's Clothing,
Accessories, Shoe Store
Average price: Inexpensive
Area: Spring Valley
Address: 5165 S Fort Apache Rd
Las Vegas, NV 89148
Phone: (702) 456-4526

#322
Celebrations Bridal & Fashion
Category: Bridal, Formal Wear
Average price: Modest
Area: Westside
Address: 3131 S Jones Blvd
Las Vegas, NV 89146
Phone: (702) 222-0507

#323
Bellagio Gallery of Fine Art
Category: Art Gallery, Museum
Average price: Modest
Area: The Strip
Address: 3600 S Las Vegas Blvd
Las Vegas, NV 89109
Phone: (702) 693-7871

#324
**Las Vegas Premium
Outlets - South**
Category: Shopping Center,
Outlet Store
Average price: Modest
Area: Southeast
Address: 7400 Las Vegas Blvd
S Las Vegas, NV 89123
Phone: (702) 896-5599

#325
Smith's Food & Drug Store
Category: Grocery, Department Store
Average price: Modest
Area: Westside
Address: 9851 W Charleston Blvd
Las Vegas, NV 89117
Phone: (702) 946-1200

#326
The Amore Cosmetics
Category: Cosmetics & Beauty
Average price: Inexpensive
Area: Chinatown
Address: 4215 Spring Mountain Rd
Las Vegas, NV 89102
Phone: (702) 259-5577

#327
French Connection
Category: Men's Clothing,
Women's Clothing
Average price: Expensive
Area: Eastside
Address: 3663 Las Vegas Blvd,
Ste 820, Las Vegas, NV 89109
Phone: (702) 733-6420

#328
Rodney Lough Jr.
Category: Art Gallery
Average price: Exclusive
Area: The Strip
Address: 3720 Las Vegas Blvd S
Las Vegas, NV 89109
Phone: (702) 522-9400

#329
Optic Gallery Family Eye Care
Category: Eyewear & Opticians,
Optometrists, Medical Supplies
Average price: Modest
Area: Westside
Address: 2580 S Decatur Blvd
Las Vegas, NV 89102
Phone: (702) 876-2020

#330
Boulevard Trophy
Category: Trophy Shop
Average price: Modest
Area: Southeast
Address: 5007 Tamarus St
Las Vegas, NV 89119
Phone: (702) 736-3130

#331
Liquid Vape House
Category: Tobacco Shop
Average price: Modest
Area: Southeast
Address: 3421 E Tropicana
Las Vegas, NV 89121
Phone: (702) 331-3030

#332
Lululemon Athletica
Category: Sport Wear,
Women's Clothing
Average price: Expensive
Area: Westside
Address: 1215 S Fort Apache Rd
Las Vegas, NV 89117
Phone: (702) 233-5923

#333
Eyes & Optics
Category: Optometrists,
Eyewear & Opticians
Average price: Modest
Area: Westside
Address: 2261 S Rainbow Blvd
Las Vegas, NV 89146
Phone: (702) 254-0332

#334
Pick N Puff
Category: Tobacco Shop
Average price: Modest
Area: Southeast
Address: 5030 Paradise Rd
Las Vegas, NV 89119
Phone: (702) 758-7709

#335
Blackbird Studio
Category: Art Gallery
Average price: Modest
Area: Downtown
Address: 1551 S Commerce St
Las Vegas, NV 89102
Phone: (702) 782-0319

#336
Backstage Beauty Salon
Category: Hair Salon,
Cosmetics & Beauty
Average price: Modest
Area: Centennial, Northwest
Address: 5643 Centennial Center Blvd
Las Vegas, NV 89149
Phone: (702) 340-4771

#337
Tadashi Shoji
Category: Bridal, Formal Wear,
Plus Size Fashion
Average price: Expensive
Area: The Strip
Address: 3500 Las Vegas Boulevard
S Las Vegas, NV 89109
Phone: (702) 733-6071

#338
Frame Fixer
Category: Eyewear & Opticians
Average price: Modest
Area: Southeast
Address: 9480 S Eastern Ave
Las Vegas, NV 89123
Phone: (702) 733-7879

#339
Forget Me Nots Floral & Gift
Category: Florist
Average price: Inexpensive
Area: Northwest
Address: 5803 W Craig Rd
Las Vegas, NV 89130
Phone: (702) 457-9200

#340
Sin City Gallery
Category: Art Gallery
Average price: Modest
Area: Downtown
Address: 107 E Charleston Blvd
Las Vegas, NV 89104
Phone: (702) 608-2461

#341
Full Circle Couture
Category: Women's Clothing,
Thrift Store
Average price: Inexpensive
Area: Westside
Address: 9440 W Sahara
Las Vegas, NV 89117
Phone: (702) 685-1901

#342
Haynes Bowling Supply
Category: Bowling, Sporting Goods
Average price: Modest
Area: Spring Valley
Address: 5255 S Decatur Blvd
Las Vegas, NV 89118
Phone: (702) 982-2255

#343
Vegas Bike Store
Category: Bike Rentals, Bikes
Average price: Modest
Area: Spring Valley
Address: 3955 S Durango Dr
Las Vegas, NV 89147
Phone: (702) 586-5500

#344
Shall We Play?...a Game
Category: Hobby Shop
Average price: Modest
Area: Centennial
Address: 7120 N Durango Dr
Las Vegas, NV 89149
Phone: (702) 721-7974

#345
Tourneau
Category: Watches, Jewelry,
Watch Repair
Average price: Exclusive
Area: The Strip
Address: 3500 Las Vegas Blvd
S Las Vegas, NV 89109
Phone: (702) 732-8463

#346
The Grand Canal Shoppes
Category: Shopping Center
Average price: Expensive
Area: Eastside
Address: 3377 Las Vegas Blvd S
Las Vegas, NV 89109
Phone: (702) 414-4525

#347
Tiffany & Co
Category: Jewelry
Average price: Modest
Area: The Strip
Address: 3200 Las Vegas Blvd
Paradise, NV 89109
Phone: (702) 734-2461

#348
Dior Beauty Boutique
Category: Cosmetics & Beauty
Average price: Expensive
Area: Eastside
Address: 3327 Las Vegas Blvd
S Las Vegas, NV 89109
Phone: (702) 734-1102

#349
Dollar General Market
Category: Discount Store
Average price: Inexpensive
Area: Spring Valley
Address: 8610 Spring Mountain Rd
Las Vegas, NV 89117
Phone: (702) 892-0295

#350
Tory Burch
Category: Women's Clothing
Average price: Expensive
Area: Eastside
Address: 3500 Las Vegas Blvd.
South Las Vegas, NV 89109
Phone: (702) 369-3459

#351
Corsa Collections
Category: Jewelry, Accessories
Average price: Exclusive
Area: The Strip
Address: 3377 Las Vegas Blvd
Las Vegas, NV 89109
Phone: (702) 733-9442

#352
Buffalo Exchange
Category: Vintage & Consignment, Men's
Clothing, Women's Clothing
Average price: Modest
Area: University, Eastside
Address: 4110 S Maryland Pkwy
Las Vegas, NV 89119
Phone: (702) 791-3960

#353
Apple Store
Category: Electronics, Computers
Average price: Expensive
Area: Southeast
Address: 6671 Las Vegas Blvd
Las Vegas, NV 89119
Phone: (702) 221-8826

#354
Victoria's Secret
Category: Cosmetics & Beauty, Lingerie
Average price: Modest
Area: The Strip
Address: 3500 Las Vegas Blvd
S Las Vegas, NV 89109
Phone: (702) 893-0903

#355
Louis Vuitton
Category: Leather Goods, Accessories
Average price: Exclusive
Area: The Strip
Address: 3600 S Las Vegas Blvd
Las Vegas, NV 89108
Phone: (702) 691-2777

#356
Aaron Brothers Art & Framing
Category: Art Supplies
Average price: Modest
Area: Westside
Address: 9765 W Charleston Boulevard
Las Vegas, NV 89117
Phone: (702) 940-5330

#357
OTM Fight Shop
Category: Sport Wear, Outdoor Gear
Average price: Modest
Area: Chinatown
Address: 3755 Spring Mountain Rd
Las Vegas, NV 89102
Phone: (702) 383-0002

#358
Childs' Play
Category: Arcade, Toy Store
Average price: Modest
Area: Centennial
Address: 7060 N Durango Dr
Las Vegas, NV 89149
Phone: (702) 834-5500

#359
Sur La Table
Category: Kitchen & Bath
Average price: Modest
Area: The Strip
Address: 3200 Las Vegas Blvd
S Las Vegas, NV 89109
Phone: (702) 732-2706

#360
Michael Kors
Category: Accessories
Average price: Expensive
Area: Eastside
Address: 3500 Las Vegas Blvd.
South, Las Vegas, NV 89109
Phone: (702) 869-0010

#361
RC Willey
Category: Furniture Store,
Appliances, Mattresses
Average price: Modest
Area: South Summerlin
Address: 3850 S Town Center Dr
Las Vegas, NV 89135
Phone: (702) 515-2600

#362
Uniform Sport
Category: Sporting Goods
Average price: Modest
Area: Southeast
Address: 7400 Las Vegas Blvd
S Ste 46, Las Vegas, NV 89123
Phone: (702) 869-1640

#363
The Art of Shaving
Category: Barbers,
Cosmetics & Beauty
Average price: Expensive
Area: The Strip
Address: 3377 Las Vegas Blvd
Las Vegas, NV 89109
Phone: (702) 836-9419

#364
Paul Smith
Category: Fashion
Average price: Expensive
Area: The Strip
Address: City Center
Las Vegas, NV 89109
Phone: (702) 796-2640

#365
JCPenney
Category: Baby Gear & Furniture,
Women's Clothing, Department Store
Average price: Modest
Area: Eastside
Address: 3542 S Maryland Parkway
Las Vegas, NV 89169
Phone: (702) 735-5131

#366
Theatre7
Category: Cinema, Art Gallery
Average price: Inexpensive
Area: Downtown
Address: 1406 S 3rd St
Las Vegas, NV 89104
Phone: (702) 568-9663

#367
D & G Dolce & Gabbana
Category: Women's Clothing, Accessories,
Men's Clothing
Average price: Exclusive
Area: The Strip
Address: 3500 Las Vegas Blvd
S Las Vegas, NV 89109
Phone: (702) 732-9292

#368
Fossil Company Store
Category: Outlet Store
Average price: Modest
Area: Southeast
Address: 7400 Las Vegas Blvd
S Ofc, Las Vegas, NV 89123
Phone: (702) 897-4770

#369
Cartridge World
Category: Office Equipment
Average price: Modest
Area: Southeast
Address: 9550 S Eastern Ave
Las Vegas, NV 89123
Phone: (702) 586-0634

#370
Direct Beauty Supply
Category: Cosmetics & Beauty
Average price: Inexpensive
Area: Chinatown
Address: 3545 S Decatur Blvd
Las Vegas, NV 89103
Phone: (702) 437-3376

#371
Pier 1 Imports
Category: Department Store
Average price: Modest
Area: Westside
Address: 8945 W Charleston
Boulevard, Las Vegas, NV 89117
Phone: (702) 255-9136

#372
Sanrio
Category: Shopping
Average price: Modest
Area: Eastside
Address: 3200 Las Vegas Blvd
S Las Vegas, NV 89109
Phone: (702) 699-9373

#373
The Home Depot
Category: Nurseries & Gardening,
Appliances, Hardware Store
Average price: Modest
Area: Southeast
Address: 2200 E Serene Ave
Las Vegas, NV 89123
Phone: (702) 837-4300

#374
Chic Cache
Category: Accessories, Jewelry
Average price: Inexpensive
Area: Westside
Address: 5191 W Charleston Blvd
Las Vegas, NV 89146
Phone: (702) 822-1046

#375
T-Bird Jewels
Category: Watches, Jewelry,
Jewelry Repair
Average price: Expensive
Area: Summerlin
Address: 1990 Village Center Cir
Las Vegas, NV 89134
Phone: (702) 256-3900

#376
Golf Galaxy
Category: Sport Wear,
Outdoor Gear, Golf Equipment
Average price: Expensive
Area: Westside
Address: 8621 W Charleston Boulevard
Las Vegas, NV 89117
Phone: (702) 932-4110

#377
**Las Vegas Cyclery
& Running Center**
Category: Bikes, Bike Rentals
Average price: Modest
Area: South Summerlin
Address: 10575 Discovery Dr
Las Vegas, NV 89135
Phone: (702) 596-2953

#378
Plato's Closet
Category: Thrift Store,
Vintage & Consignment
Average price: Modest
Area: Centennial, Northwest
Address: 5643 Centennial Center Blvd
Las Vegas, NV 89149
Phone: (702) 818-3333

#379
Donald J Pliner
Category: Shoe Store
Average price: Exclusive
Area: The Strip
Address: 3500 Las Vegas Blvd
S Las Vegas, NV 89109
Phone: (702) 796-0900

#380
Ann Taylor
Category: Accessories
Average price: Expensive
Area: Westside
Address: 1013 S Rampart Blvd
Las Vegas, NV 89145
Phone: (702) 946-5001

#381
Sweet Beads
Category: Arts & Crafts, Jewelry
Average price: Modest
Area: Westside
Address: 5734 W Charleston Blvd
Las Vegas, NV 89146
Phone: (702) 629-6010

#382
Gap
Category: Men's Clothing, Women's
Clothing, Children's Clothing
Average price: Modest
Area: Eastside
Address: 3500 Las Vegas Blvd
S Las Vegas, NV 89109
Phone: (702) 796-0010

#383
**Ulta Salon Cosmetics
& Fragrance**
Category: Cosmetics & Beauty
Average price: Modest
Area: Southeast, Anthem
Address: 9857 S Eastern Ave
Las Vegas, NV 89183
Phone: (702) 270-2410

#384
Macy's
Category: Department Store,
Men's Clothing, Women's Clothing
Average price: Modest
Area: The Strip
Address: 3200 S. Las Vegas Blvd.
Las Vegas, NV 89109
Phone: (702) 731-5111

#385
Gold & Silver Pawn Shop
Category: Pawn Shop
Average price: Expensive
Area: Downtown
Address: 713 Las Vegas Blvd
S Las Vegas, NV 89101
Phone: (702) 385-7912

#386
Tory Burch
Category: Outlet Store
Average price: Expensive
Area: Downtown
Address: 8755 S Grand Central Pkwy
Las Vegas, NV 89106
Phone: (702) 385-0679

#387
Pharmacy Boardshop
Category: Sport Wear,
Men's Clothing, Shoe Store
Average price: Modest
Area: Southeast
Address: 1920 E Serene Ave
Las Vegas, NV 89123
Phone: (702) 614-9591

#388
Pink The Boutique
Category: Women's Clothing, Accessories
Average price: Modest
Area: Westside
Address: 740 S Rampart
Las Vegas, NV 89145
Phone: (702) 932-7465

#389
DiyFlavorShack
Category: Tobacco Shop
Average price: Modest
Area: Northwest
Address: 3231 N Decatur Blvd
Las Vegas, NV 89130
Phone: (702) 807-7215

#390
Bath & Body Works
Category: Cosmetics & Beauty
Average price: Modest
Area: Westside
Address: 8800 W Charleston Boulevard
Las Vegas, NV 89117
Phone: (702) 944-4700

#391
Levi's Store
Category: Men's Clothing,
Women's Clothing, Accessories
Average price: Modest
Area: The Strip
Address: 3200 Las Vegas Boulevard
Las Vegas, NV 89109
Phone: (702) 731-1866

#392
Off 5th Saks Fifth Avenue Outlet
Category: Women's Clothing,
Department Store, Jewelry
Average price: Modest
Area: Southeast
Address: 7680 Las Vegas Blvd
S Las Vegas, NV 89123
Phone: (702) 263-7692

#393
Meadows Mall
Category: Shopping Center
Average price: Modest
Area: Westside
Address: 4300 Meadows Lane #10
Las Vegas, NV 89107
Phone: (702) 878-3331

#394
Victoria's Secret
Category: Women's Clothing, Lingerie
Average price: Modest
Area: Eastside
Address: 3327 Las Vegas Blvd
S Las Vegas, NV 89109
Phone: (702) 696-0110

#395
Kate Spade Outlet
Category: Accessories
Average price: Modest
Area: Downtown
Address: 875 S Grand Central Pkwy
Las Vegas, NV 89106
Phone: (702) 255-8777

#396
Prada
Category: Fashion
Average price: Exclusive
Area: The Strip
Address: 3720 S Las Vegas Blvd
Las Vegas, NV 89109
Phone: (702) 740-3000

#397
The Home Depot
Category: Hardware Store,
Nurseries & Gardening, Appliances
Average price: Modest
Area: Westside
Address: 9705 W Charleston Blvd
Las Vegas, NV 89117
Phone: (702) 940-2426

#398
Target
Category: Department Store
Average price: Modest
Area: Eastside
Address: 4001 S Maryland Pkwy
Las Vegas, NV 89136
Phone: (702) 732-2218

#399
Urban Outfitters
Category: Men's Clothing,
Women's Clothing
Average price: Expensive
Area: The Strip
Address: 3663 Las Vegas Blvd
S Las Vegas, NV 89109
Phone: (702) 733-0058

#400
Lowe's Home Improvement
Category: Building Supplies, Hardware
Store, Nurseries & Gardening
Average price: Modest
Area: Anthem
Address: 9955 S Eastern Ave W
Henderson, NV 89123
Phone: (702) 270-7400

#401
Bonanza General Store
Category: Flowers & Gifts
Average price: Inexpensive
Area: The Strip
Address: 2400 Las Vegas Blvd
S Las Vegas, NV 89104
Phone: (702) 384-0005

#402
Tiffany and Co.
Category: Watches, Jewelry
Average price: Exclusive
Area: Eastside
Address: 3500 Las Vegas Blvd
S Las Vegas, NV 89109
Phone: (702) 644-3065

#403
Magnolia Lane
Category: Home Decor
Average price: Expensive
Area: Anthem
Address: 2260 Village Walk Dr
Henderson, NV 89052
Phone: (702) 233-4438

#404
Tiffany & Co
Category: Jewelry,
Accessories, Watches
Average price: Exclusive
Area: The Strip
Address: 3720 Las Vegas Blvd
S Las Vegas, NV 89158
Phone: (702) 545-9090

#405
AAA Bar & Restaurant Supply
Category: Wholesale Store,
Discount Store
Average price: Modest
Area: Eastside
Address: 2025 E Sahara Ave
Las Vegas, NV 89104
Phone: (702) 678-6005

#406
Joe's Jeans Premium Outlets
Category: Women's Clothing,
Men's Clothing, Children's Clothing
Average price: Expensive
Area: Downtown
Address: 755 S Grand Central Pkwy
Las Vegas, NV 89106
Phone: (702) 382-5510

#407
Best Kept Secret Boutique
Category: Women's Clothing
Average price: Modest
Area: Summerlin
Address: 1930 Village Center Cir
Las Vegas, NV 89134
Phone: (702) 255-1100

#408
Christian Dior
Category: Women's Clothing,
Leather Goods, Accessories
Average price: Exclusive
Area: The Strip
Address: 3720 S Las Vegas Blvd
Las Vegas, NV 89109
Phone: (702) 597-0941

#409
Lamps Plus
Category: Lighting Fixtures & Equipment,
Home Decor,
Furniture Store
Average price: Modest
Area: Westside
Address: 8800 W Charleston Blvd
Las Vegas, NV 89117
Phone: (702) 242-4995

#410
Summerlin Jewelers
Category: Jewelry
Average price: Modest
Area: Summerlin
Address: 2221 N Rampart Blvd
Las Vegas, NV 89128
Phone: (702) 243-8240

#411
Cowtown Boots
Category: Shoe Store
Average price: Modest
Area: Eastside
Address: 1080 E Flamingo Rd
Las Vegas, NV 89119
Phone: (702) 737-8469

#412
The Tiger Lily Flower Shop
Category: Florist
Average price: Modest
Area: Downtown
Address: 700 E Sahara Ave
Las Vegas, NV 89104
Phone: (702) 737-7077

#413
Patty's Closet
Category: Women's Clothing
Average price: Modest
Area: Southeast
Address: 6659 Las Vegas Blvd
Las Vegas, NV 89119
Phone: (702) 617-6452

#414
The Home Depot
Category: Nurseries & Gardening,
Appliances, Hardware Store
Average price: Modest
Area: Southeast
Address: 6025 South Pecos Road
Las Vegas, NV 89120
Phone: (702) 434-1948

#415
Cycle Gear
Category: Motorcycle Repair,
Sporting Goods, Motorcycle Dealer
Average price: Modest
Address: 6280 S. Pecos Rd.
Las Vegas East, NV 89120
Phone: (702) 435-0635

#416
Williams-Sonoma
Category: Kitchen & Bath
Average price: Expensive
Area: Westside
Address: 1001 South Rampart Blvd
Las Vegas, NV 89145
Phone: (702) 938-9480

#417
John Varvatos
At the Forum Shop
Category: Accessories
Average price: Exclusive
Area: Eastside
Address: 3500 Las Vegas Blvd
S Las Vegas, NV 89109
Phone: (702) 939-0922

#418
Boutique Talulah
Category: Women's Clothing,
Men's Clothing
Average price: Exclusive
Area: The Strip
Address: 3200 Las Vegas Blvd
S Las Vegas, NV 89109
Phone: (702) 431-2288

#419
Maurices
Category: Accessories,
Women's Clothing
Average price: Modest
Area: Spring Valley
Address: 7235 Arroyo Crossing
Pkwy Ste 105, Las Vegas, NV 89113
Phone: (702) 263-4898

#420
Banana Republic
Category: Men's Clothing,
Women's Clothing
Average price: Modest
Area: Westside
Address: 1049 S Rampart Blvd
Las Vegas, NV 89145
Phone: (702) 938-7090

#421
**Michael E Minden
Diamond Jewelers**
Category: Jewelry
Average price: Modest
Area: The Strip
Address: 3200 S Las Vegas Blvd,
Ste 2475, Las Vegas, NV 89109
Phone: (702) 253-5588

#422
Kush Fine Art
Category: Art Gallery
Average price: Exclusive
Area: The Strip
Address: 3663 Las Vegas Blvd
S Las Vegas, NV 89109
Phone: (702) 363-1990

#423
Bath & Body Works
Category: Cosmetics & Beauty
Average price: Modest
Area: Summerlin
Address: 1946 Village Center Cir
Las Vegas, NV 89134
Phone: (702) 233-9841

#424
Bath & Body Works
Category: Cosmetics & Beauty
Average price: Modest
Area: Eastside
Address: 3500 Las Vegas Blvd S
Las Vegas, NV 89109
Phone: (702) 796-4902

#425
Adidas
Category: Shoe Store
Average price: Modest
Area: Southeast
Address: 7400 Las Vegas Blvd
S Ste 163, Las Vegas, NV 89123
Phone: (702) 256-3429

#426
Michael's
Category: Arts & Crafts
Average price: Modest
Area: Westside
Address: 1251 S Decatur Blvd
Las Vegas, NV 89102
Phone: (702) 259-0034

#427
99 Cents Only
Category: Shopping,
Convenience Store
Average price: Inexpensive
Area: Spring Valley
Address: 4920 S Fort Apache Rd
Las Vegas, NV 89148
Phone: (702) 876-6699

#428
Sam's Club
Category: Department Store, Grocery
Average price: Modest
Area: Southeast
Address: 5101 S Pecos Rd
Las Vegas, NV 89120
Phone: (702) 247-1129

#429
Walmart
Category: Department Store,
Grocery, Mobile Phones
Average price: Inexpensive
Area: Southeast
Address: 3075 E Tropicana Ave
Las Vegas, NV 89121
Phone: (702) 433-4267

#430
Vape Distrct
Category: Tobacco Shop
Average price: Modest
Area: Southeast
Address: 1775 E Tropicana Blvd
Las Vegas, NV 89119
Phone: (702) 476-0388

#431
Southwest Bikes
Category: Bikes, Mountain Biking,
Bike Rentals
Average price: Modest
Area: Centennial
Address: 7290 W Azure Dr #110
Las Vegas, NV 89130
Phone: (702) 227-7433

#432
Zara
Category: Women's Clothing,
Men's Clothing
Average price: Modest
Area: The Strip
Address: 3200 S Las Vegas Blvd
Las Vegas, NV 89109
Phone: (702) 733-1113

#433
Smith's Food & Drug Center
Category: Grocery, Photography Store
Average price: Modest
Area: Eastside
Address: 3850 E Flamingo Road
Las Vegas, NV 89121
Phone: (702) 451-2246

#434
Old Navy
Category: Sport Wear
Average price: Modest
Area: Southeast
Address: 6587 Las Vegas Blvd S
Las Vegas, NV 89119
Phone: (702) 361-7479

#435
Swatch
Category: Watches, Jewelry
Average price: Modest
Area: Eastside
Address: 3500 Las Vegas Blvd
S Las Vegas, NV 89109
Phone: (702) 734-1093

#436
Timberland
Category: Shoe Store
Average price: Modest
Area: Downtown
Address: 805 S Grand Central Pkwy
Las Vegas, NV 89106
Phone: (702) 386-3045

#437
Fabric Boutique
Category: Fabric Store
Average price: Modest
Area: Westside
Address: 4465 W Charleston Blvd
Las Vegas, NV 89102
Phone: (702) 878-0068

#438
Balenciaga
Category: Leather Goods
Average price: Exclusive
Area: The Strip
Address: 3720 Las Vegas Blvd S,
Ste 220, Las Vegas, NV 89109
Phone: (702) 262-1636

#439
Yes of Course
Category: Mobile Phones
Average price: Modest
Area: Westside
Address: 4660 W Charleston Blvd
Las Vegas, NV 89102
Phone: (702) 939-9993

#440
A Traders Turquoise Chief
Category: Jewelry
Average price: Inexpensive
Area: Downtown
Address: 1616 Las Vegas Blvd
S Las Vegas, NV 89104
Phone: (702) 383-6069

#441
Carlito's Way
Category: Tobacco Shop
Average price: Inexpensive
Area: Sunrise
Address: 5001 E Bonanza Rd Ste 102
Las Vegas, NV 89110
Phone: (702) 839-5001

#442
Napa Valley Pottery & Floral
Category: Home Decor
Average price: Modest
Area: Westside
Address: 4101 W Charleston
Boulevard, Las Vegas, NV 89102
Phone: (702) 877-3607

#443
Anna's Linens
Category: Home Decor, Kitchen & Bath
Average price: Modest
Area: Westside
Address: 1191 S Decatur Ave
Las Vegas, NV 89102
Phone: (702) 877-0088

#444
4 Real Intimate Apparel
Category: Lingerie
Average price: Modest
Area: Centennial
Address: 8414 Farm Rd
Las Vegas, NV 89131
Phone: (702) 258-8700

#445
Friendly Wireless
Category: Electronics Repair,
Mobile Phones
Average price: Modest
Area: Northwest
Address: 3616 N Rancho Dr
Las Vegas, NV 89130
Phone: (702) 395-6328

#446
Payless Shoes
Category: Shoe Store
Average price: Inexpensive
Area: Centennial
Address: 7950 W Tropical Pkwy
Las Vegas, NV 89149
Phone: (702) 645-1482

#447
Cowtown Guitars
Category: Musical Instruments
Average price: Expensive
Area: Downtown
Address: 1009 S Main St
Las Vegas, NV 89101
Phone: (702) 866-2600

#448
The Salvation Army
Category: Vintage & Consignment
Average price: Inexpensive
Area: Spring Valley
Address: 4196 S Durango Dr
Las Vegas, NV 89147
Phone: (702) 227-3795

#449
99 Cents Only
Category: Discount Store
Average price: Inexpensive
Area: Southwest
Address: 3835 Blue Diamond Rd
Las Vegas, NV 89139
Phone: (702) 451-0399

#450
Adidas Inline
Category: Shoe Store
Average price: Modest
Area: The Strip
Address: 3791 Las Vegas Boulevard
S Las Vegas, NV 89109
Phone: (702) 262-1373

#451
**Mixt Urban Beauty
Bar & Boutique**
Category: Cosmetics & Beaut,
Eyelash Service
Average price: Modest
Area: Westside
Address: 750 S Rampart Blvd
Las Vegas, NV 89145
Phone: (702) 541-6949

#452
Discount Shoe Factory
Category: Shoe Store
Average price: Inexpensive
Area: Westside
Address: 1701 S Rainbow Blvd
Las Vegas, NV 89146
Phone: (702) 304-1399

#453
Albertsons
Category: Drugstore,
Department Store, Grocery
Average price: Modest
Area: Southwest
Address: 7350 S Rainbow Blvd
Las Vegas, NV 89139
Phone: (702) 739-1033

#454
Bare Escentuals Outlet
Category: Cosmetics & Beauty
Average price: Modest
Area: Downtown
Address: 755 Grand Central
Pkwy, Ste 2105, Las Vegas, NV 89106
Phone: (702) 366-0781

#455
Kay Jewelers
Category: Jewelry
Average price: Modest
Area: Southeast
Address: 6659 S Las Vegas Blvd
Las Vegas, NV 89119
Phone: (702) 614-8487

#456
Giardini Garden Store
Category: Home Decor
Average price: Exclusive
Area: Eastside
Address: 3600 Las Vegas Blvd
South Las Vegas, NV 89109
Phone: (702) 693-8785

#457
Target
Category: Department Store
Average price: Modest
Area: Chinatown
Address: 3550 S Rainbow Boulevard
Las Vegas, NV 89103
Phone: (702) 253-5151

#458
Savers
Category: Thrift Store
Average price: Inexpensive
Area: Westside
Address: 2620 S Decatur Blvd
Las Vegas, NV 89102
Phone: (702) 220-7350

#459
Fones Gone Wild
Category: Mobile Phones
Average price: Modest
Area: University
Address: 4632 S Maryland Pkwy
Las Vegas, NV 89119
Phone: (702) 522-1337

#460
As They Grow
Category: Thrift Store,
Discount Store, Baby Gear & Furniture
Average price: Inexpensive
Area: Westside
Address: 230 S Decatur Blvd
Las Vegas, NV 89107
Phone: (702) 499-1438

#461
Bike World
Category: Bikes
Average price: Modest
Area: Westside
Address: 1901 S Rainbow Blvd
Las Vegas, NV 89146
Phone: (702) 254-1718

#462
White House Black Market
Category: Women's Clothing
Average price: Expensive
Area: The Strip
Address: 3663 Las Vegas Blvd
South, Ste 340, Las Vegas, NV 89109
Phone: (702) 732-2562

#463
Converse
Category: Shoe Store
Average price: Modest
Area: Southeast
Address: 7400 Las Vegas
Boulevard S Ofc,
Las Vegas, NV 89123
Phone: (702) 896-9814

#464
Bebe
Category: Accessories,
Women's Clothing
Average price: Expensive
Area: Southeast
Address: 6569 Las Vegas Blvd
S Las Vegas, NV 89119
Phone: (702) 260-6274

#465
Cotton On
Category: Women's Clothing,
Men's Clothing, Accessories
Average price: Inexpensive
Area: Westside
Address: 4300 Meadows Ln,
Shop 2510, Las Vegas, NV 89107
Phone: (702) 822-2068

#466
Fossil
Category: Outlet Store
Average price: Modest
Area: Downtown
Address: 875 S Grand Central
Parkway, Las Vegas, NV 89106
Phone: (702) 366-9366

#467
Vapors
Category: Tobacco Shop
Average price: Modest
Area: Spring Valley
Address: 4235 S Fort Apache Rd
Las Vegas, NV 89147
Phone: (702) 723-8273

#468
Fantastic Indoor Swapmeet
Category: Shopping Center
Average price: Inexpensive
Area: Westside
Address: 1717 S Decatur Blvd
Las Vegas, NV 89102
Phone: (702) 877-0087

#469
Victoria's Secret
Category: Women's Clothing
Average price: Modest
Area: Southeast
Address: 6543 Las Vegas Blvd
S Las Vegas, NV 89119
Phone: (702) 270-0088

#470
Sprint
Category: Mobile Phones
Average price: Modest
Area: Westside
Address: 3862 W Sahara Ave
Las Vegas, NV 89102
Phone: (702) 625-7759

#471
Sam's Club
Category: Department Store, Electronics
Average price: Modest
Area: Spring Valley
Address: 7175 Spring Mountain Rd
Las Vegas, NV 89117
Phone: (702) 253-0072

#472
Salvatore Ferragamo Outlet
Category: Fashion
Average price: Exclusive
Area: Downtown
Address: 855 S Grand Central Pkwy
Las Vegas, NV 89106
Phone: (702) 384-5938

#473
Walgreens
Category: Drugstore, Cosmetics & Beauty,
Convenience Store
Average price: Modest
Area: Westside
Address: 8633 W Charleston Blvd
Las Vegas, NV 89117
Phone: (702) 383-9660

#474
Michaels
Category: Arts & Crafts, Knitting Supplies,
Hobby Shop
Average price: Modest
Area: Centennial
Address: 7941 W Tropical Pkwy
Las Vegas, NV 89149
Phone: (702) 839-0140

#475
The Home Depot
Category: Nurseries & Gardening,
Appliances, Hardware Store
Average price: Modest
Area: Spring Valley
Address: 4195 S Fort Apache Rd
Las Vegas, NV 89147
Phone: (702) 220-4903

#476
Target
Category: Department Store
Average price: Modest
Area: Northwest
Address: 3210 N Tenaya Way
Las Vegas, NV 89129
Phone: (702) 645-5440

#477
JUST YOU
Home of Glamour Boutique 2
Category: Fashion
Average price: Modest
Area: Westside
Address: 3400 W Desert Inn Rd
Las Vegas, NV 89102
Phone: (702) 697-1800

#478
Vegas Vision
Category: Eyewear & Opticians
Average price: Modest
Area: Eastside
Address: 2595 S Maryland Pkwy
Las Vegas, NV 89109
Phone: (702) 220-9767

#479
Sunglass Optic Studio
Category: Eyewear & Opticians
Average price: Modest
Area: Summerlin
Address: 10300 W Charleston Blvd
Las Vegas, NV 89135
Phone: (702) 822-2199

#480
Swag Antiques
Category: Antiques
Average price: Modest
Area: Downtown
Address: 630 S Las Vegas Blvd
Las Vegas, NV 89101
Phone: (702) 464-3299

#481
Hermès Paris
Category: Shopping
Average price: Exclusive
Area: The Strip
Address: 3600 Las Vegas Blvd
S Las Vegas, NV 89109
Phone: (702) 866-2629

#482
Landero Learning Center
Category: Musical Instruments,
Tutoring Center
Average price: Modest
Area: Southeast
Address: 9620 S Las Vegas Blvd
Las Vegas, NV 89123
Phone: (702) 407-2787

#483
**Allied Charcoal
& Wood Products**
Category: Home & Garden
Average price: Modest
Area: Sunrise
Address: 2584 N Nellis Blvd
Las Vegas, NV 89115
Phone: (702) 871-8308

#484
Ace Pharmacy
Category: Drugstore
Average price: Modest
Area: Spring Valley
Address: 6085 S Fort Apache Rd
Las Vegas, NV 89148
Phone: (702) 675-3050

#485
Lowe's Home Improvement
Category: Building Supplies,
Nurseries & Gardening, Hardware Store
Average price: Modest
Area: Sunrise
Address: 2465 N Nellis Boulevard
N E Las Vegas, NV 89115
Phone: (702) 352-1836

#486
Lili Boutique
Category: Women's Clothing, Accessories
Average price: Modest
Area: Spring Valley
Address: 9484 W Flamingo Rd
Las Vegas, NV 89147
Phone: (702) 433-5454

#487
Peloton Sport
Category: Bikes
Average price: Expensive
Area: Summerlin
Address: 911 N Buffalo Dr
Las Vegas, NV 89128
Phone: (702) 363-1991

#488
Ultra Diamonds
Category: Jewelry
Average price: Modest
Area: Downtown
Address: 855 S Grand Central Parkway
Las Vegas, NV 89106
Phone: (702) 385-2206

#489
Meads Hardware
Category: Building Supplies,
Hardware Store
Average price: Inexpensive
Area: Sunrise
Address: 4438 E Lake Mead Blvd
Las Vegas, NV 89115
Phone: (702) 452-1560

#490
Westside Trains
Category: Hobby Shop
Average price: Modest
Area: Westside
Address: 2960 S Durango
Las Vegas, NV 89117
Phone: (702) 254-9475

#491
**Show-Off
Las Vegas Costume Rentals**
Category: Costume,
Professional Services
Average price: Modest
Area: Southeast
Address: 6400 S Eastern Ave
Las Vegas, NV 89119
Phone: (702) 739-6995

#492
Jason Of Beverly Hills
Category: Jewelry
Average price: Expensive
Area: The Strip
Address: 3708 Las Vegas Blvd
S 3A Las Vegas, NV 89109
Phone: (702) 698-7655

#493
Vapors East
Category: Tobacco Shop
Average price: Modest
Area: Sunrise
Address: 4530 E Charleston Blvd
Las Vegas, NV 89104
Phone: (702) 285-6052

#494
City Center Fine Art Collection
Category: Art Gallery
Average price: Exclusive
Area: The Strip
Address: 3730 S Las Vegas Blvd
Las Vegas, NV 89109
Phone: (702) 590-7111

#495
J Crimi Eyewear Boutique
Category: Eyewear & Opticians
Average price: Modest
Area: Anthem
Address: 10575 S Eastern Ave
Henderson, NV 89052
Phone: (702) 243-3937

#496
Supernova Comics
Category: Comic Book
Average price: Modest
Area: Downtown
Address: 450 E Fremont St
Las Vegas, NV 89101
Phone: (702) 721-7620

#497
Sew Little Time
Category: Fabric Store
Average price: Modest
Area: Spring Valley
Address: 5325 S Fort Apache Rd
Las Vegas, NV 89148
Phone: (702) 450-6766

#498
Dinettes & Stools Las Vegas
Category: Furniture Store
Average price: Modest
Area: Westside
Address: 5661 W Sahara Avenue
Las Vegas, NV 89146
Phone: (702) 221-9622

#499
Little Havana
Cafe & Smoke Shop
Category: Tobacco Shop,
Coffee & Tea
Average price: Modest
Area: Southeast
Address: 2381 E Windmill Ln
Las Vegas, NV 89123
Phone: (702) 896-0051

#500
Fredericks of Hollywood
Category: Adult
Average price: Inexpensive
Area: The Strip
Address: 3663 Las Vegas Blvd
Las Vegas, NV 89109
Phone: (702) 731-9360

TOP 500 RESTAURANTS

The Most Recommended by Locals and Travelers

(From #1 to #500)

#1
Bronze Cafe at The Center
Category: Vegan, Vegetarian, Coffee & Tea
Average price: Under $10
Area: Downtown
Address: 401 S Maryland Pkwy
Las Vegas, NV 89101
Phone: (702) 202-3100

#2
Soho Japanese Restaurant
Category: Japanese, Sushi Bar
Average price: $11-30
Area: Southwest
Address: 7377 S Jones Blvd
Las Vegas, NV 89139
Phone: (702) 776-7778

#3
Baguette Cafe
Category: Coffee & Tea, Sandwiches, Breakfast & Brunch
Average price: Under $10
Area: Spring Valley
Address: 8359 W Sunset Rd
Las Vegas, NV 89113
Phone: (702) 269-4781

#4
Kabuto
Category: Sushi Bar, Japanese
Average price: Above $61
Area: Chinatown
Address: 5040 Spring Mountain Rd
Las Vegas, NV 89146
Phone: (702) 676-1044

#5
Raku
Category: Japanese
Average price: $31-60
Area: Chinatown
Address: 5030 Spring Mountain Rd
Las Vegas, NV 89146
Phone: (702) 367-3511

#6
Layla Grill & Hookah
Category: Mediterranean, Hookah Bar, Lounge
Average price: $11-30
Area: Spring Valley
Address: 8665 W Flamingo Rd
Las Vegas, NV 89147
Phone: (702) 202-4930

#7
Tacos El Gordo
Category: Mexican
Average price: Under $10
Area: Downtown
Address: 1724 E Charleston Blvd
Las Vegas, NV 89104
Phone: (702) 251-8226

#8
Earl of Sandwich
Category: Sandwiches
Average price: Under $10
Area: The Strip, Eastside
Address: 3667 Las Vegas Blvd.
S. Las Vegas, NV 89109
Phone: (702) 463-0259

#9
Biaggio's Pizzeria
Category: Pizza, Italian
Average price: Under $10
Area: Spring Valley
Address: 4235 S Fort Apache Rd
Las Vegas, NV 89147
Phone: (702) 207-4992

#10
Tacos El Gordo
Category: Mexican
Average price: Under $10
Area: The Strip
Address: 3049 S Las Vegas Blvd
Las Vegas, NV 89109
Phone: (702) 641-8228

#11
Picasso
Category: French
Average price: Above $61
Area: The Strip
Address: 3600 S Las Vegas Blvd
Las Vegas, NV 89109
Phone: (702) 693-8105

#12
Strip N Dip Chicken Strips
Category: Fast Food, American, Comfort Food
Average price: Under $10
Area: Westside
Address: 873 S Rainbow Blvd
Las Vegas, NV 89145
Phone: (702) 823-2835

#13
Baladie Café
Category: Greek, Mediterranean
Average price: Under $10
Area: Northwest
Address: 4872 W Lone Mountain Rd
Las Vegas, NV 89130
Phone: (702) 658-0024

#14
JJANGA Japanese Restaurant
Category: Japanese, Sushi Bar
Average price: $11-30
Area: Chinatown
Address: 3650 S Decatur Blvd
Las Vegas, NV 89103
Phone: (702) 453-3377

#15
Fogo de Chao Las Vegas
Category: Brazilian, Steakhouses
Average price: $31-60
Area: Eastside
Address: 360 E Flamingo Rd
Las Vegas, NV 89169
Phone: (702) 431-4500

#16
Presto Cafe
Category: Salad, American, Sandwiches
Average price: Under $10
Area: Spring Valley
Address: 4950 S Rainbow Blvd
Las Vegas, NV 89118
Phone: (702) 293-3332

#17
Egg & I
Category: Breakfast & Brunch,
Burgers, Sandwiches
Average price: $11-30
Area: Westside
Address: 4533 W Sahara Ave
Las Vegas, NV 89102
Phone: (702) 364-9686

#18
Capriotti's Sandwich Shop
Category: Sandwiches, Vegetarian
Average price: Under $10
Area: The Strip
Address: 322 W Sahara Ave
Las Vegas, NV 89102
Phone: (702) 474-0229

#19
Thai Food To Go
Category: Thai
Average price: Under $10
Area: Eastside
Address: 3242 E Desert Inn Rd
Las Vegas, NV 89121
Phone: (702) 778-8898

#20
Fat Tuesday & Chippery
Category: Bar, American
Average price: $11-30
Area: The Strip
Address: 3500 Las Vegas Blvd
S Las Vegas, NV 89109
Phone: (702) 369-3265

#21
Taco y Taco
Category: Mexican, Vegetarian
Average price: Under $10
Area: Southeast, Eastside
Address: 3430 E Tropicana Ave
Las Vegas, NV 89121
Phone: (702) 331-3015

#22
Pan Asian
Category: Japanese, Thai, Chinese
Average price: Under $10
Area: Westside
Address: 2980 S Durango Dr
Las Vegas, NV 89117
Phone: (702) 629-7464

#23
Lotus of Siam
Category: Thai
Average price: $11-30
Area: Eastside, Downtown
Address: 953 E Sahara Ave
Las Vegas, NV 89104
Phone: (702) 735-3033

#24
DW Bistro
Category: Caribbean, American
Average price: $11-30
Area: Spring Valley
Address: 6115 S Ft Apache Rd
Las Vegas, NV 89148
Phone: (702) 527-5200

#25
The Barrymore
Category: American
Average price: $31-60
Area: The Strip
Address: 99 Convention Center Dr
Las Vegas, NV 89109
Phone: (702) 407-5303

#26
**La Belle Terre Bread
French Bakery Café**
Category: Coffee & Tea,
Bakeries, Cafe
Average price: Under $10
Area: Westside
Address: 8390 W Sahara Ave
Las Vegas, NV 89117
Phone: (702) 685-7712

#27
Patisserie Manon
Category: Bakeries, French
Average price: $11-30
Area: Westside
Address: 8751 W Charleston Blvd
Las Vegas, NV 89117
Phone: (702) 586-2666

#28
Viva Las Arepas
Category: Venezuelan
Average price: Under $10
Area: Downtown
Address: 1616 S Las Vegas Blvd
Las Vegas, NV 89104
Phone: (702) 366-9696

#29
Secret Pizza
Category: Pizza
Average price: Under $10
Area: The Strip
Address: 3708 Las Vegas Blvd
S Las Vegas, NV 89109
Phone: (702) 698-7860

#30
Carlos' Kitchen
Category: American, Seafood, Burgers
Average price: $11-30
Area: Spring Valley
Address: 4140 S Durango Dr
Las Vegas, NV 89147
Phone: (702) 207-6556

#31
Jean Philippe Patisserie
Category: Desserts, Cafe
Average price: $11-30
Area: The Strip
Address: 3600 S Las Vegas Blvd
Las Vegas, NV 89109
Phone: (702) 693-8788

#33
Amena Bakery & Deli
Category: Bakeries, Middle Eastern
Average price: Under $10
Area: Westside
Address: 2101 S Decatur Blvd
Las Vegas, NV 89102
Phone: (702) 382-1010

#32
Project Pie
Category: Pizza, Salad,
Do-It-Yourself Food
Average price: $11-30
Area: The Strip, Eastside
Address: 3799 S Las Vegas Blvd
Las Vegas, NV 89109
Phone: (702) 463-6200

#34
Pizza Rock
Category: Pizza
Average price: $11-30
Area: Downtown
Address: 201 N 3rd St
Las Vegas, NV 89101
Phone: (702) 385-0838

#35
**Juan's Flaming Fajitas
& Cantina**
Category: Mexican
Average price: $11-30
Area: Spring Valley
Address: 9640 W Tropicana
Las Vegas, NV 89147
Phone: (702) 823-1400

#36
Texas de Brazil
Category: Brazilian,
Steakhouses, Gluten-Free
Average price: $31-60
Area: Southeast
Address: 6533 S Las Vegas Blvd
Las Vegas, NV 89119
Phone: (702) 614-0080

#37
Joe's Seafood Prime Steak & Stone Crab
Category: Seafood, Steakhouses
Average price: $31-60
Area: The Strip
Address: 3500 Las Vegas Blvd
S, Ste R-05, Las Vegas, NV 89109
Phone: (702) 792-9222

#38
Monta Ramen
Category: Ramen
Average price: Under $10
Area: Chinatown
Address: 5030 Spring Mountain Rd
Las Vegas, NV 89146
Phone: (702) 367-4600

#39
Simply Pure
by Chef Stacey Dougan
Category: Vegan, Vegetarian
Average price: $11-30
Area: Downtown
Address: 707 Fremont St
Las Vegas, NV 89101
Phone: (702) 810-5641

#40
MTO Café
Category: Breakfast & Brunch,
Cafe, Comfort Food
Average price: $11-30
Area: Downtown
Address: 500 S Main St
Las Vegas, NV 89101
Phone: (702) 380-8229

#41
Tasty Crepes
Category: Desserts, Ice Cream,
Frozen Yogurt, Creperies
Average price: Under $10
Area: Spring Valley
Address: 4845 S Fort Apache Rd
Las Vegas, NV 89147
Phone: (702) 818-5517

#42
Custom Built Pizza
Category: Pizza, Vegan, Gluten-Free
Average price: Under $10
Area: Spring Valley
Address: 4165 S Grand Canyon Dr
Las Vegas, NV 89147
Phone: (702) 473-9918

#43
Braddah's Island Style
Category: Ethnic Food, Hawaiian
Average price: Under $10
Area: Westside
Address: 2330 S Rainbow Blvd
Las Vegas, NV 89146
Phone: (702) 222-0767

#44
Poke Express
Category: Hawaiian
Average price: $11-30
Area: Southeast
Address: 9400 S Eastern Ave
Las Vegas, NV 89123
Phone: (702) 221-1600

#45
Komol Restaurant
Category: Vegetarian, Thai, Vegan
Average price: $11-30
Area: Eastside
Address: 953 E Sahara Ave
Las Vegas, NV 89104
Phone: (702) 731-6542

#46
Pop Up Pizza
Category: Pizza
Average price: Under $10
Area: Downtown
Address: 1 S Main St
Las Vegas, NV 89101
Phone: (702) 366-0049

#47
Scarpetta
Category: Italian
Average price: $31-60
Area: The Strip
Address: 3708 Las Vegas Blvd
S Las Vegas, NV 89109
Phone: (702) 698-7960

#48
Buldogis Gourmet Hot Dogs
Category: Hot Dogs, Korean
Average price: Under $10
Area: Westside
Address: 2291 S Fort Apache Rd
Las Vegas, NV 89117
Phone: (702) 570-7560

#49
Asian BBQ & Noodles
Category: Chinese, Barbeque
Average price: Under $10
Area: Chinatown
Address: 3400 S Jones Blvd
Las Vegas, NV 89146
Phone: (702) 202-3636

#50
Ramen Sora
Category: Ramen
Average price: Under $10
Area: Chinatown
Address: 4490 Spring Mountain Rd
Las Vegas, NV 89102
Phone: (702) 685-1011

#51
Ichiza
Category: Japanese
Average price: $11-30
Area: Chinatown
Address: 4355 Spring Mountain Rd
Las Vegas, NV 89102
Phone: (702) 367-3151

#52
Fat Boy
Category: Burgers, Pizza, Mexican
Average price: Under $10
Area: Sunrise
Address: 4425 Stewart St
Las Vegas, NV 89110
Phone: (702) 434-1600

#53
Original Lindo Michoacan
Category: Mexican
Average price: $11-30
Area: Eastside
Address: 2655 E Desert Inn Rd
Las Vegas, NV 89121
Phone: (702) 735-6828

#54
Sushi Koma
Category: Japanese, Sushi Bar
Average price: $11-30
Area: Spring Valley
Address: 8665 W Flamingo Rd
Las Vegas, NV 89147
Phone: (702) 453-8897

#55
Bouchon
Category: French, Breakfast & Brunch
Average price: $31-60
Area: The Strip
Address: 3355 Las Vegas Blvd
S Las Vegas, NV 89109
Phone: (702) 414-6200

#56
Bachi Burger
Category: Burgers
Average price: $11-30
Area: Southeast
Address: 470 E Windmill Ln
Las Vegas, NV 89123
Phone: (702) 242-2244

#57
Trattoria Nakamura-Ya
Category: Italian, Japanese
Average price: $11-30
Area: Chinatown
Address: 5040 W Spring Mountain Rd
Las Vegas, NV 89146
Phone: (702) 251-0022

#58
Yassou
Category: Greek, Mediterranean
Average price: Under $10
Area: Westside
Address: 7871 W Charleston Blvd
Las Vegas, NV 89117
Phone: (702) 798-8989

#59
Bouchon Bakery
Category: French, Bakeries
Average price: Under $10
Area: The Strip
Address: 3355 Las Vegas Blvd
S Las Vegas, NV 89109
Phone: (702) 414-6203

#60
Firefly on Paradise
Category: Tapas,
Tapas Bar
Average price: $11-30
Area: Eastside
Address: 3824 Paradise Rd
Las Vegas, NV 89169
Phone: (702) 369-3971

#61
Raising Cane's
Category: Fast Food,
Chicken Wings, American
Average price: Under $10
Area: Southeast
Address: 7550 S Las Vegas Blvd
Las Vegas, NV 89123
Phone: (702) 434-3644

#62
BabyStacks Cafe
Category: Breakfast & Brunch
Average price: Under $10
Area: Summerlin
Address: 2400 N Buffalo Dr
Las Vegas, NV 89128
Phone: (702) 541-6708

#63
Capriottis Sandwich Shop
Category: Sandwiches, American
Average price: Under $10
Area: Eastside
Address: 4480 Paradise Rd
Las Vegas, NV 89169
Phone: (702) 736-6166

#64
Kyara Japanese Tapas
Category: Japanese
Average price: $11-30
Area: Spring Valley
Address: 6555 S Jones Blvd
Las Vegas, NV 89118
Phone: (702) 434-8856

#65
Spago
Category: American
Average price: $31-60
Area: The Strip
Address: 3500 Las Vegas Blvd
S, Ste G1, Las Vegas, NV 89109
Phone: (702) 369-6300

#66
Rí Rá
Category: Irish, Pub
Average price: $11-30
Area: The Strip
Address: 3930 Las Vegas Blvd
S Las Vegas, NV 89119
Phone: (702) 632-7771

#67
Fukumimi Ramen
Category: Japanese
Average price: Under $10
Area: Southeast, Eastside
Address: 4860 S Eastern Ave
Las Vegas, NV 89119
Phone: (702) 631-2933

#68
Bacchanal Buffet
Category: Buffets
Average price: $31-60
Area: The Strip
Address: 3570 Las Vegas Boulevard
South, Las Vegas, NV 89109
Phone: (702) 731-7928

#69
Eat.
Category: Breakfast & Brunch
Average price: $11-30
Area: Downtown
Address: 707 Carson Ave
Las Vegas, NV 89101
Phone: (702) 534-1515

#70
**Zaytoon Mediterranean
Market & Kabob**
Category: Mediterranean, Persian/Iranian
Average price: $11-30
Area: Spring Valley
Address: 3655 S Durango Dr
Las Vegas, NV 89147
Phone: (702) 685-1875

#71
Omelet House
Category: Breakfast & Brunch
Average price: Under $10
Area: Downtown
Address: 2160 W Charleston Blvd
Las Vegas, NV 89102
Phone: (702) 384-6868

#72
The Paiza Club
Category: Restaurant, Casino
Average price: Above $61
Area: Eastside
Address: 3355 Las Vegas Blvd
S Las Vegas, NV 89109
Phone: (702) 414-1000

#73
Mesa Grill
Category: Southern
Average price: $31-60
Area: The Strip
Address: 3570 Las Vegas Boulevard
South, Las Vegas, NV 89109
Phone: (702) 731-7731

#74
Those Guys Pies
Category: Pizza,
Cheesesteaks, Sandwiches
Average price: $11-30
Area: The Lakes
Address: 2916 Lake E Dr
Las Vegas, NV 89117
Phone: (702) 629-2626

#75
Stephano's Greek
& Mediterranean Grill
Category: Middle Eastern,
Greek, Mediterranean
Average price: Under $10
Area: University
Address: 4632 S Maryland Pkwy
Las Vegas, NV 89119
Phone: (702) 795-8444

#76
Grimaldi's Pizzeria
Category: Pizza
Average price: $11-30
Area: The Strip
Address: 3327 Las Vegas
Blvd S, Ste 2710
Las Vegas, NV 89109
Phone: (702) 754-3450

#77
Sunrise Coffee
Category: Coffee & Tea, Vegan
Average price: Under $10
Area: Southeast
Address: 3130 E Sunset Rd
Las Vegas, NV 89120
Phone: (702) 433-3304

#78
Yama Sushi
Category: Sushi Bar
Average price: $11-30
Area: Eastside
Address: 1350 E Flamingo Rd
Las Vegas, NV 89119
Phone: (702) 696-0072

#79
I-Naba
Category: Japanese
Average price: $11-30
Area: Westside
Address: 3210 S Decatur Blvd
Las Vegas, NV 89102
Phone: (702) 220-6060

#80
The Steakhouse
Category: Steakhouses
Average price: $31-60
Area: The Strip
Address: 2880 Las Vegas Blvd S
Las Vegas, NV 89109
Phone: (702) 794-3767

#81
Slidin' Thru
Category: Burgers, Food Trucks
Average price: Under $10
Area: Downtown
Address: 500 S Grand Central Pkwy
Las Vegas, NV 89155
Phone: (702) 645-1570

#82
M & M Soul Food Cafe
Category: Soul Food, Southern
Average price: $11-30
Area: Westside
Address: 3923 W Charleston Blvd
Las Vegas, NV 89102
Phone: (702) 453-7685

#83
Fleming's Prime
Steakhouse & Wine Bar
Category: Wine Bar,
Steakhouses, American
Average price: $31-60
Area: Southeast
Address: 6515 South Las Vegas Blvd.
Las Vegas, NV 89119
Phone: (702) 407-0019

#84
Bonito Michoacan
Category: Mexican
Average price: $11-30
Area: Chinatown
Address: 3715 S Decatur Blvd
Las Vegas, NV 89103
Phone: (702) 257-6810

#85
Echo & Rig
Category: Steakhouses
Average price: $11-30
Area: Westside
Address: 440 S Rampart Blvd
Las Vegas, NV 89145
Phone: (702) 489-3525

#86
Rincon De Buenos Aires
Category: Steakhouses, Argentine
Average price: $11-30
Area: Chinatown
Address: 5300 Spring Mountain Rd
Las Vegas, NV 89146
Phone: (702) 257-3331

#87
Sushi House Goyemon
Category: Japanese, Sushi Bar
Average price: $11-30
Area: Spring Valley
Address: 5255 S Decatur Blvd
Las Vegas, NV 89118
Phone: (702) 331-0333

#88
The Sparklings
Category: American
Average price: $11-30
Area: Southwest
Address: 8310 S Rainbow Blvd
Las Vegas, NV 89139
Phone: (702) 293-5003

#89
Verandah
Category: Breakfast & Brunch, Italian
Average price: $31-60
Area: The Strip
Address: 3950 S Las Vegas Blvd
Las Vegas, NV 89109
Phone: (702) 632-5000

#90
Mundo Restaurant
Category: Mexican, Spanish,
Latin American
Average price: $11-30
Area: Downtown
Address: 495 S Grand Central Pkwy
Las Vegas, NV 89106
Phone: (702) 270-4400

#91
Prommares Thai Food
Category: Thai
Average price: Under $10
Area: Westside
Address: 6362 W Sahara Ave
Las Vegas, NV 89146
Phone: (702) 221-9644

#92
Le Thai
Category: Thai
Average price: $11-30
Area: Downtown
Address: 523 Fremont St
Las Vegas, NV 89101
Phone: (702) 778-0888

#93
Capriotti's Sandwich Shop
Category: Sandwiches,
Salad, Vegetarian
Average price: Under $10
Area: Southeast
Address: 9620 Las Vegas Blvd
S Las Vegas, NV 89123
Phone: (702) 407-5602

#94
BabyStacks Cafe
Category: Breakfast & Brunch, Cafe
Average price: Under $10
Area: Spring Valley
Address: 4135 S Buffalo Dr
Las Vegas, NV 89147
Phone: (702) 207-6432

#95
Brand Steakhouse & Lounge
Category: Steakhouses
Average price: $31-60
Area: The Strip
Address: 3770 Las Vegas Blvd
S Las Vegas, NV 89109
Phone: (702) 730-6700

#96
Aloha Specialties Restaurant
Category: Hawaiian
Average price: Under $10
Area: Downtown
Address: 12 E Ogden Ave
Las Vegas, NV 89101
Phone: (702) 382-0338

#97
The Peppermill Restaurant & Fireside Lounge
Category: American,
Breakfast & Brunch, Lounge
Average price: $11-30
Area: The Strip
Address: 2985 Las Vegas Blvd
S Las Vegas, NV 89109
Phone: (702) 735-4177

#98
Abuela's Tacos
Category: Mexican
Average price: Under $10
Area: Sunrise
Address: 4225 E Sahara Ave
Las Vegas, NV 89104
Phone: (702) 431-0284

#99
Beijing Noodle Cafe
Category: Chinese
Average price: Under $10
Area: Eastside
Address: 4130 S Sandhill Rd
Las Vegas, NV 89121
Phone: (702) 641-0666

#100
Bachi Burger
Category: Burgers, Asian Fusion
Average price: $11-30
Area: Westside
Address: 9410 W Sahara Ave
Las Vegas, NV 89117
Phone: (702) 255-3055

#101
Satay Thai Bistro & Bar
Category: Thai, Chinese
Average price: $11-30
Area: Eastside
Address: 3900 Paradise Rd
Las Vegas, NV 89169
Phone: (702) 369-8788

#102
Hawaiian Style Poke
Category: Hawaiian
Average price: Under $10
Area: Chinatown
Address: 3524 Wynn Rd
Las Vegas, NV 89103
Phone: (702) 202-0729

#103
Firefly
Category: Tapas, Tapas Bar
Average price: $11-30
Area: Westside
Address: 9560 W Sahara Ave
Las Vegas, NV 89117
Phone: (702) 834-3814

#104
Yard House
Category: American
Average price: $11-30
Area: Southeast
Address: 6593 Las Vegas Blvd
S. Las Vegas, NV 89119
Phone: (702) 734-9273

#105
Manhattan Fish Grill
Category: Seafood
Average price: $11-30
Area: Spring Valley
Address: 4115 Grand Canyon Dr
Las Vegas, NV 89147
Phone: (702) 802-2993

#106
Musashi Japanese Steakhouse
Category: Japanese
Average price: $11-30
Area: Eastside
Address: 3900 Paradise Rd
Las Vegas, NV 89169
Phone: (702) 735-4744

#107
Crab Corner
Category: Seafood
Average price: $11-30
Area: Eastside
Address: 4161 S Eastern Ave
Las Vegas, NV 89119
Phone: (702) 489-4646

#108
E-Jo Korean Restaurant
Category: Korean
Average price: $11-30
Area: Downtown
Address: 700 E Sahara Ave
Las Vegas, NV 89104
Phone: (702) 796-1004

#109
Todd English's Olives
Category: Mediterranean
Average price: $31-60
Area: The Strip
Address: 3600 S Las Vegas Blvd
Las Vegas, NV 89109
Phone: (702) 693-8181

#110
Tableau
Category: American
Average price: $31-60
Area: The Strip
Address: 3131 Las Vegas Blvd
S Las Vegas, NV 89109
Phone: (702) 770-3330

#111
Grand Lux Cafe
Category: American,
Desserts, American
Average price: $11-30
Area: The Strip
Address: 3355 Las Vegas Blvd
S Las Vegas, NV 89109
Phone: (702) 414-3888

#112
Due Forni
Category: Pizza, Italian
Average price: $11-30
Area: South Summerlin
Address: 3555 S Town Center Dr
Las Vegas, NV 89135
Phone: (702) 586-6500

#113
The Original Sunrise Cafe
Category: Breakfast & Brunch
Average price: $11-30
Area: Southeast
Address: 8975 S Eastern Ave
Las Vegas, NV 89123
Phone: (702) 257-8877

#114
Gordon Ramsay BurGR
Category: Burgers
Average price: $11-30
Area: The Strip
Address: 3667 Las Vegas Boulevard
South, Las Vegas, NV 89109
Phone: (702) 785-5555

#115
SUSHISAMBA Las Vegas
Category: Asian Fusion, Bar, Dim Sum
Average price: $31-60
Area: The Strip
Address: 3327 Las Vegas Blvd S
Las Vegas, NV 89109
Phone: (702) 607-0700

#116
La Cave Wine & Food Hideaway
Category: Tapas Bar
Average price: $31-60
Area: The Strip
Address: 3131 Las Vegas Blvd.
South, Las Vegas, NV 89109
Phone: (702) 770-7375

#117
Maggiano's Little Italy
Category: Italian
Average price: $11-30
Area: The Strip
Address: 3200 Las Vegas Blvd
S Las Vegas, NV 89109
Phone: (702) 732-2550

#118
Burger Bar
Category: Burgers, American
Average price: $11-30
Area: The Strip
Address: 3930 S Las Vegas Boulevard
Las Vegas, NV 89119
Phone: (702) 632-9364

#119
Vintner Grill
Category: American
Average price: $31-60
Area: Summerlin
Address: 10100 W Charleston Blvd
Las Vegas, NV 89135
Phone: (702) 214-5590

#120
Lola's
Category: Cajun/Creole
Average price: $11-30
Area: Downtown
Address: 241 W Charleston Blvd
Las Vegas, NV 89102
Phone: (702) 227-5652

#121
Las Vegas Jerkys
Category: Specialty Food, Hawaiian
Average price: Under $10
Area: Downtown
Address: 18 E Fremont St
Las Vegas, NV 89101
Phone: (702) 385-7991

#122
Hot N Juicy Crawfish
Category: Cajun/Creole, Seafood
Average price: $11-30
Area: Chinatown
Address: 3863 Spring Mountain Rd
Las Vegas, NV 89102
Phone: (702) 750-2428

#123
Sakana
Category: Japanese, Sushi Bar
Average price: $11-30
Area: Eastside
Address: 3949 S Maryland Pkwy
Las Vegas, NV 89119
Phone: (702) 733-0066

#124
Baja Bar & Grill
Category: Mexican
Average price: Under $10
Area: University
Address: 4755 S Maryland Pkwy
Las Vegas, NV 89119
Phone: (702) 736-8830

#125
Hokaido Sushi
Category: Sushi Bar
Average price: $11-30
Area: Spring Valley
Address: 6015 S Fort Apache Rd
Las Vegas, NV 89148
Phone: (702) 262-2213

#126
Hash House A Go Go
Category: Breakfast & Brunch
Average price: $11-30
Area: Westside
Address: 6800 W Sahara Ave
Las Vegas, NV 89146
Phone: (702) 804-4646

#127
Miko's Izakaya
Category: Japanese, Sushi Bar
Average price: $11-30
Area: Southeast
Address: 500 E Windmill Ln
Las Vegas, NV 89123
Phone: (702) 823-2779

#128
Social House
Category: Japanese, Lounge,
Asian Fusion
Average price: $31-60
Area: The Strip
Address: 3720 Las Vegas Blvd
S Las Vegas, NV 89158
Phone: (702) 736-1122

#129
Ellis Island Casino & Brewery
Category: Casino, American
Average price: Under $10
Area: Eastside
Address: 4178 Koval Ln
Las Vegas, NV 89109
Phone: (702) 733-8901

#130
Wicked Spoon
Category: Buffets
Average price: $31-60
Area: The Strip
Address: 3708 Las Vegas Blvd
S Las Vegas, NV 89109
Phone: (702) 698-7000

#131
The Martini
Category: American, Lounge
Average price: $11-30
Area: Westside
Address: 1205 S Fort Apache Rd
Las Vegas, NV 89117
Phone: (702) 227-8464

#132
Chile Verde Express
Category: Mexican
Average price: Under $10
Area: Southwest
Address: 8095 S Rainbow Blvd
Las Vegas, NV 89113
Phone: (702) 260-7758

#133
MIX
Category: French, American, Lounge
Average price: Above $61
Area: The Strip
Address: 3950 Las Vegas Boulevard
Las Vegas, NV 89119
Phone: (702) 632-9500

#134
Holsteins Shakes & Buns
Category: Burgers, American
Average price: $11-30
Area: The Strip
Address: 3708 Las Vegas Blvd
S Las Vegas, NV 89109
Phone: (702) 698-7940

#135
Off The Strip Bistro & Bar
Category: American
Average price: $11-30
Area: Southwest
Address: 10670 Southern Highlands Pkwy
Las Vegas, NV 89141
Phone: (702) 202-2448

#136
Gallagher's Steakhouse
Category: Steakhouses
Average price: $31-60
Area: The Strip
Address: 3790 Las Vegas Blvd
S Las Vegas, NV 89109
Phone: (702) 740-6450

#137
The Buffet
Category: Buffets
Average price: $31-60
Area: The Strip
Address: 3131 Las Vegas Blvd
S Las Vegas, NV 89109
Phone: (702) 770-3340

#138
K-bop Korean Tapas Restaurant
Category: Korean, Tapas Bar
Average price: $11-30
Area: Spring Valley
Address: 4235 S Fort Apache Rd
Las Vegas, NV 89147
Phone: (702) 740-5267

#139
Raising Cane's
Category: Fast Food,
Chicken Wings, American
Average price: Under $10
Area: Eastside
Address: 1120 E Flamingo Rd
Las Vegas, NV 89119
Phone: (702) 453-2263

#140
Trattoria Reggiano
Category: Italian
Average price: $11-30
Area: The Strip
Address: 3355 Las Vegas Blvd
S Las Vegas, NV 89109
Phone: (702) 369-2053

#141
Sensi
Category: Asian Fusion
Average price: $31-60
Area: The Strip
Address: 3600 S Las Vegas Blvd
Las Vegas, NV 89109
Phone: (702) 693-8800

#142
Foundation Room
Category: Lounge,
Dance Club, American
Average price: $31-60
Area: Eastside
Address: 3950 S Las Vegas Blvd
Las Vegas, NV 89109
Phone: (702) 632-7614

#143
Gangnam Asian BBQ Dining
Category: Japanese, Korean, Barbeque
Average price: $11-30
Area: Eastside
Address: 4480 Paradise Rd
Las Vegas, NV 89169
Phone: (702) 802-5508

#144
**Red Square Restaurant
& Vodka Lounge**
Category: American, Steakhouses
Average price: $31-60
Area: Southeast
Address: 3950 Las Vegas Blvd
S Las Vegas, NV 89119
Phone: (702) 693-8300

#145
Andrea's
Category: Asian Fusion, Bar
Average price: Above $61
Area: The Strip
Address: 3131 Las Vegas Blvd
S Las Vegas, NV 89109
Phone: (702) 770-5340

#146
Nine Fine Irishmen
Category: Pub, Irish
Average price: $11-30
Area: The Strip
Address: 3790 Las Vegas Blvd
S Las Vegas, NV 89109
Phone: (702) 740-6463

#147
Big Wong Restaurant
Category: Chinese, Taiwanese, Malaysian
Average price: Under $10
Area: Chinatown
Address: 5040 Spring Mountain Rd
Las Vegas, NV 89146
Phone: (702) 368-6808

#148
Honey Salt
Category: American, Cafe
Average price: $11-30
Area: Westside
Address: 1031 S Rampart Blvd
Las Vegas, NV 89145
Phone: (702) 445-6100

#149
Hash House A Go Go
Category: Breakfast & Brunch
Average price: $11-30
Area: The Strip
Address: 3535 Las Vegas Blvd
S Las Vegas, NV 89109
Phone: (702) 254-4646

#150
Palm Restaurant
Category: Steakhouses,
Seafood, American
Average price: $31-60
Area: The Strip
Address: 3500 Las Vegas Blvd
S Las Vegas, NV 89109
Phone: (702) 732-7256

#151
Fat Choy
Category: American,
Chinese, Asian Fusion
Average price: $11-30
Area: Eastside, Downtown
Address: 595 E Sahara Ave
Las Vegas, NV 89104
Phone: (702) 794-3464

#152
Roy's Restaurant
Category: Asian Fusion, Hawaiian
Average price: $31-60
Area: University, Eastside
Address: 620 E Flamingo Rd
Las Vegas, NV 89119
Phone: (702) 691-2053

#153
The Bagel Cafe
Category: Cafe
Average price: $11-30
Area: Westside
Address: 301 N Buffalo Dr
Las Vegas, NV 89145
Phone: (702) 255-3444

#154
DJ's Taco Bar
Category: Mexican
Average price: Under $10
Area: The Strip
Address: 3743 S Las Vegas Blvd
Las Vegas, NV 89109
Phone: (702) 778-3051

#155
Top of the World Restaurant
Category: American
Average price: Above $61
Area: The Strip
Address: 2000 Las Vegas Blvd
S Las Vegas, NV 89104
Phone: (702) 380-7711

#156
Wine 5 Cafe
Category: American,
Specialty Food, African
Average price: $11-30
Area: Northwest
Address: 3250 N Tenaya Ave
Las Vegas, NV 89129
Phone: (702) 462-9463

#157
Los Tacos
Category: Mexican
Average price: Under $10
Area: Downtown
Address: 1710 E Charleston Blvd
Las Vegas, NV 89104
Phone: (702) 471-7447

#158
Raising Cane's
Category: Chicken Wings,
Fast Food, American
Average price: Under $10
Area: Westside
Address: 4655 W Charleston
Las Vegas, NV 89102
Phone: (702) 294-2263

#159
Fleur by Hubert Keller
Category: Tapas
Average price: Above $61
Area: The Strip
Address: 3950 Las Vegas Blvd
Las Vegas, NV 89119
Phone: (702) 632-9400

#160
Sushi Mon
Category: Japanese, Sushi Bar
Average price: $11-30
Area: Southeast
Address: 9770 S Maryland Pkwy
Las Vegas, NV 89183
Phone: (702) 617-0241

#161
Nosh & Swig
Category: Tapas
Average price: $11-30
Area: Eastside
Address: 3620 E Flamingo Rd
Las Vegas, NV 89121
Phone: (702) 456-6674

#162
Coffee Pub
Category: Coffee & Tea,
Breakfast & Brunch, Sandwiches
Average price: Under $10
Area: Westside
Address: 2800 W Sahara Ave
Las Vegas, NV 89102
Phone: (702) 367-1913

#163
Los Tacos
Category: Mexican
Average price: Under $10
Area: Westside
Address: 4001 W Sahara Ave
Las Vegas, NV 89102
Phone: (702) 252-0100

#164
Sakina Thai Cuisine
Category: Halal, Thai, Cantonese
Average price: $11-30
Area: Westside
Address: 4251 W Sahara
Las Vegas, NV 89102
Phone: (702) 754-4999

#165
The Cracked Egg
Category: Breakfast & Brunch
Average price: $11-30
Area: Spring Valley
Address: 6435 S Rainbow Blvd
Las Vegas, NV 89118
Phone: (702) 220-6449

#166
**Paymon's Mediterranean
Cafe & Lounge**
Category: Vegetarian, Greek, Mediterranean
Average price: $11-30
Area: University, Eastside
Address: 4147 S Maryland Pkwy
Las Vegas, NV 89119
Phone: (702) 731-6030

#167
Geisha Steakhouse
Category: Japanese, Steakhouses
Average price: $11-30
Area: Eastside
Address: 3751 E Desert Inn Rd
Las Vegas, NV 89121
Phone: (702) 451-9814

#168
RePete's
Category: American, Bar
Average price: $11-30
Area: Southeast
Address: 2460 W Warm Springs Rd
Las Vegas, NV 89119
Phone: (702) 410-5600

#169
Booming Spot Mini Pot
Category: Chinese
Average price: $11-30
Area: Chinatown
Address: 3466 S Decatur Blvd
Las Vegas, NV 89102
Phone: (702) 294-0008

#170
Grand Lux Cafe
Category: American, Desserts
Average price: $11-30
Area: The Strip
Address: 3327 Las Vegas Blvd S,
Ste 1580 Las Vegas, NV 89109
Phone: (702) 733-7411

#171
Mandarin Oriental Tea Lounge
Category: Tea Rooms, Tapas Bar
Average price: $31-60
Area: The Strip
Address: 3752 Las Vegas Blvd
S Las Vegas, NV 89158
Phone: (702) 590-8888

#172
Firehouse Subs
Category: Fast Food, Deli, Sandwiches
Average price: Under $10
Area: Southeast
Address: 5905 S. Eastern Ave.
Las Vegas, NV 89119
Phone: (702) 262-7805

#173
Payard Pâtisserie & Bistro
Category: French
Average price: $11-30
Area: The Strip
Address: 3570 Las Vegas Boulevard
South, Las Vegas, NV 89109
Phone: (702) 731-7292

#174
Gold Spike
Category: Cafe, Lounge
Average price: $11-30
Area: Downtown
Address: 217 Las Vegas Blvd
N Las Vegas, NV 89101
Phone: (702) 476-1082

#175
Rise & Shine,
a Steak & Egg Place
Category: Breakfast & Brunch,
Steakhouses, American
Average price: $11-30
Area: Southwest
Address: 10690 Southern Highlands Pwy,
Las Vegas, NV 89141
Phone: (702) 202-4646

#176
STK
Category: Steakhouses
Average price: Above $61
Area: The Strip
Address: 3708 Las Vegas Blvd
S Las Vegas, NV 89109
Phone: (702) 698-7990

#177
Public House
Category: GastroPub
Average price: $31-60
Area: The Strip
Address: 3355 Las Vegas Blvd
S Las Vegas, NV 89109
Phone: (702) 407-5310

#178
Nittaya's Secret Kitchen
Category: Thai
Average price: $11-30
Area: Summerlin
Address: 2110 N Rampart
Las Vegas, NV 89128
Phone: (702) 360-8885

#179
Border Grill
Category: Mexican
Average price: $11-30
Area: The Strip
Address: 3950 S Las Vegas Boulevard
Las Vegas, NV 89119
Phone: (702) 632-7403

#180
Pam Real Thai Las Vegas
Category: Thai
Average price: Under $10
Area: Chinatown
Address: 3650 S Decatur Blvd
Las Vegas, NV 89103
Phone: (702) 802-3377

#181
KoMex Fusion
Category: Korean, Mexican,
Asian Fusion
Average price: Under $10
Area: Spring Valley
Address: 4155 S Buffalo Dr
Las Vegas, NV 89147
Phone: (702) 778-5566

#182
Culinary Dropout
Category: Bar, American, Fondue
Average price: $11-30
Area: Eastside
Address: 4455 Paradise Rd
Las Vegas, NV 89169
Phone: (702) 522-8100

#183
Saffron Flavors of India
Category: Indian, Vegetarian
Average price: $11-30
Area: Northwest
Address: 4450 N Tenaya Way
Las Vegas, NV 89129
Phone: (702) 489-7900

#184
Pho Bosa
Category: Vietnamese, Soup
Average price: Under $10
Area: Chinatown
Address: 3355 Spring Mountain Rd
Las Vegas, NV 89102
Phone: (702) 418-1931

#185
Yard House
Category: American, American,
Vegetarian, Asian Fusion
Average price: $11-30
Area: The Strip
Address: 3545 Las Vegas Blvd.
Las Vegas, NV 89109
Phone: (702) 597-0434

#186
Kinh Do
Category: Vietnamese
Average price: Under $10
Area: Chinatown
Address: 4300 Spring Mountain Rd
Las Vegas, NV 89102
Phone: (702) 253-0199

#187
Volcano Grille
Category: Japanese
Average price: Under $10
Area: Southwest
Address: 7315 W Warm Springs Rd
Las Vegas, NV 89113
Phone: (702) 260-7571

#188
**Wolfgang Puck
Pizzeria & Cucina**
Category: Italian
Average price: $11-30
Area: The Strip
Address: 3720 Las Vegas Blvd
Las Vegas, NV 89158
Phone: (702) 238-1000

#189
Piero's Italian Cuisine
Category: Italian, Seafood
Average price: Above $61
Area: Eastside
Address: 355 Convention Center Dr
Las Vegas, NV 89109
Phone: (702) 369-2305

#190
MadHouse Coffee
Category: Coffee & Tea, Bakeries,
Sandwiches
Average price: Under $10
Area: Westside
Address: 8470 W Desert Inn Rd
Las Vegas, NV 89117
Phone: (702) 360-4232

#191
Kabob Korner
Category: Mediterranean,
Pakistani, Halal
Average price: Under $10
Area: Downtown
Address: 507 E Fremont St
Las Vegas, NV 89101
Phone: (702) 384-7722

#192
Firehouse Subs
Category: Fast Food, Deli
Average price: Under $10
Area: Westside
Address: 9921 W Charleston Blvd
Las Vegas, NV 89117
Phone: (702) 463-9800

#193
Du-Par's Restaurant & Bakery
Category: American, Breakfast & Brunch
Average price: $11-30
Area: Downtown
Address: 1 Fremont St
Las Vegas, NV 89101
Phone: (702) 385-1906

#194
Tournament of Kings
Category: American
Average price: $31-60
Area: The Strip
Address: 3850 Las Vegas Blvd
S Las Vegas, NV 89109
Phone: (702) 597-7600

#195
Cuba Cafe Restaurant
Category: Cuban
Average price: $11-30
Area: Southeast, Eastside
Address: 2055 E Tropicana Ave
Las Vegas, NV 89119
Phone: (702) 795-7070

#196
808 Tapas East-West Infusion
Category: Asian Fusion,
Japanese, Sushi Bar
Average price: $11-30
Area: Westside
Address: 9350 W Sahara Ave
Las Vegas, NV 89117
Phone: (702) 485-3433

#197
Strip House Steak House
Category: Steakhouses, Desserts
Average price: Above $61
Area: The Strip
Address: Planet Hollywood Resort and
Casino, Las Vegas, NV 89109
Phone: (702) 737-5200

#198
Casa Di Amore
Category: Italian, American
Average price: $11-30
Area: Southeast, Eastside
Address: 2850 E Tropicana Ave
Las Vegas, NV 89121
Phone: (702) 433-4967

#199
Amore Taste of Chicago
Category: Italian, Pizza
Average price: $11-30
Area: Spring Valley
Address: 3945 S Durango Dr
Las Vegas, NV 89147
Phone: (702) 562-9000

#200
Triple George Grill
Category: Steakhouses, Seafood
Average price: $11-30
Area: Downtown
Address: 201 N 3rd St
Las Vegas, NV 89101
Phone: (702) 384-2761

#201
The Buffet at Bellagio
Category: Buffets
Average price: $31-60
Area: The Strip
Address: 3600 S Las Vegas Blvd
Las Vegas, NV 89109
Phone: (702) 693-8111

#202
Stripburger
Category: Burgers
Average price: $11-30
Area: The Strip
Address: 3200 Las Vegas Blvd
S Las Vegas, NV 89109
Phone: (702) 737-8747

#203
Thai Style Noodle House
Category: Thai, Vegan
Average price: Under $10
Area: Summerlin
Address: 2267 N Rampart Blvd
Las Vegas, NV 89134
Phone: (702) 749-7991

#204
Table 34
Category: American
Average price: $31-60
Area: Southeast
Address: 600 E Warm Springs Rd
Las Vegas, NV 89119
Phone: (702) 263-0034

#205
Kabob Express
Category: Afghan, Persian/Iranian
Average price: Under $10
Area: Southeast
Address: 4912 S Eastern Ave
Las Vegas, NV 89119
Phone: (702) 433-7499

#206
Metro Pizza
Category: Pizza, Italian
Average price: $11-30
Area: Southeast
Address: 1395 E Tropicana Ave
Las Vegas, NV 89119
Phone: (702) 736-1955

#207
The Cracked Egg
Category: American, Breakfast & Brunch
Average price: $11-30
Area: Northwest
Address: 7660 W Cheyenne Ave
Las Vegas, NV 89129
Phone: (702) 395-7981

#208
Sicilian Ristorante
Category: Italian
Average price: $11-30
Area: Southeast, Eastside
Address: 3520 E Tropicana Ave
Las Vegas, NV 89121
Phone: (702) 458-2004

#209
Mr Tofu
Category: Korean
Average price: Under $10
Area: Chinatown
Address: 3889 Spring Mountain Rd
Las Vegas, NV 89102
Phone: (702) 388-7733

#210
Nobu
Category: Japanese
Average price: Above $61
Area: The Strip
Address: 3570 Las Vegas Boulevard
South Las Vegas, NV 89109
Phone: (702) 785-6628

#211
Five Guys Burgers & Fries
Category: Burgers, Fast Food
Average price: Under $10
Area: Southeast
Address: 7580 S Las Vegas Blvd
Las Vegas, NV 89123
Phone: (702) 431-0055

#212
Naka Sushi
Category: Sushi Bar
Average price: $11-30
Area: Summerlin
Address: 8540 W Lake Mead Blvd
Las Vegas, NV 89128
Phone: (702) 233-5900

#213
Badger Cafe
Category: American
Average price: Under $10
Area: Southeast, Eastside
Address: 1801 E Tropicana Ave
Las Vegas, NV 89119
Phone: (702) 798-7594

#214
Sasa Sushi
Category: Japanese, Sushi Bar
Average price: $11-30
Area: Northwest
Address: 7450 W Cheyenne Ave
Las Vegas, NV 89129
Phone: (702) 396-9760

#215
Greens and Proteins
Category: American,
Juice Bar & Smoothies
Average price: $11-30
Area: Southeast
Address: 8975 S Eastern Ave
Las Vegas, NV 89123
Phone: (702) 541-7800

#216
Café Casera
Category: Mexican, Cafe
Average price: Under $10
Area: Southwest
Address: 7720 S Jones Blvd
Las Vegas, NV 89139
Phone: (702) 722-6005

#217
Fish N Bowl
Category: Sushi Bar,
Seafood, Asian Fusion
Average price: $11-30
Area: Southwest, Spring Valley
Address: 7225 S Durango Dr
Las Vegas, NV 89113
Phone: (702) 739-3474

#218
Egg Works
Category: Breakfast & Brunch
Average price: $11-30
Area: Spring Valley
Address: 6960 S Rainbow Blvd
Las Vegas, NV 89118
Phone: (702) 361-3447

#219
Sno Shack Hawaiian Shave Ice
Category: Hawaiian, Desserts,
Shaved Ice
Average price: Under $10
Area: Westside
Address: 1717 S Decatur Blvd
Las Vegas, NV 89102
Phone: (702) 321-6466

#220
Hank's Philly Steaks
Category: Cheesesteaks
Average price: Under $10
Area: Southeast
Address: 467 E Silverado Ranch Blvd
Las Vegas, NV 89183
Phone: (702) 778-8353

#221
Q Bistro
Category: Korean,
Chicken Wings, Barbeque
Average price: $11-30
Area: Chinatown
Address: 3400 S Jones Blvd
Las Vegas, NV 89146
Phone: (702) 685-9876

#222
Society Cafe Encore
Category: American
Average price: $11-30
Area: The Strip
Address: 3131 Las Vegas Blvd
South Las Vegas, NV 89109
Phone: (702) 770-5300

#223
Merkato Ethiopian Cafe
Category: Ethiopian
Average price: Under $10
Area: Eastside
Address: 855 E Twain Ave
Las Vegas, NV 89162
Phone: (702) 796-1231

#224
The Cheesecake Factory
Category: American, Desserts
Average price: $11-30
Area: The Strip
Address: 3500 South Las Vegas Blvd.
Las Vegas, NV 89109
Phone: (702) 792-6888

#225
Mama Maria's Mexican Restaurant
Category: Mexican
Average price: Under $10
Area: Sunrise
Address: 6055 E Lake Mead Blvd
Las Vegas, NV 89156
Phone: (702) 453-3111

#226
Blueberry Hill Family Restaurant
Category: Diners, Breakfast & Brunch
Average price: Under $10
Area: Eastside
Address: 3790 E Flamingo Rd
Las Vegas, NV 89121
Phone: (702) 433-9999

#227
Delhi Indian Cuisine
Category: Indian, Buffets
Average price: $11-30
Area: Eastside
Address: 4022 S Maryland Pkwy
Las Vegas, NV 89119
Phone: (702) 383-4900

#228
Mashisoyo
Category: Korean, Desserts, Soup
Average price: $11-30
Area: Spring Valley
Address: 5035 S Fort Apache Rd
Las Vegas, NV 89148
Phone: (702) 684-7263

#229
Thai Style Noodle House 2
Category: Thai, Chinese
Average price: Under $10
Area: Spring Valley
Address: 5135 S Fort Apache Ave
Las Vegas, NV 89148
Phone: (702) 823-2882

#230
Kaizen Fusion Roll & Sushi
Category: Sushi Bar, Japanese
Average price: $11-30
Area: Eastside
Address: 4480 S Paradise Rd
Las Vegas, NV 89109
Phone: (702) 641-7772

#231
KJ Kitchen
Category: Chinese
Average price: $11-30
Area: Chinatown
Address: 5960 Spring Mountain Rd
Las Vegas, NV 89146
Phone: (702) 221-0456

#232
Viva Mercado's
Mexican Bar & Grill
Category: Mexican
Average price: $11-30
Area: Westside
Address: 9440 W Sahara Ave
Las Vegas, NV 89117
Phone: (702) 454-8482

#233
Greenberg's Deli
Category: Deli, Pizza, Sandwiches
Average price: $11-30
Area: The Strip
Address: 3790 Las Vegas Blvd
S Las Vegas, NV 89136
Phone: (702) 740-6969

#234
Gina's Bistro
Category: Italian
Average price: $11-30
Area: Spring Valley
Address: 4226 S Durango Dr
Las Vegas, NV 89117
Phone: (702) 341-1800

#235
Dom DeMarco's Pizzeria & Bar
Category: Pizza, Wine Bar, Italian
Average price: $11-30
Area: Westside
Address: 9785 W Charleston Blvd
Las Vegas, NV 89117
Phone: (702) 570-7000

#236
Rocco's NY Pizzeria
Category: Pizza
Average price: $11-30
Area: Summerlin
Address: 10860 W Charleston Blvd
Las Vegas, NV 89135
Phone: (702) 796-0111

#237
Sushi Kaya
Category: Japanese, Sushi Bar
Average price: $11-30
Area: Chinatown
Address: 4355 Spring Mountain Rd
Las Vegas, NV 89103
Phone: (702) 257-9496

#238
India Masala
Category: Indian
Average price: $11-30
Area: The Strip
Address: 2901 Las Vegas Blvd
S Las Vegas, NV 89109
Phone: (702) 794-9436

#239
Yanni's Gyros
Category: Greek
Average price: $11-30
Area: Southeast
Address: 9770 S Maryland Pkwy
Las Vegas, NV 89183
Phone: (702) 260-9397

#240
Cheffinis Hot Dogs
Category: Hot Dogs
Average price: Under $10
Area: Downtown
Address: 520 Fremont St
Las Vegas, NV 89101
Phone: (702) 629-0396

#241
Taco Tijuana
Category: Mexican
Average price: Under $10
Area: Southeast, Eastside
Address: 2554 E Tropicana Ave
Las Vegas, NV 89121
Phone: (702) 547-9163

#242
Market Street Cafe
Category: American, Hawaiian
Average price: Under $10
Area: Downtown
Address: 12 East Ogden Ave
Las Vegas, NV 89101
Phone: (702) 385-1222

#243
Jimmy John's
Gourmet Sandwiches
Category: Sandwiches,
Food Delivery Services, Deli
Average price: Under $10
Area: University
Address: 4800 S Maryland Pkwy
Las Vegas, NV 89119
Phone: (702) 740-0305

#244
50s Diner
Category: Breakfast & Brunch,
Diners, Comfort Food
Average price: Under $10
Area: Eastside
Address: 3050 E Desert Inn Rd
Las Vegas, NV 89121
Phone: (702) 737-0377

#245
Dakao Sandwiches
Category: Vietnamese
Average price: Under $10
Area: Chinatown
Address: 5700 W Spring Mountain Rd
Las Vegas, NV 89146
Phone: (702) 221-0930

#246
Well Being In The Box
Category: Korean, Japanese
Average price: $11-30
Area: Westside
Address: 2555 S Jones Blvd
Las Vegas, NV 89146
Phone: (702) 253-5222

#247
China One
Category: Chinese
Average price: Under $10
Area: Westside
Address: 921 S Rainbow Blvd
Las Vegas, NV 89145
Phone: (702) 822-2228

#248
Chop Chop Wok
Category: Chinese
Average price: Under $10
Area: Northwest
Address: 6812 W Cheyenne Ave
Las Vegas, NV 89108
Phone: (702) 658-2467

#249
Forte European
Tapas Bar & Bistro
Category: Tapas Bar, Spanish, Ukrainian
Average price: $11-30
Area: Spring Valley
Address: 4180 Rainbow Blvd
Las Vegas, NV 89103
Phone: (702) 220-3876

#250
Greens and Proteins
Category: Pizza, American,
Juice Bar & Smoothies
Average price: $11-30
Area: Spring Valley
Address: 9809 W Flamingo Rd
Las Vegas, NV 89147
Phone: (702) 541-6400

#251
Aloha Kitchen
Category: Hawaiian
Average price: Under $10
Area: Sunrise
Address: 4466 E Charleston Blvd
Las Vegas, NV 89104
Phone: (702) 437-4426

#252
Naked City Pizza on Arville
Category: Pizza, Chicken Wings, Italian
Average price: $11-30
Area: Westside
Address: 3240 S Arville St
Las Vegas, NV 89102
Phone: (702) 243-6277

#253
Rachel's Kitchen
Category: Breakfast & Brunch,
Juice Bar & Smoothies, Sandwiches
Average price: $11-30
Area: Downtown
Address: 150 Las Vegas Blvd N
Las Vegas, NV 89101
Phone: (702) 778-8800

#254
Bahama Breeze
Category: Caribbean, Bar, Seafood
Average price: $11-30
Area: Eastside
Address: 375 Hughes Center Dr
Las Vegas, NV 89109
Phone: (702) 731-3252

#255
Brio Tuscan Grille
Category: Italian
Average price: $11-30
Area: Westside
Address: 420 S Rampart Blvd
Las Vegas, NV 89145
Phone: (702) 433-1233

#256
Sammy's Woodfired
Pizza and Grill
Category: Pizza, Gluten-Free
Average price: $11-30
Area: Westside
Address: 6500 W Sahara Ave
Las Vegas, NV 89146
Phone: (702) 227-6000

#257
Capriotti's Sandwich Shop
Category: Sandwiches
Average price: Under $10
Area: Centennial
Address: 7240 Azure Dr
Las Vegas, NV 89130
Phone: (702) 655-1234

#258
Tao Asian Bistro
Category: Asian Fusion
Average price: $31-60
Area: The Strip
Address: 3355 Las Vegas Blvd
S Las Vegas, NV 89109
Phone: (702) 388-8338

#259
Casa Don Juan
Category: Mexican
Average price: $11-30
Area: Downtown
Address: 1204 S Main St
Las Vegas, NV 89104
Phone: (702) 384-8070

#260
Todd English P.U.B.
Category: GastroPub, British
Average price: $11-30
Area: The Strip
Address: 3720 Las Vegas Blvd
S Las Vegas, NV 89109
Phone: (702) 489-8080

#261
The View Wine Bar & Kitchen
Category: Wine Bar, Tapas
Average price: $11-30
Area: Westside
Address: 420 S Rampart Blvd
Las Vegas, NV 89145
Phone: (702) 280-7390

#262
Pizza Natali
Category: Pizza
Average price: $11-30
Area: Southeast
Address: 580 E Windmill Ln
Las Vegas, NV 89123
Phone: (702) 248-6262

#263
Island Sushi & Grill Express
Category: Sushi Bar, Hawaiian
Average price: $11-30
Area: Downtown
Address: 1st S Main St
Las Vegas, NV 89101
Phone: (702) 386-1600

#264
Grimaldi's Pizzeria
Category: Pizza
Average price: $11-30
Area: Westside
Address: 750 S Rampart Blvd
Las Vegas, NV 89145
Phone: (702) 479-1351

#265
Oyshi Sushi
Category: Sushi Bar
Average price: $11-30
Area: Southwest
Address: 7775 S Rainbow Blvd
Las Vegas, NV 89113
Phone: (702) 646-9744

#266
Surang's Thai Kitchen
Category: Thai
Average price: Under $10
Area: Spring Valley
Address: 5455 S Fort Apache Rd
Las Vegas, NV 89148
Phone: (702) 385-0021

#267
Sura BBQ Buffet
Category: Korean, Buffets, Barbeque
Average price: $11-30
Area: Chinatown
Address: 4480 Spring Mountain Rd
Las Vegas, NV 89102
Phone: (702) 365-9888

#268
Lima Limon
Category: Peruvian
Average price: $11-30
Area: Westside
Address: 222 S Decatur Blvd
Las Vegas, NV 89107
Phone: (702) 463-0002

#269
Firehouse Subs
Category: Sandwiches, Deli
Average price: Under $10
Area: Spring Valley
Address: 6070 S. Rainbow Blvd.
Las Vegas, NV 89118
Phone: (702) 463-3900

#270
Yu-Yu
Category: Japanese
Average price: $11-30
Area: Chinatown
Address: 4115 Spring Mountain Rd
Las Vegas, NV 89102
Phone: (702) 220-4223

#271
Yard House
Category: American, American
Average price: $11-30
Area: South Summerlin
Address: 11027 W Charleston Blvd
Las Vegas, NV 89135
Phone: (702) 363-9273

#272
The Henry
Category: American
Average price: $11-30
Area: The Strip
Address: 3700 Las Vegas Blvd
S Las Vegas, NV 89109
Phone: (702) 698-7000

#273
Lulu's Bread & Breakfast
Category: Breakfast & Brunch,
Cafe, Bakeries
Average price: $11-30
Area: Centennial
Address: 6720 Skypointe Dr
Las Vegas, NV 89131
Phone: (702) 437-5858

#274
Windy City Beefs N Pizza
Category: Hot Dogs, Pizza
Average price: Under $10
Area: Southeast
Address: 9711 S Eastern Ave
Las Vegas, NV 89183
Phone: (702) 388-4300

#275
**Sammy's LA Pastrami
& Burgers**
Category: Fast Food,
Sandwiches, Burgers
Average price: $11-30
Area: Southeast, Eastside
Address: 2191 E Tropicana Ave
Las Vegas, NV 89119
Phone: (702) 736-1698

#276
Embers
Category: American, Cocktail Bar
Average price: $11-30
Area: Westside
Address: 740 S Rampart Blvd
Las Vegas, NV 89145
Phone: (702) 778-2160

#277
Buddy V's Ristorante
Category: Italian
Average price: $11-30
Area: The Strip
Address: 3339 Las Vegas Blvd
S Las Vegas, NV 89109
Phone: (702) 607-2355

#278
Lakes Lounge
Category: American
Average price: Under $10
Area: The Lakes
Address: 2920 Lake East Dr
Las Vegas, NV 89117
Phone: (702) 363-9733

#279
Hyde Bellagio
Category: Lounge, Italian
Average price: $31-60
Area: The Strip
Address: 3600 S Las Vegas Blvd
Las Vegas, NV 89109
Phone: (702) 693-8700

#280
Pho Sing Sing
Category: Vietnamese
Average price: Under $10
Area: Chinatown
Address: 3409 S Jones Blvd
Las Vegas, NV 89146
Phone: (702) 380-2999

#281
Kauai Cafe
Category: Hawaiian
Average price: Under $10
Area: Spring Valley
Address: 10140 W Tropicana Ave
Las Vegas, NV 89147
Phone: (702) 754-3559

#282
Geisha House Steak & Sushi
Category: Sushi Bar, Japanese,
Steakhouses
Average price: $11-30
Area: Spring Valley
Address: 9719 W Flamingo Rd
Las Vegas, NV 89147
Phone: (702) 369-9637

#283
R Steak & Seafood
Category: Seafood, Steakhouses
Average price: $31-60
Area: The Strip
Address: 2901 S Las Vegas Blvd
S Las Vegas, NV 89109
Phone: (702) 794-9233

#284
Pho Kim Long
Category: Vietnamese, Chinese
Average price: Under $10
Area: Chinatown
Address: 4029 Spring Mountain Rd
Las Vegas, NV 89102
Phone: (702) 220-3613

#285
Novecento Pizzeria
Category: Pizza, Italian
Average price: $11-30
Area: Centennial, Northwest
Address: 5705 Centennial Center Blvd
Las Vegas, NV 89149
Phone: (702) 685-4900

#286
Kona Grill
Category: American, Sushi Bar
Average price: $11-30
Area: Westside
Address: 750 S Rampart Blvd
Las Vegas, NV 89145
Phone: (702) 547-5552

#287
Tom Colicchio's Heritage Steak
Category: Diners, Steakhouses
Average price: Above $61
Area: The Strip
Address: 3400 Las Vegas Blvd
S Las Vegas, NV 89109
Phone: (702) 791-7111

#288
Pita House
Category: Mediterranean
Average price: Under $10
Area: Southeast
Address: 1310 E Silverado Ranch Blvd
Las Vegas, NV 89123
Phone: (702) 778-7100

#289
Jimmy John's
Category: Sandwiches, Deli
Average price: Under $10
Area: Downtown
Address: 2204 W Charleston Blvd
Las Vegas, NV 89102
Phone: (702) 363-5469

#290
Capriotti's Sandwich Shop
Category: Sandwiches
Average price: Under $10
Area: Spring Valley
Address: 8090 Blue Diamond Rd
Las Vegas, NV 89113
Phone: (702) 240-3354

#291
Zenshin Asian Restaurant
Category: Sushi Bar, Japanese,
Asian Fusion
Average price: $11-30
Area: Southeast
Address: 9777 S Las Vegas Blvd
Las Vegas, NV 89183
Phone: (702) 797-8538

#292
Red Velvet Cafe
Category: Vegan, Vegetarian
Average price: $11-30
Area: Westside
Address: 7875 W Sahara Ave
Las Vegas, NV 89117
Phone: (702) 360-1972

#293
Pho Annie
Category: Vietnamese
Average price: Under $10
Area: Southwest
Address: 8390 S Rainbow Blvd
Las Vegas, NV 89139
Phone: (702) 776-7017

#294
Pho Saigon 8
Category: Vietnamese
Average price: Under $10
Area: Chinatown
Address: 5650 Spring Mountain Rd
Las Vegas, NV 89146
Phone: (702) 248-6663

#295
**Sammy's Woodfired
Pizza and Grill**
Category: Pizza, Gluten-Free
Average price: $11-30
Area: Spring Valley
Address: 7345 Arroyo Crossing Pkwy
Las Vegas, NV 89147
Phone: (702) 263-7171

#296
**Paymon's Mediterranean
Cafe & Hookah Lounge**
Category: Greek, Mediterranean,
Middle Eastern
Average price: $11-30
Area: Westside
Address: 8380 W Sahara Ave
Las Vegas, NV 89117
Phone: (702) 804-0293

#297
Full House BBQ
Category: Filipino, Asian Fusion
Average price: Under $10
Area: Southeast
Address: 9890 S Maryland Pkwy
Las Vegas, NV 89183
Phone: (702) 227-4663

#298
Tacos El Compita #2
Category: Mexican
Average price: Under $10
Area: Westside
Address: 7622 Westcliff Dr
Las Vegas, NV 89145
Phone: (702) 319-8283

#299
Los Antojos
Category: Mexican
Average price: Under $10
Area: Eastside, Downtown
Address: 2520 S Eastern Ave
Las Vegas, NV 89169
Phone: (702) 457-3505

#300
Fellini's Ristorante
Category: Italian
Average price: $11-30
Area: The Strip
Address: 2000 Las Vegas Blvd
S Las Vegas, NV 89104
Phone: (702) 383-4860

#301
Desnudo Tacos
Category: Mexican
Average price: $11-30
Area: Westside
Address: 3240 Arville St
Las Vegas, NV 89102
Phone: (702) 243-6277

#302
Swish Shabu Shabu
Category: Japanese,
Sushi Bar, Hot Pot
Average price: $11-30
Area: Chinatown
Address: 5115 W Spring Mountain Rd
Las Vegas, NV 89146
Phone: (702) 522-9345

#303
Sushi Yamaguchi
Category: Japanese, Sushi Bar
Average price: $11-30
Area: Westside
Address: 5900 W Charleston Blvd
Las Vegas, NV 89146
Phone: (702) 646-0300

#304
Cous Cous Mediterranean Cafe
Category: Mediterranean,
Vegetarian, Burgers
Average price: Under $10
Area: Downtown
Address: 450 Fremont St
Las Vegas, NV 89101
Phone: (702) 366-9501

#305
Ocha Cuisine
Category: Thai, Chinese
Average price: Under $10
Area: Downtown
Address: 1201 Las Vegas Blvd
S Las Vegas, NV 89104
Phone: (702) 386-8631

#306
Steiner's A Nevada Style Pub
Category: Restaurant, Pub
Average price: $11-30
Area: Southeast
Address: 8168 Las Vegas Blvd
S Las Vegas, NV 89123
Phone: (702) 214-6700

#307
Coco's Family Restaurant
Category: Bakeries, American
Average price: Under $10
Area: Southeast
Address: 169 E Tropicana Rd
Las Vegas, NV 89119
Phone: (702) 736-3936

#308
Go Raw Cafe
Category: Vegan, Juice Bar & Smoothies,
Vegetarian
Average price: $11-30
Area: Southeast
Address: 2381 E Windmill Ln
Las Vegas, NV 89123
Phone: (702) 450-9007

#309
Mastrioni's
Category: Italian, Seafood
Average price: $11-30
Area: Spring Valley, South Summerlin
Address: 3330 S Hualapai Way
Las Vegas, NV 89117
Phone: (702) 367-7511

#310
WILD
Category: American, Pizza,
Juice Bar & Smoothies
Average price: $11-30
Area: Downtown
Address: 150 N Las Vegas Blvd
Las Vegas, NV 89101
Phone: (702) 527-7717

#311
**Tamba Indian Cuisine
& Lounge**
Category: Indian
Average price: $11-30
Area: The Strip
Address: 3743 S Las Vegas Blvd,
Ste 205, Las Vegas, NV 89109
Phone: (702) 798-7889

#312
Parsley Mediterranean Grill
Category: Mediterranean
Average price: Under $10
Area: Southeast
Address: 6420 S Pecos Rd
Las Vegas, NV 89120
Phone: (702) 489-3189

#313
Carlito's Burritos
Category: Mexican
Average price: Under $10
Area: Southeast
Address: 3345 E Patrick Ln
Las Vegas, NV 89120
Phone: (702) 547-3592

#314
Fausto's Mexican Grill
Category: Mexican
Average price: Under $10
Area: Southwest
Address: 7835 S Rainbow Blvd
Las Vegas, NV 89139
Phone: (702) 407-9445

#315
Waffles Cafe
Category: Coffee & Tea,
Breakfast & Brunch
Average price: Under $10
Area: Centennial
Address: 6446 N Durango Dr
Las Vegas, NV 89149
Phone: (702) 727-3267

#316
Capriotti's Sandwich Shop
Category: Sandwiches, Salad, Burgers
Average price: Under $10
Area: Sunrise
Address: 325 N Nellis Blvd
Las Vegas, NV 89110
Phone: (702) 437-2100

#317
Park On Fremont
Category: American,
GastroPub, Lounge
Average price: $11-30
Area: Downtown
Address: 506 E Fremont
Las Vegas, NV 89101
Phone: (702) 834-3160

#318
Tiffany's
Category: Cafe
Average price: Under $10
Area: Downtown
Address: 1700 Las Vegas Blvd
S Las Vegas, NV 89104
Phone: (702) 444-4459

#319
Stake Out
Category: Restaurant, Pub
Average price: Under $10
Area: University
Address: 4800 S Maryland Pkwy
Las Vegas, NV 89119
Phone: (702) 798-8383

#320
Great Harvest Bread Company
Category: Bakeries, Sandwiches
Average price: Under $10
Area: Spring Valley
Address: 10180 W Tropicana Ave
Las Vegas, NV 89147
Phone: (702) 221-5623

#321
Noodle Pot
Category: Chinese, Taiwanese
Average price: Under $10
Area: Chinatown
Address: 4215 Spring Mountain Rd
Las Vegas, NV 89102
Phone: (702) 522-8989

#322
Rx Boiler Room
Category: American
Average price: $31-60
Area: The Strip
Address: 3930 Las Vegas Blvd
Las Vegas, NV 89119
Phone: (702) 632-9900

#323
El Panzon Tacos Y Tortas
Category: Mexican
Average price: Under $10
Area: Southeast
Address: 3720 E Sunset Rd
Las Vegas, NV 89120
Phone: (702) 368-6219

#324
Freddy's Frozen Custard & Steakburgers
Category: Burgers, Ice Cream,
Frozen Yogurt
Average price: Under $10
Area: Southeast
Address: 9809 S Eastern Ave
Las Vegas, NV 89183
Phone: (702) 434-3733

#325
Orchids Garden Chinese Restaurant
Category: Dim Sum
Average price: $11-30
Area: Westside
Address: 5485 W Sahara Ave
Las Vegas, NV 89146
Phone: (702) 631-3839

#326
The Olive Mediterranean Grill
Category: Mediterranean, Hookah Bar
Average price: $11-30
Area: Southeast
Address: 3850 E Sunset Rd
Las Vegas, NV 89120
Phone: (702) 451-8805

#327
China A Go Go
Category: Chinese
Average price: Under $10
Area: Southeast
Address: 505 E Windmill Ave
Las Vegas, NV 89123
Phone: (702) 733-8887

#328
Leticia's Mexican Cocina
Category: Mexican
Average price: $11-30
Area: Centennial
Address: 7585 Norman Rockwell Ln
Las Vegas, NV 89143
Phone: (702) 445-7722

#329
Firehouse Subs
Category: Sandwiches, Deli
Average price: Under $10
Area: University
Address: 4761 S Maryland Pkwy
Las Vegas, NV 89119
Phone: (702) 262-1222

#330
808 Sushi
Category: Sushi Bar
Average price: $11-30
Area: Southwest
Address: 7435 S Durango Dr
Las Vegas, NV 89113
Phone: (702) 541-7874

#331
Mob Bar
Category: Italian, Lounge
Average price: $11-30
Area: Downtown
Address: 240 N 3rd St
Las Vegas, NV 89101
Phone: (702) 259-9700

#332
Luna Lounge - Hookah Lounge
Category: Hookah Bar, Lounge, Tapas Bar
Average price: $11-30
Area: The Strip
Address: 3057 S Las Vegas Blvd
Las Vegas, NV 89109
Phone: (702) 462-9991

#333
Sushi Tower & Steakhouse
Category: Sushi Bar, Steakhouses
Average price: $11-30
Area: Spring Valley
Address: 4145 S Grand Canyon Dr
Las Vegas, NV 89147
Phone: (702) 368-4336

#334
Sababa
Category: Middle Eastern, Kosher
Average price: $11-30
Area: Westside
Address: 3220 S Durango Dr
Las Vegas, NV 89117
Phone: (702) 547-5556

#335
Ping Pong Thai
Category: Thai, Vegetarian
Average price: Under $10
Area: Southeast
Address: 2955 E Sunset Rd
Las Vegas, NV 89120
Phone: (702) 228-9988

#336
Redwood Bar and Grill
Category: Steakhouses
Average price: $11-30
Area: Downtown
Address: 12 E Ogden Ave
Las Vegas, NV 89101
Phone: (702) 385-1222

#337
Lobster Me
Miracle Mile Shop
Category: Seafood
Average price: $11-30
Area: The Strip
Address: 3663 S Las Vegas Blvd
Las Vegas, NV 89109
Phone: (702) 562-7837

#338
Blueberry Hill Family Restaurant
Category: Diners
Average price: Under $10
Area: University, Eastside
Address: 1505 E Flamingo Rd
Las Vegas, NV 89119
Phone: (702) 696-9666

#339
Market Grille Cafe
Category: Greek, Mediterranean
Average price: $11-30
Area: Centennial
Address: 7070 N Durango Dr
Las Vegas, NV 89149
Phone: (702) 396-0070

#340
Chicago Brewing Company
Category: American, Breweries
Average price: $11-30
Area: Westside
Address: 2201 S Fort Apache Rd
Las Vegas, NV 89117
Phone: (702) 254-3333

#341
Hot N Juicy Crawfish
Category: Seafood, Cajun/Creole
Average price: $11-30
Area: Southeast
Address: 9560 S Eastern Ave
Las Vegas, NV 89123
Phone: (702) 776-3030

#342
Noodle Asia
Category: Chinese
Average price: $11-30
Area: The Strip
Address: 3355 Las Vegas Blvd
S Las Vegas, NV 89109
Phone: (702) 414-1444

#343
Sicili's Pizza
Category: Pizza
Average price: Under $10
Area: Eastside
Address: 529 E Twain Ave
Las Vegas, NV 89169
Phone: (702) 792-2929

#344
Smashburger
Category: Burgers
Average price: $11-30
Area: The Lakes
Address: 9101 W Sahara Ave
Las Vegas, NV 89117
Phone: (702) 462-5500

#345
Fatburger
Category: Fast Food, Burgers
Average price: $11-30
Area: The Strip
Address: 3763 Las Vegas Blvd
S Las Vegas, NV 89019
Phone: (702) 736-4733

#346
Margaritaville
Category: African
Average price: $11-30
Area: The Strip
Address: 3555 South Las Vegas Boulevard
Las Vegas, NV 89109
Phone: (702) 733-3302

#347
Swish
Category: Japanese
Average price: $11-30
Area: Westside
Address: 7875 W Sahara Ave
Las Vegas, NV 89117
Phone: (702) 586-7947

#348
BLT Burger
Category: Burgers
Average price: $11-30
Area: The Strip
Address: 3400 Las Vegas Blvd
S Las Vegas, NV 89109
Phone: (702) 792-7888

#349
Our Families Country Cafe
Category: Breakfast & Brunch
Average price: $11-30
Area: Southwest
Address: 10591 S Rainbow Blvd
Las Vegas, NV 89179
Phone: (702) 270-8700

#350
Russo's Pizza Kitchen
Category: Pizza
Average price: $11-30
Area: Spring Valley
Address: 4950 S Rainbow Blvd
Las Vegas, NV 89118
Phone: (702) 489-4444

#351
Cantina Laredo
Category: Mexican, Specialty Food
Average price: $11-30
Area: Westside
Address: 440 S Rampart Blvd
Las Vegas, NV 89145
Phone: (702) 202-4511

#352
Five Guys Burgers & Fries
Category: Burgers, Fast Food
Average price: Under $10
Area: Spring Valley
Address: 9484 W Flamingo Rd
Las Vegas, NV 89147
Phone: (702) 463-4424

#353
Wing King
Category: Chicken Wings
Average price: Under $10
Area: Westside
Address: 6475 W Charleston Blvd
Las Vegas, NV 89146
Phone: (702) 431-9464

#354
Benihana
Category: Japanese
Average price: $31-60
Area: Eastside
Address: 3000 Paradise Rd
Las Vegas, NV 89109
Phone: (702) 732-5334

#355
Kabob Grill
Category: Middle Eastern, Mediterranean,
Persian/Iranian
Average price: Under $10
Area: Southeast
Address: 9550 S Eastern Ave
Las Vegas, NV 89123
Phone: (702) 435-2262

#356
Rosati's Pizza Pub
Category: Pizza, Sandwiches
Average price: $11-30
Area: Southwest
Address: 8060 S Rainbow Blvd
Las Vegas, NV 89139
Phone: (702) 463-1777

#357
Buffalo Wild Wings
Category: Chicken Wings,
Sport Bar, American
Average price: $11-30
Area: Southwest
Address: 7345 S Durango Dr
Las Vegas, NV 89113
Phone: (702) 260-4800

#358
Marché Bacchus
Category: French, Wine Bar
Average price: $31-60
Area: Summerlin
Address: 2620 Regatta Dr
Las Vegas, NV 89128
Phone: (702) 804-8008

#359
The Lodge Coffee
House & Tavern
Category: Coffee & Tea,
Cocktail Bar
Average price: Under $10
Area: Spring Valley
Address: 5745 S Durango Dr
Las Vegas, NV 89113
Phone: (702) 220-8880

#360
Lao Thai Kitchen
Category: Thai
Average price: Under $10
Area: Sunrise
Address: 1000 N Nellis Blvd
Las Vegas, NV 89110
Phone: (702) 453-9188

#361
India Masala Bar & Grill
Category: Indian
Average price: $11-30
Area: Eastside
Address: 1040 E Flamingo Rd
Las Vegas, NV 89119
Phone: (702) 431-8313

#362
The Bar @ Tropicana & Durango
Category: American
Average price: $11-30
Area: Spring Valley
Address: 4705 S Durango
Las Vegas, NV 89147
Phone: (702) 331-3178

#363
Chao Thai Restaurant
Category: Thai
Average price: Under $10
Area: University
Address: 4550 S Maryland Pkwy
Las Vegas, NV 89119
Phone: (702) 431-2445

#364
Sushi On Rainbow
Category: Japanese, Sushi Bar
Average price: $11-30
Area: Chinatown
Address: 6870 Spring Mountain Rd
Las Vegas, NV 89146
Phone: (702) 247-8977

#365
Cafe Zupas
Category: Salad, Sandwiches, Soup
Average price: Under $10
Area: Southeast
Address: 9460 S Eastern Ave
Las Vegas, NV 89123
Phone: (702) 763-6415

#366
Fresh Mama
Category: Cafe
Average price: Under $10
Area: Spring Valley
Address: 5875 S Rainbow Blvd
Las Vegas, NV 89118
Phone: (702) 726-2621

#367
Ohana Hawaiian Bbq
Category: Hawaiian, Barbeque
Average price: Under $10
Area: Southeast
Address: 7435 S Eastern Ave
Las Vegas, NV 89123
Phone: (702) 676-2098

#368
Chicago Joes
Category: Italian
Average price: $11-30
Area: Downtown
Address: 820 S 4th St
Las Vegas, NV 89101
Phone: (702) 382-5637

#369
Famous Daves
Category: Barbeque, Sandwiches
Average price: $11-30
Area: Southwest
Address: 4390 Blue Diamond Rd
Las Vegas, NV 89139
Phone: (702) 633-7427

#370
Biscuits 2 Burgers
Category: Burgers, Breakfast & Brunch
Average price: Under $10
Area: Spring Valley
Address: 9700 W Tropicana Ave
Las Vegas, NV 89147
Phone: (702) 570-6877

#371
TC's Rib Crib
Category: Barbeque, Soul Food
Average price: $11-30
Area: Spring Valley
Address: 3655 South Durango
Las Vegas, NV 89147
Phone: (702) 451-7427

#372
Crown & Anchor British Pub
Category: Pub, British
Average price: $11-30
Area: University
Address: 1350 E Tropicana Ave
Las Vegas, NV 89119
Phone: (702) 739-8676

#373
Serrano's Mexican Fast Food
Category: Mexican
Average price: Under $10
Area: Westside
Address: 136 S Rainbow Blvd
Las Vegas, NV 89145
Phone: (702) 243-4552

#374
Allegro
Category: Restaurant
Average price: $31-60
Area: The Strip
Address: 3131 Las Vegas Blvd
S Las Vegas, NV 89109
Phone: (702) 770-2040

#375
Wahoo's Fish Tacos
Category: Mexican, Seafood
Average price: Under $10
Area: Westside
Address: 1000 S. Rampart
Las Vegas, NV 89145
Phone: (702) 776-7600

#376
Elements Kitchen & Martini Bar
Category: American, Italian
Average price: $11-30
Area: Spring Valley
Address: 4950 S Rainbow Blvd
Las Vegas, NV 89118
Phone: (702) 750-2991

#377
Rising Sun
Category: Japanese, Sushi Bar
Average price: $11-30
Area: Eastside
Address: 280 E Flamingo Rd
Las Vegas, NV 89169
Phone: (702) 248-7070

#378
Smashburger
Category: Burgers
Average price: Under $10
Area: University
Address: 4725 S Maryland Pkwy
Las Vegas, NV 89119
Phone: (702) 385-0043

#379
Wingstop
Category: American
Average price: $11-30
Area: Chinatown
Address: 7017 Spring Mountain Rd
Las Vegas, NV 89117
Phone: (702) 307-9464

#380
Yi Mei Champion Taiwan Deli
Category: Taiwanese, Chinese
Average price: Under $10
Area: Chinatown
Address: 3435 S Jones Blvd
Las Vegas, NV 89146
Phone: (702) 222-3435

#381
Chipotle Mexican Grill
Category: Mexican
Average price: Under $10
Area: Southeast
Address: 7370 Las Vegas Blvd
S Las Vegas, NV 89123
Phone: (702) 270-1973

#382
Kailyn's Kitchen
Category: American,
Breakfast & Brunch, Burgers
Average price: Under $10
Area: Southeast, Eastside
Address: 3430 E Tropicana Ave
Las Vegas, NV 89121
Phone: (702) 301-6448

#383
Sedona Lounge
Category: American
Average price: $11-30
Area: Spring Valley
Address: 9580 W Flamingo Rd
Las Vegas, NV 89147
Phone: (702) 320-4700

#384
Capriotti's Sandwich Shop
Category: Sandwiches
Average price: Under $10
Area: South Summerlin
Address: 11011 West Charleston Blvd
Las Vegas, NV 89135
Phone: (702) 257-3337

#385
The Diner at LVM Resort
Category: American,
Breakfast & Brunch, Diners
Average price: Under $10
Area: Southwest
Address: 8175 Arville St
Las Vegas, NV 89139
Phone: (702) 263-0146

#386
Aloha Kitchen & Bar
Category: Hawaiian, Karaoke, Bar
Average price: Under $10
Area: Westside
Address: 2605 S Decatur Blvd
Las Vegas, NV 89102
Phone: (702) 364-0064

#387
Krung Siam Thai Restaurant
Category: Thai
Average price: $11-30
Area: Chinatown
Address: 3755 Spring Mountain Rd
Las Vegas, NV 89102
Phone: (702) 735-9485

#388
Big Dog's Draft House
Category: American, Breweries
Average price: $11-30
Area: Northwest
Address: 4543 N Rancho Dr
Las Vegas, NV 89130
Phone: (702) 645-1404

#389
Cravings Buffet at Mirage
Category: Buffets
Average price: $11-30
Area: The Strip
Address: 3400 Las Vegas Blvd S
Las Vegas, NV 89109
Phone: (702) 791-7111

#390
Yanni's Greek Grill
Category: Greek
Average price: Under $10
Area: Southeast
Address: 9620 S Las Vegas Blvd
Las Vegas, NV 89123
Phone: (702) 754-4898

#391
Baja Taco
Category: Mexican
Average price: Under $10
Area: Spring Valley
Address: 4225 S Fort Apache Rd
Las Vegas, NV 89147
Phone: (702) 432-8225

#392
Wake Up Coffee Cafe
Category: Cafe
Average price: Under $10
Area: Westside
Address: 6350 W Charleston Blvd
Las Vegas, NV 89146
Phone: (702) 822-6885

#393
Chicago Brewing Co.
Category: Breweries, Pizza
Average price: Under $10
Area: Downtown
Address: 202 Fremont St
Las Vegas, NV 89101
Phone: (702) 385-4011

#394
White Cross Drugs
Category: Cafe
Average price: Under $10
Area: Downtown
Address: 1700 Las Vegas Blvd
S Las Vegas, NV 89104
Phone: (702) 444-4459

#395
Fresh Grill & Bar
Category: Sandwiches, American
Average price: Under $10
Area: The Strip, Eastside
Address: 3663 S Las Vegas Blvd
Las Vegas, NV 89109
Phone: (702) 734-9727

#396
Sonio's Cafe
Category: American, Hot Dogs, Cafe
Average price: Under $10
Area: Westside
Address: 3900 W Charleston Blvd
Las Vegas, NV 89102
Phone: (702) 307-2177

#397
Jimmy John's
Category: Sandwiches, Food Delivery
Services, Deli
Average price: Under $10
Area: Spring Valley
Address: 5469 S Rainbow Blvd
Las Vegas, NV 89118
Phone: (702) 247-8813

#398
21 Restaurant & Lounge
Category: Lounge,
Asian Fusion, Karaoke
Average price: $11-30
Area: Westside
Address: 6145 W Sahara Ave
Las Vegas, NV 89146
Phone: (702) 523-6286

#399
Pink Taco
Category: Mexican
Average price: $11-30
Area: Eastside
Address: 4455 Paradise Rd
Las Vegas, NV 89109
Phone: (702) 693-5525

#400
Sakun Thai
Category: Thai, Ethnic Food
Average price: $11-30
Area: Southeast
Address: 1725 E Warm Springs Rd
Las Vegas, NV 89119
Phone: (702) 270-2899

#401
Wazuzu
Category: Diners
Average price: $31-60
Area: The Strip
Address: 3131 Las Vegas Blvd
S Las Vegas, NV 89109
Phone: (702) 770-5388

#402
Pita Pit
Category: Mediterranean,
Fast Food, Greek
Average price: Under $10
Area: University
Address: 4680 S Maryland Pkwy
Las Vegas, NV 89119
Phone: (702) 431-6675

#403
India Palace
Category: Indian
Average price: $11-30
Area: Eastside
Address: 505 E Twain Ave
Las Vegas, NV 89169
Phone: (702) 796-4177

#404
Kaba Curry
Category: Japanese, Asian Fusion
Average price: Under $10
Area: Chinatown
Address: 5115 Spring Mountain Rd
Las Vegas, NV 89146
Phone: (702) 589-0370

#405
Rice n Noodle
Category: Chinese
Average price: Under $10
Area: Southwest
Address: 7910 S Rainbow Blvd
Las Vegas, NV 89139
Phone: (702) 614-1335

#406
Island Sushi and Grill
Category: Sushi Bar, Hawaiian
Average price: $11-30
Area: Southeast
Address: 9400 S Eastern Ave
Las Vegas, NV 89123
Phone: (702) 221-1600

#407
Frank & Fina's Cocina
Category: Mexican
Average price: $11-30
Area: Spring Valley
Address: 4175 S Grand Canyon Dr
Las Vegas, NV 89147
Phone: (702) 579-3017

#408
Taco Azteca
Category: Mexican
Average price: Under $10
Area: Eastside
Address: 4800 S Nellis Blvd
Las Vegas, NV 89122
Phone: (702) 769-3135

#409
Mac Shack Spring Valley
Category: Italian
Average price: $11-30
Area: Southwest
Address: 8680 W Warm Springs Rd
Las Vegas, NV 89148
Phone: (702) 463-2433

#410
Weeziana Gumbo & More
Category: Southern
Average price: Under $10
Area: Westside
Address: 6475 W Charleston Blvd
Las Vegas, NV 89146
Phone: (702) 822-4626

#411
Prima Pizza & Cafe
Category: Pizza
Average price: $11-30
Area: Southwest
Address: 7750 S Jones Blvd
Las Vegas, NV 89139
Phone: (702) 269-9944

#412
House of Blues
Category: Music Venues,
American, Hotel
Average price: $11-30
Area: The Strip
Address: 3950 Las Vegas Blvd
S Las Vegas, NV 89119
Phone: (702) 632-7607

#413
Scooter's Pub
Category: Sport Bar, American
Average price: $11-30
Area: Spring Valley
Address: 6200 S Rainbow Blvd
Las Vegas, NV 89118
Phone: (702) 227-9047

#414
KGB: Kerry's Gourmet Burgers
Category: Burgers
Average price: $11-30
Area: The Strip
Address: 3475 Las Vegas Blvd
South Las Vegas, NV 89109
Phone: (702) 369-5000

#415
7777 Bar & Grill
Category: Sport Bar, Chinese
Average price: Under $10
Area: Westside
Address: 7777 W Sahara Ave
Las Vegas, NV 89117
Phone: (702) 388-7777

#416
Uncle Joe's Pizza
Category: Pizza
Average price: Under $10
Area: Downtown
Address: 505 Fremont St
Las Vegas, NV 89101
Phone: (702) 385-2162

#417
Big Sur Oyster Bar
Category: Seafood
Average price: $11-30
Area: Southeast
Address: 9777 Las Vegas Blvd
S Las Vegas, NV 89183
Phone: (702) 796-7111

#418
Potato Corner
Category: American, Fast Food
Average price: Under $10
Area: Westside
Address: 4300 Meadow Ln
Las Vegas, NV 89107
Phone: (702) 822-6838

#419
Mac Shack
Category: Italian, Gluten-Free, Vegan
Average price: $11-30
Area: Westside
Address: 8975 W Charleston Blvd
Las Vegas, NV 89117
Phone: (702) 243-1722

#420
DJ Bibingkahan
Category: Filipino
Average price: Under $10
Area: Eastside
Address: 2680 S Maryland Pkwy
Las Vegas, NV 89109
Phone: (702) 732-9121

#421
Pho Thanh Huong
Category: Vietnamese, American
Average price: Under $10
Area: Southeast
Address: 1131 E Tropicana Ave
Las Vegas, NV 89119
Phone: (702) 739-8703

#422
Bob's East Side Deli
Category: Deli, Sandwiches
Average price: Under $10
Area: Southeast
Address: 2900 E Patrick Ln
Las Vegas, NV 89120
Phone: (702) 739-5860

#423
TJ's Steakhouse
Category: Steakhouses
Average price: $31-60
Area: Eastside
Address: 3000 Paradise Rd
Las Vegas, NV 89109
Phone: (702) 732-5645

#424
Cafe El Mundo Cubano
Category: Cuban
Average price: $11-30
Area: Westside
Address: 5781 W Sahara Ave
Las Vegas, NV 89146
Phone: (702) 472-8225

#425
Gordon Biersch Brewery Restaurant
Category: American, Bar, Breweries
Average price: $11-30
Area: Eastside
Address: 3987 Paradise Rd
Las Vegas, NV 89169
Phone: (702) 312-5247

#426
Buffalo Wild Wings
Category: Sport Bar,
Chicken Wings, American
Average price: $11-30
Area: Spring Valley
Address: 4280 Hualapi
Las Vegas, NV 89147
Phone: (702) 251-3911

#427
Lazy Joe's Fish & Chips
Category: Fish & Chips, Seafood
Average price: $11-30
Area: Southwest
Address: 7835 S Rainbow Blvd
Las Vegas, NV 89139
Phone: (702) 489-6523

#428
El Regio
Category: Mexican
Average price: Under $10
Area: Centennial, Northwest
Address: 5601 N Tenaya Way
Las Vegas, NV 89130
Phone: (702) 655-1333

#429
Bar + Bistro @ the Arts Factory
Category: American, Spanish,
Breakfast & Brunch
Average price: $11-30
Area: Downtown
Address: 107 E Charleston Blvd
Las Vegas, NV 89104
Phone: (702) 202-6060

#430
Rambo's Kitchen
Category: American
Average price: $11-30
Area: Spring Valley
Address: 6085 S Fort Apache Rd
Las Vegas, NV 89148
Phone: (702) 722-2626

#431
T&T - Tacos and Tequila
Category: Mexican
Average price: $11-30
Area: The Strip
Address: 3900 Las Vegas Blvd
Las Vegas, NV 89119
Phone: (702) 262-5225

#432
Pizza Company
Category: Pizza
Average price: Under $10
Area: Southeast
Address: 2275 E Sunset Rd
Las Vegas, NV 89119
Phone: (702) 363-9300

#433
A Thyme For All Seasons
Category: Cafe
Average price: $11-30
Area: Southeast
Address: 310 E Warm Springs Rd
Las Vegas, NV 89119
Phone: (702) 614-0023

#434
Steak 'n Shake
Category: Burgers, Fast Food
Average price: Under $10
Area: Southeast
Address: 9777 Las Vegas Blvd
S Las Vegas, NV 89183
Phone: (702) 796-7111

#435
Kumi Japanese Restaurant + Bar
Category: Japanese, Sushi Bar
Average price: $31-60
Area: The Strip
Address: 3950 Las Vegas Blvd
S Las Vegas, NV 89119
Phone: (702) 693-8300

#436
Bobby's Burger Palace
Category: Burgers, American
Average price: $11-30
Area: The Strip
Address: 3750 S Las Vegas Blvd
Las Vegas, NV 89109
Phone: (702) 598-0191

#437
Joe's New York Pizza
Category: Pizza
Average price: Under $10
Area: Eastside
Address: 4480 Paradise Rd
Las Vegas, NV 89169
Phone: (702) 792-9001

#438
North End Pizza
Category: Pizza, Italian
Average price: $11-30
Area: Centennial
Address: 6440 N Durango Dr
Las Vegas, NV 89149
Phone: (702) 645-9006

#439
Jason's Deli
Category: Deli, Salad, Sandwiches
Average price: Under $10
Area: Downtown
Address: 100 City Pkwy
Las Vegas, NV 89101
Phone: (702) 366-0130

#440
Crazy Pita Rotisserie & Grill
Category: Mediterranean
Average price: $11-30
Area: Southeast
Address: 6587 S Las Vegas Blvd,
Ste 190, Las Vegas, NV 89119
Phone: (702) 778-3310

#441
Rock'N'oodles
Category: American
Average price: $11-30
Area: Downtown
Address: 1108 S 3rd St
Las Vegas, NV 89104
Phone: (702) 522-9953

#442
Bob Taylor's Ranch House
Category: Steakhouses, American
Average price: $31-60
Area: Centennial
Address: 6250 Rio Vista St
Las Vegas, NV 89130
Phone: (702) 645-1399

#443
Fuji Japanese Restaurant
Category: Japanese, Steakhouses
Average price: $11-30
Area: Eastside
Address: 3430 E Tropicana Ave
Las Vegas, NV 89121
Phone: (702) 435-8838

#444
Sushi Bomb
Category: Sushi Bar, Japanese
Average price: $11-30
Area: Northwest, Summerlin
Address: 10470 W Cheyenne Ave
Las Vegas, NV 89129
Phone: (702) 272-1000

#445
Fireside Restaurant & Tavern
Category: Bar, American
Average price: $11-30
Area: Southeast
Address: 1785 E Cactus Ave
Las Vegas, NV 89183
Phone: (702) 307-7000

#446
Daisho Sushi
Category: Sushi Bar
Average price: $11-30
Area: Southeast
Address: 7435 S Eastern Ave
Las Vegas, NV 89123
Phone: (702) 570-5600

#447
Tacos La Mexicana
Category: Mexican,
Food Delivery Services
Average price: Under $10
Area: Spring Valley
Address: 3555 S Durango Dr
Las Vegas, NV 89147
Phone: (702) 233-5070

#448
Zabas Mexican Grill
Category: Mexican
Average price: Under $10
Area: Southeast, Anthem
Address: 9905 S Eastern Ave
Las Vegas, NV 89183
Phone: (702) 453-9222

#449
Khoury's Mediterranean Restaurant
Category: Greek, Middle Eastern,
Mediterranean
Average price: $11-30
Area: Spring Valley
Address: 6115 S Fort Apache Rd
Las Vegas, NV 89148
Phone: (702) 671-0005

#450
Original Pancake House
Category: Breakfast & Brunch
Average price: $11-30
Area: Spring Valley
Address: 4170 S Ft Apache Rd
Las Vegas, NV 89147
Phone: (702) 433-5800

#451
Mr. Lucky's Cafe Vegas
Category: Diners, American
Average price: $11-30
Area: Eastside
Address: 4455 Paradise Rd
Las Vegas, NV 89136
Phone: (702) 693-5000

#452
Canyon Ranch
SpaClub Las Vegas
Category: Breakfast & Brunch,
Cafe, Desserts
Average price: $11-30
Area: The Strip
Address: 3355 Las Vegas Blvd.
South Suite 1159, Las Vegas, NV 89109
Phone: (702) 414-3600

#453
Zaba's Mexican Grill
Category: Mexican
Average price: Under $10
Area: Eastside
Address: 3318 E Flamingo Rd
Las Vegas, NV 89121
Phone: (702) 435-9222

#454
Mulligan's Border Bar & Grill
Category: American
Average price: Under $10
Area: Southeast
Address: 1235 E Pebble Rd
Las Vegas, NV 89123
Phone: (702) 614-6660

#455
Dona Maria Tamales Restaurant
Category: Mexican
Average price: $11-30
Area: Downtown
Address: 910 Las Vegas Blvd
S Las Vegas, NV 89101
Phone: (702) 382-6538

#456
Mi Ga
Category: Korean, Hawaiian
Average price: Under $10
Area: Chinatown
Address: 6850 Spring Mt Rd
Las Vegas, NV 89146
Phone: (702) 220-4516

#457
Taiga Modern Japanese & Thai Restaurant
Category: Japanese, Thai
Average price: $11-30
Area: Southeast
Address: 3130 E Sunset Rd
Las Vegas, NV 89120
Phone: (702) 388-8884

#458
Pizza Lounge
Category: Pizza, Italian
Average price: $11-30
Area: Westside
Address: 420 S Rampart Blvd
Las Vegas, NV 89145
Phone: (702) 778-0400

#459
Sushiko
Category: Japanese, Sushi Bar
Average price: $11-30
Area: Northwest
Address: 7101 W Craig Rd
Las Vegas, NV 89129
Phone: (702) 655-5782

#460
Gonzalez Y Gonzalez Mexican Restaurant
Category: Mexican
Average price: $11-30
Area: The Strip
Address: 3790 Las Vegas Blvd
S Las Vegas, NV 89109
Phone: (702) 740-6455

#461
D.O.C.G.
Category: Italian
Average price: $31-60
Area: The Strip
Address: 3708 Las Vegas Blvd
S Las Vegas, NV 89109
Phone: (702) 698-7920

#462
Barcelona Tapas Restaurant
Category: Spanish, Tapas Bar
Average price: $11-30
Area: Southwest
Address: 10690 Southern Highlands Pkwy,
Las Vegas, NV 89141
Phone: (702) 483-5764

#463
Battista's Hole In the Wall
Category: Italian
Average price: $11-30
Area: The Strip
Address: 4041 Audrie St
Las Vegas, NV 89109
Phone: (702) 732-1424

#464
Dae Jang Keum Korean BBQ & Tofu Restaurant
Category: Korean
Average price: $11-30
Area: Chinatown
Address: 3943 Spring Mountain Rd
Las Vegas, NV 89102
Phone: (702) 638-2222

#465
SmashBurger
Category: Burgers
Average price: Under $10
Area: Centennial, Northwest
Address: 5655 Centennial Center Blvd
Las Vegas, NV 89149
Phone: (702) 462-5503

#466
Carnegie
Category: Deli, Sandwiches, American
Average price: $11-30
Area: The Strip
Address: 3400 Las Vegas Blvd S
Las Vegas, NV 89109
Phone: (702) 791-7310

#467
Backstage Deli
Category: Breakfast & Brunch, Sandwiches
Average price: $11-30
Area: The Strip
Address: 3900 Las Vegas Blvd
S Las Vegas, NV 89109
Phone: (702) 262-4778

#468
Kabuki Japanese Restaurant
Category: Japanese,
Sushi Bar, Asian Fusion
Average price: $11-30
Area: Westside
Address: 400 S Rampart Blvd
Las Vegas, NV 89145
Phone: (702) 685-7776

#469
Del Frisco's Double Eagle Steak House
Category: Steakhouses
Average price: Above $61
Area: Eastside
Address: 3925 Paradise Rd
Las Vegas, NV 89169
Phone: (702) 796-0063

#470
Angie's Soul Food Kitchen IJN
Category: Soul Food
Average price: Under $10
Area: Eastside
Address: 860 E Twain
Las Vegas, NV 89169
Phone: (702) 296-8173

#471
Egg Works
Category: American,
Breakfast & Brunch, Brasseries
Average price: $11-30
Area: Spring Valley
Address: 9355 W Flamingo Rd
Las Vegas, NV 89147
Phone: (702) 368-3447

#472
Wahoo's Fish Tacos
Category: Mexican, Seafood
Average price: Under $10
Area: Spring Valley
Address: 7020 W. Sunset Rd
Las Vegas, NV 89113
Phone: (702) 399-1665

#473
Rounders
Category: American, Sport Bar
Average price: $11-30
Area: Southwest
Address: 8030 Blue Diamond Rd
Las Vegas, NV 89113
Phone: (702) 212-0594

#474
Carmine's
Category: Italian
Average price: $31-60
Area: The Strip
Address: 3500 S Las Vegas Blvd
Las Vegas, NV 89109
Phone: (702) 473-9700

#475
Lahaina Grill
Category: Sushi Bar
Average price: $11-30
Area: Spring Valley, South Summerlin
Address: 4570 S Hualapai Way
Las Vegas, NV 89147
Phone: (702) 309-9911

#476
T-Bird Lounge & Restaurant
Category: Sport Bar, Diners
Average price: $11-30
Area: Southwest, Spring Valley
Address: 6560 W Warm Springs Rd
Las Vegas, NV 89118
Phone: (702) 617-6775

#477
Teriyaki Madness
Category: Japanese,
Asian Fusion, Hawaiian
Average price: Under $10
Area: Southeast
Address: 9845 S Maryland Pkwy
Las Vegas, NV 89183
Phone: (702) 252-8623

#478
Los Jarochos Restaurant
Category: Mexican
Average price: Under $10
Area: Spring Valley
Address: 4811 S Rainbow Blvd
Las Vegas, NV 89147
Phone: (702) 646-0125

#479
STRIPSTEAK
Category: Steakhouses, Cheesesteaks
Average price: Above $61
Area: The Strip
Address: 3950 S Las Vegas Boulevard
Las Vegas, NV 89119
Phone: (702) 632-7200

#480
Olive Garden Italian Restaurant
Category: Italian
Average price: $11-30
Area: University
Address: 1545 E Flamingo Rd
Las Vegas, NV 89119
Phone: (702) 735-0082

#481
Baan Mae Toy
Category: Thai
Average price: Under $10
Area: Westside
Address: 4105 W Sahara Ave
Las Vegas, NV 89102
Phone: (702) 362-3624

#482
Sierra Gold
Category: American, Sport Bar, Pub
Average price: $11-30
Area: Summerlin
Address: 2400 N Buffalo Dr
Las Vegas, NV 89128
Phone: (702) 724-7004

#483
Chipotle
Category: Mexican
Average price: Under $10
Area: University
Address: 4530 S Maryland Pkwy
Las Vegas, NV 89119
Phone: (702) 436-9177

#484
Doh Sushi & Tapas
Category: Sushi Bar
Average price: $11-30
Area: Chinatown
Address: 3909 Spring Mt Rd
Las Vegas, NV 89102
Phone: (702) 257-1100

#485
Pin Up Pizza
Category: Pizza
Average price: Under $10
Area: The Strip
Address: 3667 Las Vegas Blvd S
Las Vegas, NV 89109
Phone: (702) 785-5888

#486
Spice Market Buffet
Category: Buffets
Average price: $11-30
Area: The Strip
Address: 3667 Las Vegas Boulevard South,
Las Vegas, NV 89109
Phone: (702) 785-5555

#487
Mr.
Category: Chinese
Average price: Under $10
Area: Eastside
Address: 730 E Flamingo Rd
Las Vegas, NV 89119
Phone: (702) 633-8883

#488
Teriyaki House
Category: Japanese
Average price: Under $10
Area: Spring Valley
Address: 6181 S. Rainbow Blvd
Las Vegas, NV 89118
Phone: (702) 365-9292

#489
Rhythm Kitchen
Category: Seafood, Steakhouses,
Cajun/Creole
Average price: $11-30
Area: Spring Valley
Address: 6435 S Decatur Blvd
Las Vegas, NV 89118
Phone: (702) 767-8438

#490
Second Street Grill
Category: American, American
Average price: $31-60
Area: Downtown
Address: 200 Fremont St
Las Vegas, NV 89101
Phone: (702) 385-6277

#491
Raising Cane's
Category: Fast Food, Chicken Wings
Average price: Under $10
Area: Southwest, Spring Valley
Address: 7135 S Rainbow Blvd
Las Vegas, NV 89118
Phone: (702) 233-2263

#492
China A Go Go
Category: Chinese
Average price: Under $10
Area: Sunrise
Address: 5841 E Charleston Blvd
Las Vegas, NV 89142
Phone: (702) 432-0234

#493
The Hush Puppy
Category: Seafood, Southern
Average price: $11-30
Area: Westside
Address: 7185 W Charleston Blvd
Las Vegas, NV 89117
Phone: (702) 363-5988

#494
The Cracked Egg
Category: Breakfast & Brunch
Average price: $11-30
Area: Centennial, Northwest
Address: 5570 Painted Mirage
Las Vegas, NV 89149
Phone: (702) 645-9438

#495
Sun's Thai Food & Jerky
Category: Thai, Food
Average price: $11-30
Area: Northwest
Address: 4941 W Craig Rd
Las Vegas, NV 89130
Phone: (702) 272-1381

#496
Mr.
Category: Thai, Chinese
Average price: Under $10
Area: Southeast
Address: 5075 S Pecos Rd
Las Vegas, NV 89120
Phone: (702) 456-2020

#497
Cafe Bellagio
Category: American, Cafe
Average price: $11-30
Area: The Strip
Address: 3600 S Las Vegas Blvd
Las Vegas, NV 89109
Phone: (702) 693-7356

#498
Fu Restaurant
Category: Asian Fusion, Cantonese
Average price: $11-30
Area: Eastside
Address: 4455 Paradise Rd
Las Vegas, NV 89169
Phone: (702) 522-8188

#499
China Gourmet
Category: Chinese
Average price: Under $10
Area: Sunrise
Address: 2585 S. Nellis Blvd
Las Vegas, NV 89121
Phone: (702) 431-8090

#500
Capriotti's Sandwich Shop
Category: Deli, Sandwiches
Average price: $11-30
Area: Eastside
Address: 3830 E Flamingo Rd
Las Vegas, NV 89121
Phone: (702) 454-2430

TOP 400
ARTS & ENTERTAINMENT
The Most Recommended by Locals and Travelers
(From #1 to #400)

#1
Absinthe
Category: Performing Arts
Area: The Strip
Address: Flamingo Rd and
Las Vegas Blvd
Las Vegas, NV 89109
Phone: (800) 745-3000

#2
Neon Museum
Category: Museum
Area: Downtown
Address: 770 Las Vegas Blvd
N Las Vegas, NV 89101
Phone: (702) 387-6366

#3
JABBAWOCKEEZ
Category: Performing Arts
Area: The Strip
Address: 3900 Las Vegas Blvd
S Las Vegas, NV 89119
Phone: (877) 386-4658

#4
Conservatory & Botanical Garden
Category: Botanical Garden
Area: The Strip
Address: 3600 S Las Vegas Blvd
Las Vegas, NV 89109
Phone: (702) 650-9459

#5
Cirque du Soleil
Michael Jackson One
Category: Performing Arts
Area: The Strip
Address: 3950 S Las Vegas Boulevard
Las Vegas, NV 89109
Phone: (877) 632-7400

#6
Cirque du Soleil
The Beatles LOVE
Category: Performing Arts
Area: The Strip
Address: 3400 Las Vegas Blvd
S Las Vegas, NV 89109
Phone: (866) 963-9634

#7
Cirque du Soleil - O
Category: Performing Arts
Area: The Strip
Address: 3600 S Las Vegas Blvd
Las Vegas, NV 89109
Phone: (702) 796-9999

#8
Trapeze Las Vegas
Category: Performing Arts,
Recreation Center
Area: Southeast
Address: 121 E. Sunset rd.
Las Vegas, NV 89119
Phone: (702) 551-4858

#9
Carrot Top
Category: Performing Arts
Area: The Strip
Address: 3900 Las Vegas Blvd
S Las Vegas, NV 89109
Phone: (702) 262-4400

#10
The Mob Museum
Category: Museum
Area: Downtown
Address: 300 Stewart Ave
Las Vegas, NV 89101
Phone: (702) 229-2734

#11
Titanic - The Artifact Exhibition
Category: Museum
Area: The Strip
Address: 3900 Las Vegas Blvd
S Las Vegas, NV 89109
Phone: (800) 288-1000

#12
Human Nature
Category: Performing Arts
Area: The Strip
Address: 3355 Las Vegas Blvd S,
Sands Showroom
Las Vegas, NV 89109
Phone: (866) 641-7469

#13
Le Re've - The Dream
Category: Performing Arts
Area: The Strip
Address: 3131 Las Vegas Blvd
S Las Vegas, NV 89109
Phone: (888) 320-7110

#14
Pinball Hall Of Fame
Category: Museum, Arcade
Area: University
Address: 1610 E Tropicana Ave
Las Vegas, NV 89119
Phone: (702) 597-2627

#15
Double Down Saloon
Category: Music Venues
Area: Eastside
Address: 4640 Paradise Rd
Las Vegas, NV 89109
Phone: (702) 791-5775

#16
Cirque du Soleil - Mystère
Category: Performing Arts
Area: The Strip
Address: 3300 S Las Vegas Blvd
Las Vegas, NV 89109
Phone: (800) 392-1999

#17
The Mac King Comedy Magic Show
Category: Performing Arts
Area: The Strip
Address: 3475 Las Vegas Blvd
S Las Vegas, NV 89109
Phone: (702) 693-6143

#18
Raiding The Rock Vault
Category: Performing Arts, Music Venues
Area: The Strip
Address: 3000 Paradise Rd
Las Vegas, NV 89109
Phone: (702) 889-2705

#19
Cirque du Soleil - Zumanity
Category: Performing Arts, Adult Entertainment
Area: The Strip
Address: 3790 Las Vegas Blvd
S Las Vegas, NV 89109
Phone: (702) 740-6815

#20
Erotic Heritage Museum
Category: Museum
Area: The Strip
Address: 3275 Industrial Rd
Las Vegas, NV 89109
Phone: (702) 794-4000

#21
The Smith Center
Category: Performing Arts
Area: Downtown
Address: 361 Symphony Park Ave
Las Vegas, NV 89106
Phone: (702) 749-2012

#22
Recycled Percussion
Category: Performing Arts
Area: The Strip
Address: 3535 Las Vegas Blvd
Las Vegas, NV 89109
Phone: (702) 794-3261

#23
Freakin' Frog
Category: Music Venues, Pub
Area: University
Address: 4700 S Maryland Pkwy
Las Vegas, NV 89119
Phone: (702) 597-9702

#24
BODIES...
Category: Museum
Area: The Strip
Address: 3900 Las Vegas Blvd
S Las Vegas, NV 89119
Phone: (800) 829-9034

#25
National Atomic Testing Museum
Category: Museum
Area: University, Eastside
Address: 755 E Flamingo Rd
Las Vegas, NV 89119
Phone: (702) 794-5151

#26
Springs Preserve
Category: Botanical Garden, Park, Venues & Event Space
Area: Westside
Address: 333 S Valley View Blvd
Las Vegas, NV 89136
Phone: (702) 822-7700

#27
Madame Tussauds
Category: Museum
Area: Eastside
Address: 3377 Las Vegas Blvd
S Las Vegas, NV 89109
Phone: (702) 862-7800

#28
MO5AIC
Category: Performing Arts
Area: Eastside
Address: 3000 Paradise Rd
Las Vegas, NV 89109
Phone: (800) 222-5361

#29
Rock Of Ages
At The Venetian Las Vegas
Category: Performing Arts
Area: The Strip
Address: 3355 S Las Vegas Blvd
Las Vegas, NV 89109
Phone: (702) 414-9000

#30
Rose.
Category: Bar, Performing Arts
Area: The Strip
Address: 3708 Las Vegas Blvd S
Las Vegas, NV 89109
Phone: (877) 667-0585

#31
Design & Wine
Category: Party & Event Planning
Area: Southwest, Spring Valley
Address: 7250 S Durango Dr
Las Vegas, NV 89148
Phone: (702) 327-7325

#32
Art-Hropologie
Category: Art Gallery
Area: University
Address: 1516 Tropicanna
Las Vegas, NV 89119
Phone: (702) 321-1960

#33
Insert Coins
Category: Bar, Arcade
Area: Downtown
Address: 512 Fremont St
Las Vegas, NV 89101
Phone: (702) 477-2525

#34
The Arts Factory
Category: Art Gallery
Area: Downtown
Address: 107 E Charleston Blvd
Las Vegas, NV 89104
Phone: (702) 676-1111

#35
Pearl Concert Theater
At Palms Casino Resort
Category: Music Venues
Area: Chinatown
Address: 4321 W Flamingo Rd
Las Vegas, NV 89103
Phone: (866) 942-7777

#36
Gene Woods Racing Experience
Category: Race Track,
 Amusement Park, Go Karts
Area: Southeast
Address: 121 E Sunset Rd
Las Vegas, NV 89119
Phone: (702) 270-8100

#37
Press Start Gaming Center
Category: Arcade, Party & Event Planning
Area: Spring Valley
Address: 4840 S Fort Apache Rd
Las Vegas, NV 89147
Phone: (702) 227-4263

#38
Fremont Street Experience
Category: Bar, Casino
Area: Downtown
Address: 425 Fremont St
Las Vegas, NV 89101
Phone: (702) 678-5600

#39
The Colosseum
At Caesars Palace
Category: Music Venues
Area: The Strip
Address: 3570 South Las Vegas Blvd
Las Vegas, NV 89109
Phone: (702) 731-7208

#40
Illusions By Jan Rouven
Category: Performing Arts
Area: The Strip
Address: 2901 Las Vegas Blvd. South
Las Vegas, NV 89109
Phone: (702) 800-5888

#41
Shania: Still the One
Category: Performing Arts
Area: The Strip
Address: 3570 Las Vegas Blvd
Las Vegas, NV 89109
Phone: (866) 574-3851

#42
VEGAS! The Show
Category: Performing Arts
Area: The Strip
Address: 3663 Las Vegas Blvd S
Las Vegas, NV 89109
Phone: (866) 932-1818

#43
Veronic Voices
Category: Performing Arts
Area: The Strip
Address: 3645 Las Vegas Boulevard S
Las Vegas, NV 89109
Phone: (702) 777-2782

#44
Sigma Derby
Category: Horse Racing, Casino
Area: Eastside
Address: 3799 Las Vegas Bl S
Las Vegas, NV 89109
Phone: (702) 880-0880

#45
Cellar Lounge
Category: Bar, Music Venues
Area: Westside
Address: 3601 W Sahara Ave
Las Vegas, NV 89102
Phone: (702) 362-6268

#46
Freakling Bros
The Trilogy of Terror
Category: Performing Arts
Area: Northwest
Address: 2321 N Rainbow Blvd
Las Vegas, NV 89108
Phone: (702) 362-3327

#47
Panda!
Category: Performing Arts
Area: The Strip
Address: 3325 S Las Vegas Blvd
Las Vegas, NV 89109
Phone: (702) 414-9000

#48
Las Vegas Little Theatre
Category: Performing Arts
Area: Chinatown
Address: 3920 Schiff Dr
Las Vegas, NV 89103
Phone: (702) 362-7996

#49
Las Vegas Greek Festival
Category: Festival, Food
Area: Spring Valley
Address: 5300 S El Camino Rd
Las Vegas, NV 89118
Phone: (702) 221-8245

#50
Brooklyn Bowl
Category: Bowling, Music Venues
Area: The Strip
Address: 3545 Las Vegas Blvd S
Las Vegas, NV 89109
Phone: (702) 862-2695

#51
Las Vegas Natural History Museum
Category: Museum
Area: Downtown
Address: 900 Las Vegas Blvd N
Las Vegas, NV 89101
Phone: (702) 384-3466

#52
Terry Cavaretta Trapeze Experience
Category: Recreation Center
Area: Summerlin
Address: 1400 N Rampart Blvd
Las Vegas, NV 89128
Phone: (702) 496-9237

#53
Pure Aloha Festival
Category: Festival
Area: Chinatown
Address: 3700 W Flamingo Rd
Las Vegas, NV 89103
Phone: (702) 777-7777

#54
Rehab
Category: Swimming Pool
Area: Eastside
Address: 4455 Paradise Rd
Las Vegas, NV 89169
Phone: (702) 693-5000

#55
Marc Savard Comedy Hypnosis
Category: Performing Arts
Area: The Strip
Address: 3663 Las Vegas Blvd S
Las Vegas, NV 89109
Phone: (702) 260-7200

#56
Evil Dead the Musical 4D
Category: Performing Arts
Area: The Strip
Address: 3663 Las Vegas Blvd
Las Vegas, NV 89109
Phone: (866) 932-1818

#57
Pinball Classics
Category: Arcade
Area: Downtown
Address: 1400 S Main St
Las Vegas, NV 89104
Phone: (702) 985-7778

#58
B - A TRIBUTE to The Beatles
Category: Performing Arts
Area: The Strip
Address: 3663 Las Vegas Blvd
Las Vegas, NV 89109
Phone: (866) 932-1818

#59
Zombie Burlesque
Category: Performing Arts
Area: The Strip
Address: 3663 S Las Vegas Blvd
Las Vegas, NV 89109
Phone: (866) 260-7200

#60
The Lady Silvia
Category: Music Venues
Area: Downtown
Address: 900 Las Vegas Blvd S
Las Vegas, NV 89101
Phone: (702) 405-0816

#61
Brenden Theatres
Category: Cinema
Area: Chinatown
Address: 4321 W Flamingo Rd
Las Vegas, NV 89103
Phone: (702) 507-4849

#62
The Paiza Club
Category: Restaurant, Casino
Area: Eastside
Address: 3355 Las Vegas Blvd S
Las Vegas, NV 89109
Phone: (702) 414-1000

#63
Leatherneck Club
of Greater NV 186
Category: Social Club
Area: Chinatown
Address: 4360 Spring Mountain Rd
Las Vegas, NV 89102
Phone: (702) 368-1775

#64
The Mentalist
Category: Performing Arts
Area: The Strip
Address: 3663 Las Vegas Blvd
Las Vegas, NV 89109
Phone: (702) 260-7200

#65
David Copperfield
Category: Performing Arts
Area: The Strip, Eastside
Address: 3799 Las Vegas Blvd S
Las Vegas, NV 89109
Phone: (702) 891-7777

#66
Commonwealth
Category: Cocktail Bar, Music Venues
Area: Downtown
Address: 525 E Fremont St
Las Vegas, NV 89101
Phone: (702) 445-6400

#67
Thomas & Mack Center
Category: Stadium
Area: University
Address: Swenson & Thomas and Mack Dr
Las Vegas, NV 89154
Phone: (702) 895-3761

#68
Zarkana by Cirque du Soleil
Category: Performing Arts
Area: The Strip
Address: 3730 Las Vegas Blvd S
Las Vegas, NV 89158
Phone: (855) 927-5262

#69
Count's Vamp'd
Category: Music Venues
Area: Westside
Address: 6750 W Sahara Ave
Las Vegas, NV 89146
Phone: (702) 220-8849

#70
The Price is Right, Live!
Category: Performing Arts
Area: The Strip
Address: 3645 Las Vegas Blvd S
Las Vegas, NV 89109
Phone: (702) 967-4567

#71
Jeff Civillico
Comedy In Action Show
Category: Comedy Club
Area: The Strip
Address: 3535 Las Vegas Blvd S
Las Vegas, NV 89109
Phone: (702) 794-3296

#72
Viva Las Vegas Rockabilly Weekend
Category: Festival, Local Flavor
Area: Chinatown
Address: 4500 W Tropicana Ave
Las Vegas, NV 89103
Phone: (702) 365-7111

#73
The Burlesque Hall of Fame
Category: Performing Arts
Area: Downtown
Address: 520 Fremont St
Las Vegas, NV 89101
Phone: (888) 661-6465

#74
Popovich Comedy Pet Theater
Category: Performing Arts
Area: The Strip
Address: 3663 Las Vegas Blvd S
Las Vegas, NV 89109
Phone: (866) 932-1818

#75
The Living Garden Show
Category: Performing Arts
Area: Westside
Address: 3325 Las Vegas Blvd S
Las Vegas, NV 89109
Phone: (702) 607-7777

#76
Wynn Las Vegas
Category: Hotel, Casino, Resort
Area: The Strip
Address: 3131 Las Vegas Blvd. South
Las Vegas, NV 89109
Phone: (702) 770-7000

#77
AMC Town Square 18
Category: Cinema
Area: Southeast
Address: 6587 Las Vegas Blvd S
Las Vegas, NV 89119
Phone: (702) 362-7283

#78
Wolf Theater
Category: Performing Arts,
Music Venues, Comedy Club
Area: Eastside
Address: 305 Convention Center Dr
Las Vegas, NV 89109
Phone: (702) 990-1524

#79
Sin City Gallery
Category: Art Gallery
Area: Downtown
Address: 107 E Charleston Blvd
Las Vegas, NV 89104
Phone: (702) 608-2461

#80
The Sci-Fi Center
Category: Cinema, Comic Book
Area: Downtown
Address: 600 East Sahara Ave
Las Vegas, NV 89104
Phone: (702) 792-4335

#81
The Pointe Dance Center
Category: Performing Arts,
Dance Studio
Area: Spring Valley
Address: 9340 W Flamingo Rd
Las Vegas, NV 89147
Phone: (702) 363-3070

#82
Score! Interactive Sport Exhibit
Category: Museum
Area: The Strip
Address: 3900 Las Vegas Blvd S
Las Vegas, NV 89109
Phone: (702) 262-4200

#83
Great Vegas Festival of Beer
Category: Festival
Area: Downtown
Address: 601 Fremont Ave
Las Vegas, NV 89101
Phone: (702) 685-9319

#84
Childs' Play
Category: Arcade, Toy Store
Area: Centennial
Address: 7060 N Durango Dr
Las Vegas, NV 89149
Phone: (702) 834-5500

#85
Tropicana Cinemas
Category: Cinema
Area: Eastside
Address: 3330 E Tropicana Ave
Las Vegas, NV 89121
Phone: (702) 438-3456

#86
Mystere Theatre At Treasure Island Hotel And Casino
Category: Music Venues
Area: The Strip
Address: 3300 Las Vegas Blvd S
Las Vegas, NV 89193
Phone: (213) 480-2323

#87
The Rat Pack is Back
Category: Performing Arts
Area: Chinatown
Address: 3700 W Flamingo Road
Las Vegas, NV 89103
Phone: (702) 777-7776

#88
Gold Diggers
Category: Dance Club, Lounge, Music Venues
Area: Downtown
Address: 129 E Fremont St
Las Vegas, NV 89101
Phone: (702) 385-7111

#89
MIX 94.1's Bite Of Las Vegas
Category: Music Venues
Area: Spring Valley
Address: 8275 W Spring Mtn Rd
Las Vegas, NV 89117
Phone: (702) 566-7387

#90
The Roller Coaster
Category: Amusement Park
Area: The Strip
Address: 3790 S Las Vegas Blvd
Las Vegas, NV 89119
Phone: (702) 740-6969

#91
Downtown Brew Festival
Category: Festival
Area: Downtown
Address: 500 S Grand Central Pkwy
Las Vegas, NV 89106
Phone: (702) 685-9319

#92
Defending the Caveman
Category: Performing Arts
Area: Downtown
Address: 3475 Las Vegas Blvd
Las Vegas, NV 89101
Phone: (800) 214-9110

#93
Blackbird Studio
Category: Art Gallery
Area: Downtown
Address: 1551 S Commerce St
Las Vegas, NV 89102
Phone: (702) 782-0319

#94
Celine
Category: Performing Arts
Area: The Strip
Address: 3570 Las Vegas Blvd S
Las Vegas, NV 89109
Phone: (702) 866-1400

#95
Wynn Theater At Wynn Las Vegas
Category: Performing Arts
Area: The Strip
Address: 3131 Las Vegas Blvd
Las Vegas, NV 89109
Phone: (702) 770-9966

#96
The Phat Pack
Category: Performing Arts
Area: The Strip
Address: 3655 Las Vegas Blvd S
Las Vegas, NV 89101
Phone: (702) 892-7575

#97
3d Mini Golf & Family Fun Center
Category: Mini Golf, Arcade
Area: Southeast
Address: 3315 E Russell Rd
Las Vegas, NV 89120
Phone: (702) 608-4653

#98
Big League Dreams Sport Park
Category: Amateur Sport Team, Stadium
Area: Downtown
Address: 3151 E Washington Ave
Las Vegas, NV 89101
Phone: (702) 642-4448

#99
Tribute Royalty
Category: Performing Arts
Area: The Strip
Address: 3663 Las Vegas Blvd S
Las Vegas, NV 89109
Phone: (702) 260-7200

#100
Nevada State Museum,
Las Vegas
Category: Museum
Area: Westside
Address: 309 S Valley View Blvd
Las Vegas, NV 89107
Phone: (702) 486-5205

#101
Kids Planet
Category: Venues & Event Space,
Arcade
Area: Spring Valley
Address: 4215 S Durango Dr
Las Vegas, NV 89147
Phone: (702) 456-5454

#102
Sgt. Pepper Live
Category: Performing Arts
Area: The Strip
Address: 3655 Las Vegas Blvd S
Las Vegas, NV 89109
Phone: (888) 727-4758

#103
Pin Up
Category: Music Venues
Area: The Strip
Address: 2000 Las Vegas Blvd
Las Vegas, NV 89104
Phone: (702) 380-7777

#104
SQUAWK! the Show
Category: Performing Arts
Area: Eastside
Address: 3500 Paradise Rd At Edison Cir.
Las Vegas, NV 89169
Phone: (702) 966-9770

#105
Nirvana Pool
Category: Music Venues,
Swimming Pool, Bar
Area: Eastside
Address: 4455 Paradise Rd
Las Vegas, NV 89169
Phone: (702) 639-5022

#106
London Dance Academy
Category: Performing Arts
Area: Eastside
Address: 2585 E Flamingo Road
Las Vegas, NV 89121
Phone: (702) 737-1202

#107
Wayne Brady - Making %@it Up
Category: Performing Arts
Area: Downtown
Address: 3355 Las Vegas Blvd S
Las Vegas, NV 89101
Phone: (702) 414-9000

#108
Killer Klowns Rehashed
Haunted House
Category: Performing Arts
Area: Westside
Address: 409 Upland Blvd.
Las Vegas, NV 89107
Phone: (702) 834-4180

#109
Olivia Newton-John
Summer Nights
Category: Performing Arts
Area: Eastside
Address: 3555 Las Vegas Blvd S
Las Vegas, NV 89109
Phone: (702) 777-2782

#110
The Cosmopolitan
Boulevard Pool
Category: Swimming Pool, Music Venues
Area: The Strip
Address: 3708 Las Vegas Blvd S
Las Vegas, NV 89109
Phone: (702) 698-7000

#111
MJ Live A Michael Jackson Tribute
Category: Performing Arts
Area: Chinatown
Address: 3700 W Flamingo Rd
Las Vegas, NV 89103
Phone: (866) 746-7671

#112
V - The Ultimate Variety Show
Category: Performing Arts
Area: The Strip
Address: 3663 Las Vegas Blvd S
Las Vegas, NV 89109
Phone: (702) 260-7200

#113
Surf The Musical Songs
Of The Beach Boys
Category: Music Venues
Area: The Strip
Address: 3667 Las Vegas Blvd S
Las Vegas, NV 89109
Phone: (800) 745-3000

#114
Chippendales
Category: Performing Arts,
Adult Entertainment
Area: Chinatown
Address: 3700 W Flamingo Rd
Las Vegas, NV 89103
Phone: (866) 244-7999

#115
Galavantier
Category: Party & Event Planning
Area: Southwest
Address: 7660 Dean Martin Dr
Las Vegas, NV 89139
Phone: (877) 425-2826

#116
Slots A Fun
Category: Amusement Park,
Hotel, Casino
Area: The Strip
Address: 2800 Las Vegas Blvd S
Las Vegas, NV 89109
Phone: (702) 734-0410

#117
Remembering Red
A Tribute to Red Skelton
Category: Performing Arts
Area: Eastside
Address: 160 E Flamingo Rd
Las Vegas, NV 89109
Phone: (724) 513-4031

#118
The Dive Bar
Category: Dive Bar, Music Venues
Area: University, Eastside
Address: 4110 S Maryland Pkwy
Las Vegas, NV 89119
Phone: (702) 586-3483

#119
Icewine Tasting with Famed Vintner
Donald Ziraldo
Category: Winery
Area: The Strip
Address: 2000 Fashion Show Dr
Las Vegas, NV 89109
Phone: (702) 982-0000

#120
Cockroach Theatre
Category: Performing Arts
Area: Downtown
Address: 1025 S 1st St
Las Vegas, NV 89101
Phone: (702) 818-3422

#121
Mike Hammer
Comedy Magic Show
Category: Performing Arts
Area: Downtown
Address: 202 Fremont St
Las Vegas, NV 89101
Phone: (877) 935-2844

#122
Men Of X
Category: Adult Entertainment
Area: Eastside
Address: 115 E Tropicana Ave
Las Vegas, NV 89109
Phone: (702) 241-4010

#123
Vegas Valley
Comic Book Festival
Category: Festival
Area: University, Eastside
Address: 1401 E Flamingo Rd
Las Vegas, NV 89119
Phone: (702) 507-3459

#124
Exclusive Collections Gallery
Category: Art Gallery
Area: The Strip
Address: 3500 Las Vegas Blvd
Las Vegas, NV 89109
Phone: (702) 432-1154

#125
Paranormal
Category: Performing Arts
Area: The Strip
Address: 3645 Las Vegas Blvd S
Las Vegas, NV 89109
Phone: (877) 374-7469

#126
City Center Fine Art Collection
Category: Art Gallery
Area: The Strip
Address: 3730 S Las Vegas Blvd
Las Vegas, NV 89109
Phone: (702) 590-7111

#127
Elton John
The Million Dollar Piano
Category: Music Venues
Area: The Strip
Address: 3570 Las Vegas Blvd S
Las Vegas, NV 89109
Phone: (888) 435-8665

#128
The Art of Music
Category: Art Gallery
Area: The Strip
Address: 3400 Las Vegas Blvd S
Las Vegas, NV 89109
Phone: (702) 791-7111

#129
Peccole Ranch Community
Association
Category: Social Club
Area: Westside
Address: 9501 Red Hills Rd
Las Vegas, NV 89117
Phone: (702) 255-3351

#130
The Boulevard Theater
Category: Performing Arts,
Event Planning & Services
Area: The Strip
Address: 3765 Las Vegas Blvd S
Las Vegas, NV 89109
Phone: (702) 473-9300

#131
Harris Squares
Category: Performing Arts
Area: Eastside
Address: 4775 Topaz St
Las Vegas, NV 89121
Phone: (702) 369-0943

#132
Asylum and Hotel
Fear Haunted House
Category: Festival
Area: Westside
Address: 4300 Meadows Ln
Las Vegas, NV 89107
Phone: (702) 636-9515

#133
Century 16 South Point
Category: Cinema
Area: Southeast
Address: 9777 S Las Vegas Blvd
Las Vegas, NV 89123
Phone: (702) 260-4061

#134
AMC Rainbow Promenade 10
Category: Cinema
Area: Northwest
Address: 2321 North Rainbow Boulevard
Las Vegas, NV 89108
Phone: (702) 636-2869

#135
Fast Frame
Category: Art Gallery
Area: Southeast
Address: 3827 E Sunset Rd
Las Vegas, NV 89120
Phone: (702) 456-3278

#136
World Series of Poker
Category: Festival
Area: Chinatown
Address: 3700 W Flamingo Rd
Las Vegas, NV 89103
Phone: (702) 777-7777

#137
Palms Place
Category: Hotel, Resort, Casino
Area: Chinatown
Address: 4381 W Flamingo Rd
Las Vegas, NV 89103
Phone: (866) 942-7779

#138
Boyz II Men
Category: Performing Arts
Area: The Strip
Address: 3400 Las Vegas Blvd
Las Vegas, NV 89109
Phone: (702) 791-7111

#139
Hypnotiq
Category: Performing Arts
Area: The Strip
Address: Harmon Theater
Las Vegas, NV 89109
Phone: (702) 836-0836

#140
Signature Productions
Category: Performing Arts
Area: Northwest
Address: 3255 N Mustang St
Las Vegas, NV 89108
Phone: (702) 878-7529

#141
Jeff Mitchum Gallery
Category: Art Gallery
Area: The Strip, Eastside
Address: 3799 S Las Vegas Blvd
Las Vegas, NV 89109
Phone: (702) 304-0007

#142
City of the World
Category: Art Gallery, Cultural Center
Area: Downtown
Address: 1229 Casino Center Blvd
Las Vegas, NV 89104
Phone: (702) 409-7549

#143
Vegas Loves Brazil Festival
Category: Festival
Area: Downtown
Address: 500 S Grand Central Pkwy
Las Vegas, NV 89155
Phone: (702) 201-2506

#144
Battle Of The Dance
Category: Performing Arts
Area: Eastside
Address: 3555 Las Vegas Blvd S
Las Vegas, NV 89109
Phone: (702) 733-3333

#145
Big Elvis
Category: Performing Arts
Area: The Strip
Address: 3595 Las Vegas Blvd S
Las Vegas, NV 89109
Phone: (702) 737-2100

#146
222 Imperial
Category: Art Gallery
Area: Downtown
Address: 222 E Imperial
Las Vegas, NV 89104
Phone: (702) 271-2844

#147
Palazzo Race & Sport Book
Category: Sport Bar, Casino
Area: The Strip
Address: 3325 Las Vegas Blvd S
Las Vegas, NV 89109
Phone: (702) 414-1000

#148
The Auto Collections
At The Quad
Category: Museum, Automotive
Area: The Strip
Address: 3535 Las Vegas Blvd S
Las Vegas, NV 89109
Phone: (702) 794-3174

#149
Saxe Theater
Category: Performing Arts
Area: The Strip
Address: 3663 Las Vegas Blvd
Las Vegas, NV 89109
Phone: (866) 932-1818

#150
UA Showcase 8
Category: Cinema
Area: The Strip
Address: 3769 S Las Vegas Blvd
Las Vegas, NV 89109
Phone: (702) 740-4511

#151
Wyland Gallery
Category: Art Gallery
Area: The Strip
Address: 3663 Las Vegas Boulevard S
Las Vegas, NV 89109
Phone: (702) 699-5363

#152
Coney Island Emporium
Category: Amusement Park, Arcade
Area: The Strip
Address: 3790 Las Vegas Blvd S
Las Vegas, NV 89109
Phone: (702) 736-4100

#153
**Summerlin Library
& Performing Arts Center**
Category: Performing Arts, Library
Area: Summerlin
Address: 1771 Inner Circle Dr
Las Vegas, NV 89134
Phone: (702) 507-3860

#154
V Theater
Category: Performing Arts, Theater, Venues
& Event Space
Area: The Strip
Address: 3663 Las Vegas Blvd
Las Vegas, NV 89109
Phone: (702) 260-7200

#155
Century Orleans 18
Category: Cinema
Area: Chinatown
Address: 4500 W Tropicana Ave
Las Vegas, NV 89103
Phone: (702) 227-3456

#156
Gordie Brown
Category: Performing Arts,
Comedy Club
Area: Downtown
Address: 129 E Fremont St
Las Vegas, NV 89101
Phone: (702) 385-7111

#157
The Rock Center For Dance
Category: Dance Studio,
Performing Arts
Area: Southeast
Address: 8210 S Maryland Pkwy
Las Vegas, NV 89123
Phone: (702) 341-7625

#158
Psychic Eye Book Shop
Category: Booktore, Gift Shop
Area: Southeast
Address: 5835 S Eastern Ave
Las Vegas, NV 89119
Phone: (702) 451-5777

#159
The Axis
Category: Performing Arts,
Music Venues
Area: Eastside
Address: 3667 Las Vegas Blvd S
Las Vegas, NV 89109
Phone: (888) 800-8264

#160
Rita Rudner
Category: Performing Arts,
Comedy Club
Area: The Strip
Address: 3355 Las Vegas Blvd S
Las Vegas, NV 89109
Phone: (702) 414-9000

#161
**Love Theatre At The Mirage
Hotel And Casino**
Category: Music Venues
Area: The Strip
Address: 3400 Las Vegas Blvd South
Las Vegas, NV 89109
Phone: (800) 745-3000

#162
Lake of Dreams
Category: Performing Arts
Area: The Strip
Address: 3131 Las Vegas Blvd. South
Las Vegas, NV 89109
Phone: (702) 770-3392

#163
Soul2Soul Tim McGraw
& Faith Hill
Category: Music Venues
Area: Eastside
Address: 3355 Las Vegas Blvd S
Las Vegas, NV 89109
Phone: (702) 414-1000

#164
Las Vegas Historical Society
Category: Museum
Area: Downtown
Address: 1114 S Main St
Las Vegas, NV 89104
Phone: (702) 580-5760

#165
Beacher's Madhouse
Category: Comedy Club,
Performing Arts
Area: The Strip, Eastside
Address: 3799 S Las Vegas Blvd
Las Vegas, NV 89109
Phone: (323) 785-3036

#166
Cashman Center
Category: Venues & Event Space
Area: Downtown
Address: 850 Las Vegas Blvd N
Las Vegas, NV 89101
Phone: (702) 386-7100

#167
Aki Matsuri Festival
Category: Festival, Local Flavor
Area: Chinatown
Address: 4983 W Flamingo Rd
Las Vegas, NV 89103
Phone: (702) 685-8358

#168
VZ Dance Studio
Category: Performing Arts
Area: Westside
Address: 7207 W Sahara Ave
Las Vegas, NV 89117
Phone: (702) 685-8989

#169
Village Pub Bar & Grill
Category: Pub
Area: Eastside
Address: 3455 E Flamingo Road
Las Vegas, NV 89121
Phone: (702) 436-2488

#170
Sam Boyd Stadium
Category: Stadium, Music Venues
Area: Southeast
Address: 7000 E Russell Rd
Las Vegas, NV 89122
Phone: (702) 895-3761

#171
The Magic and Tigers
of Rick Thomas
Category: Performing Arts
Area: The Strip
Address: 3663 Las Vegas Blvd S
Las Vegas, NV 89109
Phone: (702) 260-7200

#172
All Shook Up
Category: Performing Arts
Area: The Strip
Address: 3663 Las Vegas Blvd, Ste 360
Las Vegas, NV 89109
Phone: (702) 260-7200

#173
Zumanity Theatre At New York New
York Hotel And Casino
Category: Music Venues
Area: The Strip
Address: 3790 Las Vegas Blvd South
Las Vegas, NV 89109
Phone: (800) 745-3000

#174
Cox Pavilion
Category: Stadium
Area: Southeast, University
Address: 4505 S Maryland Pkwy
Las Vegas, NV 89101
Phone: (702) 895-3761

#175
Century 16 Santa Fe Station
Category: Cinema
Area: Northwest
Address: 4949 N Rancho Dr
Las Vegas, NV 89130
Phone: (702) 655-8178

#176
Pho Da Nang
Category: Vietnamese, Hotel, Casino
Area: Chinatown
Address: 3700 W Flamingo Rd
Las Vegas, NV 89103
Phone: (702) 777-7962

#177
Bellagio Poker Room
Category: Casino, Hotel
Area: Eastside
Address: 3600 S Las Vegas Blvd
Las Vegas, NV 89109
Phone: (888) 987-6667

#178
Randall's Fine Art Custom Framing
Category: Art Gallery, Framing
Area: Chinatown
Address: 3585 South Decatur Blvd
Las Vegas, NV 89103
Phone: (702) 873-3224

#179
Nashville Unplugged Live
Category: Performing Arts
Area: The Strip
Address: 3535 S Las Vegas Blvd
Las Vegas, NV 89109
Phone: (702) 794-3261

#180
The Will Edwards Show
Category: Performing Arts
Area: Eastside
Address: 160 E Flamingo Rd
Las Vegas, NV 89109
Phone: (702) 946-8907

#181
The Las Vegas Tenors
Category: Performing Arts
Area: Eastside
Address: 3000 Paradise Ed
Las Vegas, NV 89109
Phone: (702) 732-5111

#182
Photo Bang Bang
Category: Art Gallery,
Photography Store
Area: Downtown
Address: 224 E Imperial Ave
Las Vegas, NV 89104
Phone: (702) 518-7427

#183
Contemporary Arts Center
Category: Art Gallery
Area: Downtown
Address: 1217 S Main St
Las Vegas, NV 89104
Phone: (702) 496-0569

#184
Golden Rainbow
Category: Music Venues
Area: Eastside
Address: 3645 Las Vegas Blvd S
Las Vegas, NV 89109
Phone: (702) 384-2899

#185
Tony and Tina's Wedding
Category: Performing Arts
Area: The Strip
Address: 3645 Las Vegas Blvd S
Las Vegas, NV 89109
Phone: (702) 260-7200

#186
Distorted-Reflections
Category: Cultural Center
Area: Spring Valley
Address: 8777 W Maule Ave
Las Vegas, NV 89148
Phone: (775) 293-3918

#187
Matt Hennager's Guitar Lessons
Category: Performing Arts,
Private Tutor
Area: Downtown
Address: 1640 E Sahara Ave
Las Vegas, NV 89104
Phone: (702) 533-3611

#188
The King's Ransom Museum
Category: Museum
Area: Downtown
Address: 128 Fremont St
Las Vegas, NV 89101
Phone: (702) 366-7307

#189
Icandy Burlesque
Category: Performing Arts
Area: The Strip
Address: 3663 Las Vegas Blvd
Las Vegas, NV 89109
Phone: (866) 932-1818

#190
**The Las Vegas
Halloween Parade**
Category: Festival
Area: Downtown
Address: Fremont St E
Las Vegas, NV 89101
Phone: (702) 582-5007

#191
**Step By Step School
of Ballroom Dancing**
Category: Performing Arts
Area: Southeast, Eastside
Address: 1801 E Tropicana Ave
Las Vegas, NV 89119
Phone: (702) 795-0041

#192
Caricature Cinema
Category: Cinema
Area: Downtown
Address: Fremont St Experience
Las Vegas, NV 89101
Phone: (702) 755-0828

#193
Belmont Ballroom
Category: Music Venues
Area: The Strip
Address: 3708 Las Vegas Blvd S
Las Vegas, NV 89109
Phone: (702) 698-7000

#194
Sin City Ink
Category: Tattoo, Piercing
Area: Eastside
Address: 3430 E Tropicana Ave
Las Vegas, NV 89121
Phone: (702) 818-3500

#195
Rodney Reyes Live
Category: Party & Event Planning,
Performing Arts, Magicians
Area: Summerlin
Address: 1611 Spring Gate Ln
Las Vegas, NV 89134
Phone: (858) 952-9645

#196
Southern Highlands Golf Club
Category: Social Club
Area: Southwest
Address: 1 Robert Trent Jones S
Las Vegas, NV 89141
Phone: (702) 263-1000

#197
Stage Deli
Category: Deli, Hotel, Casino
Area: Eastside
Address: 3799 Las Vegas Blvd S
Las Vegas, NV 89109
Phone: (702) 891-7777

#198
Hard Rock Live
Category: Music Venues
Area: The Strip
Address: 3771 Las Vegas Blvd S
Las Vegas, NV 89109
Phone: (702) 733-7625

#199
HellPop!
Category: Comic Book
Area: Downtown
Address: 107 East Charleston Blvd
Las Vegas, NV 89104
Phone: (702) 353-3228

#200
The Amazing Johnathan
Category: Comedy Club,
Performing Arts
Area: The Strip
Address: 3663 Las Vegas Blvd S
Las Vegas, NV 89109
Phone: (702) 836-0836

#201
One Drunk Puppy
Category: Local Flavor, Winery
Area: Southwest
Address: 3333 Blue Diamond Rd
Las Vegas, NV 89139
Phone: (702) 263-7777

#202
CSI: The Experience
Category: Arts & Entertainment
Area: The Strip
Address: 3799 Las Vegas Blvd S
Las Vegas, NV 89109
Phone: (877) 660-0660

#203
Field of Dreams
Category: Hobby Shop, Art Gallery
Area: The Strip
Address: 3500 Las Vegas Blvd S
Las Vegas, NV 89109
Phone: (702) 792-8233

#204
**VOICES starring Lani Misalucha
at Hilton Las Vegas**
Category: Performing Arts
Area: Eastside
Address: 3000 Paradise Road
Las Vegas, NV 89109
Phone: (702) 732-5111

#205
Vinyl
Category: Music Venues
Area: Eastside
Address: 4455 Paradise Rd
Las Vegas, NV 89169
Phone: (702) 693-5222

#206
Oh My Godard Gallery
Category: Art Gallery
Area: The Strip
Address: 3663 Las Vegas Boulevard S
Las Vegas, NV 89109
Phone: (702) 699-9099

#207
The Arts Factory
Category: Art Gallery
Area: Downtown
Address: 107 E Charleston Blvd
Las Vegas, NV 89104
Phone: (702) 676-1111

#208
The Soprano's Last Supper
Category: Performing Arts
Area: The Strip
Address: 3801 Las Vegas Blvd S
Las Vegas, NV 89109
Phone: (702) 733-8669

#209
Feng Shui Gallery
Category: Art Gallery
Area: Chinatown
Address: 3548 Wynn Road
Las Vegas, NV 89103
Phone: (702) 368-3926

#210
The Rat Pack Is Back
Category: Performing Arts
Area: Downtown
Address: 3700 Flamingo Rd
Las Vegas, NV 89101
Phone: (702) 777-7776

#211
Naked Boys Singing
Category: Performing Arts
Area: The Strip
Address: 953 ES Sahara
Las Vegas, NV 89109
Phone: (702) 732-7225

#212
Fuego Raw Talent
Category: Performing Arts
Area: The Strip
Address: 2535 S. Las Vegas Blvd.
Las Vegas, NV 89109
Phone: (866) 382-8884

#213
Venetian Phantom Theater
Category: Music Venues
Area: Eastside
Address: 3355 Las Vegas Blvd S
Las Vegas, NV 89109
Phone: (702) 474-4000

#214
Alios
Category: Art Gallery
Area: Downtown
Address: 1217 S Main St
Las Vegas, NV 89104
Phone: (702) 478-9636

#215
Gracie's Who's on Third?
Category: Music Venues
Area: Downtown
Address: 1310 South 3rd St
Las Vegas, NV 89104
Phone: (702) 684-7634

#216
Five Star Tavern
Category: Bar, Casino
Area: Northwest
Address: 1905 N Decatur Blvd
Las Vegas, NV 89108
Phone: (702) 645-9961

#217
The Society of Seven
with Lani Misalucha
Category: Performing Arts
Area: Downtown
Address: 3555 Las Vegas Blvd S
Las Vegas, NV 89101
Phone: (702) 733-3333

#218
Lonnie Hammargren's
Museum Home
Category: Museum
Area: Eastside
Address: 4300 Ridgecrest Dr
Las Vegas, NV 89121
Phone: (702) 596-6669

#219
Laugh Factory
Category: Comedy Club
Area: The Strip
Address: 3801 S Las Vegas Blvd
Las Vegas, NV 89109
Phone: (702) 739-2222

#220
Guided Brush
Category: Art Gallery
Area: Spring Valley
Address: 6445 S Tenaya Way
Las Vegas, NV 89113
Phone: (702) 625-1278

#221
Hard Rock Cafe
Category: Music Venues
Area: The Strip
Address: 3771 Las Vegas Blvd S
Las Vegas, NV 89109
Phone: (702) 733-7625

#222
Spazmatics
Category: Music Venues
Area: Southeast
Address: 9777 Las Vegas Blvd S
Las Vegas, NV 89183
Phone: (702) 796-7111

#223
Magic of Paris
Category: Performing Arts
Area: The Strip
Address: 3655 Las Vegas Boulevard S.
Las Vegas, NV 89109
Phone: (702) 946-7000

#224
Xtreme Magic
Starring Dirk Arthur
Category: Performing Arts
Area: Downtown
Address: 3801 Las Vegas Blvd S
Las Vegas, NV 89101
Phone: (702) 739-2411

#225
Crazy Girls
Category: Adult Entertainment, Cabaret
Area: The Strip
Address: 2901 Las Vegas Blvd S
Las Vegas, NV 89109
Phone: (702) 794-9433

#226
United Artist Theatre
Category: Cinema
Area: Northwest
Address: 2321 N Rainbow Blvd
Las Vegas, NV 89108
Phone: (702) 636-2869

#227
Michael Turco's Magic
& Mayhem
Category: Magicians, Performing Arts
Area: Eastside
Address: 3663 Las Vegas Blvd S
Las Vegas, NV 89109
Phone: (702) 260-7200

#228
Frank Caliendo
Category: Performing Arts
Area: The Strip
Address: 3770 Las Vegas Blvd S
Las Vegas, NV 89109
Phone: (877) 386-8224

#229
The Edwards Twins
Category: Performing Arts
Area: Sunrise
Address: 425 Fremont Street
Las Vegas, NV 89104
Phone: (702) 205-5313

#230
Priscilla Queen of the Desert
Category: Performing Arts
Area: The Strip
Address: 3355 S Las Vegas Blvd
Las Vegas, NV 89109
Phone: (702) 414-9000

#231
Paint Balls Of Fury
Category: Paintball
Area: Southeast
Address: 6270 Kimberly Ave
Las Vegas, NV 89122
Phone: (702) 202-4011

#232
Art At Your Door Gallery II
Category: Art Gallery
Area: Westside, The Lakes
Address: 8605 W Sahara Ave
Las Vegas, NV 89117
Phone: (702) 256-7278

#233
Dancing Queen
Category: Performing Arts
Area: The Strip
Address: 3790 Las Vegas Blvd S
Las Vegas, NV 89109
Phone: (866) 919-7472

#234
Paul Vigil Magic & Mentalism
Category: Performing Arts
Area: The Strip
Address: 3400 S Las Vegas Blvd
Las Vegas, NV 89109
Phone: (702) 369-9567

#235
Sands Showroom
Category: Performing Arts
Area: The Strip
Address: 3355 Las Vegas Blvd S
Las Vegas, NV 89109
Phone: (888) 505-5211

#236
Neonopolis
Category: Shopping Center, Cinema
Area: Downtown
Address: 450 Fremont St
Las Vegas, NV 89101
Phone: (702) 477-0470

#237
Terry Fator
Category: Performing Arts
Area: The Strip
Address: 3400 Las Vegas Blvd South
Las Vegas, NV 89109
Phone: (800) 963-9634

#238
Marjorie Barrick Museum
Category: Museum
Area: University
Address: 4500 S Maryland Pkwy
Las Vegas, NV 89119
Phone: (702) 895-3381

#239
THE 80s SHOW
Category: Performing Arts
Area: The Strip
Address: 3663 Las Vegas Blvd
Las Vegas, NV 89109
Phone: (866) 932-1818

#240
Thunderbird Gallery
Category: Art Gallery
Area: Northwest
Address: 6010 W Cheyenne
Las Vegas, NV 89108
Phone: (702) 463-4903

#241
Brews & Blues Festival
Category: Festival
Area: Westside
Address: 333 S Valley View Blvd
Las Vegas, NV 89152
Phone: (702) 822-7700

#242
Cashetta
The Extra Large Medium
Category: Performing Arts
Area: Eastside
Address: 305 Convention Center Dr
Las Vegas, NV 89109
Phone: (702) 990-1524

#243
Country Superstars
Category: Performing Arts
Area: The Strip
Address: 3663 Las Vegas Blvd S
Las Vegas, NV 89109
Phone: (702) 260-7200

#244
The Magic Shop
Category: Local Flavor, Hobby Shop
Area: Westside
Address: 3111 S. Valley View Blvd.
Las Vegas, NV 89102
Phone: (702) 204-7481

#245
Nathan Burton Comedy Magic
Category: Performing Arts
Area: The Strip
Address: 3663 Las Vegas Blvd South
Las Vegas, NV 89109
Phone: (800) 715-9219

#246
Saxe Lounge
Category: Lounge, Performing Arts
Area: The Strip
Address: 3663 Las Vegas Blvd S
Las Vegas, NV 89109
Phone: (702) 260-7200

#247
Charleston Heights Arts Center
Category: Performing Arts,
Dance School
Area: Westside
Address: 800 Brush St
Las Vegas, NV 89107
Phone: (702) 229-6383

#248
L' Oracle Las Vegas
Category: Gymnastics, Performing Arts
Area: Southwest
Address: 7020 W Warm Springs Rd
Las Vegas, NV 89113
Phone: (702) 462-2080

#249
Creative Studio LV
Category: Performing Arts
Area: Spring Valley
Address: 6415 S Tenaya Way
Las Vegas, NV 89118
Phone: (702) 376-9650

#250
Dust Inc
Category: Art Gallery
Area: Downtown
Address: 109 E Charleston Blvd
Las Vegas, NV 89104
Phone: (702) 880-3878

#251
Masters of Rock
Category: Performing Arts
Area: The Strip
Address: 2901 S. Las Vegas Blvd.
Las Vegas, NV 89109
Phone: (877) 892-7469

#252
Jerry Greenberg Presents Bringing Back the Music
Category: Performing Arts
Area: The Strip
Address: 3000 Paradise Rd
Las Vegas, NV 89109
Phone: (888) 732-7117

#253
Las Vegas Epicurean Affaire
Category: Festival
Area: The Strip
Address: 39-47 Sands Ave
Las Vegas, NV 89109
Phone: (702) 878-2313

#254
Lassen Galerie
Category: Art Gallery
Area: The Strip
Address: 3500 Las Vegas Boulevard S
Las Vegas, NV 89109
Phone: (702) 731-6900

#255
Showroom At The Quad
Category: Music Venues
Area: The Strip
Address: 3535 South Las Vegas Boulevard.
Las Vegas, NV 89109
Phone: (800) 745-3000

#256
Anything Nightlife
Category: Music Venues
Area: The Strip
Address: 3565 Las Vegas Blvd S
Las Vegas, NV 89109
Phone: (919) 410-2953

#257
Divorce Party Las Vegas
Category: Arts & Entertainment
Area: The Strip
Address: 3645 Las Vegas Blvd S
Las Vegas, NV 89109
Phone: (702) 967-4111

#258
The Art of Richard Macdonald
Category: Opera & Ballet,
Performing Arts, Art Gallery
Area: The Strip
Address: 3600 Las Vegas Blvd, S
Las Vegas, NV 89109
Phone: (702) 730-3990

#259
S2 Art Group
Category: Art Gallery
Area: Downtown
Address: 1 E Charleston Blvd
Las Vegas, NV 89104
Phone: (702) 868-7880

#260
Rick Faugno's Body & Soul
Category: Performing Arts
Area: Eastside
Address: 3000 Paradise Rd
Las Vegas, NV 89109
Phone: (800) 222-5361

#261
Atrium
Category: Botanical Garden
Area: The Strip
Address: 3400 Las Vegas Blvd S
Las Vegas, NV 89109
Phone: (702) 791-7111

#262
Brett Thompson Tattoo
& Body Piercing
Category: Tattoo, Piercing, Art Gallery
Area: Eastside
Address: 3550 Paradise Rd
Las Vegas, NV 89169
Phone: (702) 848-9680

#263
Circadian Gallery
Category: Art Gallery
Area: Downtown
Address: 1551 S. Commerce Street
Las Vegas, NV 89102
Phone: (702) 525-2850

#264
Cob4lt Blu3 Studio Gallery
Category: Art Gallery
Area: Downtown
Address: 1400 S 3rd St
Las Vegas, NV 89104
Phone: (702) 771-0032

#265
Studio 307
Category: Art Gallery
Area: Eastside, Downtown
Address: 2618 State St
Las Vegas, NV 89109
Phone: (702) 270-3007

#266
Studio de Deathbringer
Category: Art Gallery
Area: Downtown
Address: 1114 S Casino Center Blvd
Las Vegas, NV 89104
Phone: (702) 249-3282

#267
Ryan Gallery & Custom Framing
Category: Art Gallery, Framing
Area: Westside
Address: 2972 S Rainbow Blvd
Las Vegas, NV 89146
Phone: (702) 368-0545

#268
Stifler
Category: Performing Arts
Area: The Strip
Address: 3801 S Las Vegas Blvd
Las Vegas, NV 89109
Phone: (702) 739-2222

#269
Pearl Concert Theater
At Palms Casino Resort
Category: Music Venues
Area: Chinatown
Address: 4321 W Flamingo Rd
Las Vegas, NV 89103
Phone: (866) 942-7777

#270
Karnival
Category: Performing Arts
Area: Eastside
Address: 953 E Sahara Ave, Ste 16
Las Vegas, NV 89109
Phone: (702) 732-7225

#271
Amanda Harris Gallery
of Contemporary Art
Category: Art Gallery
Area: Downtown
Address: 900 S Las Vegas Blvd
Las Vegas, NV 89101
Phone: (702) 769-6036

#272
303 North Studio
Category: Art Gallery
Area: Downtown
Address: 107 East Charleston Blvd
Las Vegas, NV 89104
Phone: (702) 742-4021

#273
Press Start Gaming Center
Category: Arcade,
Party & Event Planning
Area: Spring Valley
Address: 4840 S Fort Apache Rd
Las Vegas, NV 89147
Phone: (702) 227-4263

#274
DobeZ Designz
Category: Art Gallery, Jewelry
Area: Downtown
Address: 520 Fremont St
Las Vegas, NV 89101
Phone: (702) 279-5025

#275
Celebrity Night Club
Category: Lounge, Music Venues
Area: Downtown
Address: 201 N. 3rd Street
Las Vegas, NV 89101
Phone: (702) 384-2582

#276
ActionRED
Category: Art Gallery
Area: Downtown
Address: 1110 Fremont St
I as Vegas, NV 89101
Phone: (702) 366-0175

#277
**DanceCenter Ballroom
& Latin Dance Studio**
Category: Performing Arts,
Music Venues
Area: Southeast
Address: 3686 E Sunset Rd
Las Vegas, NV 89120
Phone: (702) 434-8800

#278
Rodney Lough Jr.
Category: Art Gallery
Area: The Strip
Address: 3720 Las Vegas Blvd S
Las Vegas, NV 89109
Phone: (702) 522-9400

#279
Studio 8 Ten
Category: Arts & Crafts, Art Gallery
Area: Downtown
Address: 810 Las Vegas Blvd S
Las Vegas, NV 89101
Phone: (702) 644-9418

#280
**Thirsty 3rd Thursday
Downtown Pub Crawl**
Category: Bar, Music Venues
Area: Downtown
Address: 425 Fremont Street
Las Vegas, NV 89101
Phone: (702) 382-4421

#281
i luv 88 keys studio
Category: Music Lessons
Area: Northwest
Address: 5639 Madre Mesa Dr
Las Vegas, NV 89108
Phone: (702) 497-6752

#282
Marjorie Barrick Museum
Category: Museum
Area: University
Address: 4500 S Maryland Pkwy
Las Vegas, NV 89119
Phone: (702) 895-3381

#283
Brunz Rosowsky Gallery
Category: Art Gallery
Area: Downtown
Address: 103 E Charleston Blvd
Las Vegas, NV 89104
Phone: (702) 474-4123

#284
CeeLo Green is Loberace
Category: Performing Arts
Area: The Strip, Eastside
Address: 3667 Las Vegas Blvd S
Las Vegas, NV 89109
Phone: (800) 745-3000

#285
Rock Star Beer Festival
Category: Festival, Beer, Wine & Spirits
Area: Eastside
Address: 4455 Paradise Rd
Las Vegas, NV 89169
Phone: (714) 721-2670

#286
Toni Braxton - Revealed
Category: Performing Arts
Area: The Strip
Address: 3555 Las Vegas Blvd S
Las Vegas, NV 89109
Phone: (888) 902-9929

#287
Venetian Theatre
At The Venetian Las Vegas
Category: Music Venues
Area: The Strip
Address: 3355 Las Vegas Blvd S
Las Vegas, NV 89109
Phone: (800) 745-3000

#288
Windows At Bally's Las Vegas
Category: Music Venues
Area: The Strip
Address: 3655 Las Vegas Blvd. South
Las Vegas, NV 89109
Phone: (800) 745-3000

#289
Jason Alexander as Donny Clay
Category: Performing Arts
Area: The Strip
Address: 3667 Las Vegas Blvd S
Las Vegas, NV 89109
Phone: (702) 785-5555

#290
Saddle 'n' Spurs Saloon
Category: Performing Arts
Area: Northwest
Address: 2333 N Jones Blvd
Las Vegas, NV 89108
Phone: (702) 646-6292

#291
Tropicana Cinema Inc
Category: Cinema
Area: Eastside
Address: 3330 E Tropicana Ave
Las Vegas, NV 89121
Phone: (702) 454-8603

#292
The Inspire Theatre
Category: Performing Arts,
Venues & Event Space
Area: Downtown
Address: 501 Fremont St
Las Vegas, NV 89101
Phone: (702) 910-2388

#293
Plaka
Category: Music Venues
Area: Westside
Address: 2550 S Rainbow Blvd
Las Vegas, NV 89146
Phone: (702) 471-0270

#294
BMX Nationals
Category: Race Track
Area: Southeast
Address: 9777 Las Vegas Blvd S
Las Vegas, NV 89183
Phone: (702) 796-7111

#295
Blue Man Group
Category: Performing Arts
Area: The Strip
Address: 3770 Las Vegas Blvd S
Las Vegas, NV 89109
Phone: (866) 678-2582

#296
American Crown Circus
Circo Osorio
Category: Performing Arts
Area: Northwest
Address: 4088 Pleasant Rd
Las Vegas, NV 89108
Phone: (702) 638-8183

#297
Cirque du Soleil
Criss Angel Believe
Category: Performing Arts
Area: The Strip
Address: 3900 Las Vegas Blvd S
Las Vegas, NV 89109
Phone: (800) 557-7428

#298
The Las Vegas Comedy Show
Category: Comedy Club,
Performing Arts
Area: Eastside
Address: 255 East Flamingo Road
Las Vegas, NV 89169
Phone: (702) 629-0715

#299
Santa's Wonderland
At Bass Pro Shop
Category: Festival
Area: Southwest
Address: 8200 Dean Martin Dr
Las Vegas, NV 89139
Phone: (702) 730-5200

#300
The Venetian Showroom
Category: Performing Arts
Area: The Strip
Address: 3355 Las Vegas Blvd S
Las Vegas, NV 89109
Phone: (702) 414-1000

#301
Amadeus School of Music
Category: Performing Arts
Area: Eastside
Address: 900 Karen Ave
Las Vegas, NV 89109
Phone: (702) 733-3028

#302
Aussie Improv Comedy Explosion
Category: Performing Arts
Area: Eastside
Address: 3663 Las Vegas Blvd S
Las Vegas, NV 89109
Phone: (888) 800-8284

#303
Disney Fine Art
Category: Art Gallery
Area: Downtown
Address: 707 E Fremont St
Las Vegas, NV 89101
Phone: (702) 331-9955

#304
The Joe Show
Category: Performing Arts,
Comedy Club
Area: The Strip
Address: 255 E Flamingo
Las Vegas, NV 89109
Phone: (702) 893-8933

#305
The Dirty Joke Show
Category: Performing Arts
Area: The Strip
Address: 115 East Tropicana Avenue
Las Vegas, NV 89109
Phone: (888) 527-8342

#306
Ripa De Monti Venetian Glass
Category: Flowers & Gifts, Art Gallery
Area: The Strip
Address: 3355 Las Vegas Blvd S
Las Vegas, NV 89109
Phone: (702) 733-1004

#307
Menopause The Musical
Category: Performing Arts
Area: The Strip
Address: 3900 Las Vegas Blvd S
Las Vegas, NV 89109
Phone: (702) 262-4420

#308
Art of Dance
Category: Performing Arts
Area: Southwest
Address: 8090 S Durango Drive
Las Vegas, NV 89113
Phone: (702) 871-2226

#309
Jubilee!
Category: Performing Arts
Area: Eastside
Address: 3645 Las Vegas Boulevard South.
Las Vegas, NV 89109
Phone: (702) 777-2782

#310
Jack Gallery
Category: Art Gallery
Area: The Strip
Address: 3200 Las Vegas Blvd S
Las Vegas, NV 89109
Phone: (702) 731-0074

#311
Art Square Theatre
Category: Performing Arts
Area: Downtown
Address: 1025 S 1st St
Las Vegas, NV 89101
Phone: (702) 818-3422

#312
Marriage Can Be Murder
Category: Performing Arts
Area: Downtown
Address: 301 Fremont Street
Las Vegas, NV 89101
Phone: (702) 388-2111

#313
Zuffa, LLC
Category: Professional Sport Team
Area: Westside
Address: 2800 W Sahara Ave
Las Vegas, NV 89102
Phone: (702) 222-9097

#314
Cazino Lounge And Gallery
Category: Music Venues, Hookah Bar
Area: Chinatown
Address: 5150 Spring Mountain Rd
Las Vegas, NV 89146
Phone: (702) 624-3095

#315
Art Factory Outlet
Category: Art Gallery
Area: Westside
Address: 1717 S Decatur Boulevard
Las Vegas, NV 89102
Phone: (702) 309-9891

#316
Main Gallery
Category: Art Gallery
Area: Downtown
Address: 1009 S Main St
Las Vegas, NV 89101
Phone: (702) 257-6246

#317
Tropfest International Las Vegas
Category: Music Venues, Cinema
Area: The Strip
Address: 3708 Las Vegas Boulevard S
Las Vegas, NV 89109
Phone: (702) 698-7000

#318
Qi-Feng Shui Gallery
Category: Art Gallery
Area: Westside
Address: 3311 S Rainbow Blvd
Las Vegas, NV 89146
Phone: (702) 222-4718

#319
Center Piece Gallery
Category: Art Gallery
Area: The Strip
Address: 3720 Las Vegas Blvd
Las Vegas, NV 89109
Phone: (702) 729-3314

#320
Hispanic Museum of Nevada
Category: Museum
Area: Westside
Address: 330 S Valley View Blvd
Las Vegas, NV 89107
Phone: (702) 773-2203

#321
Hip Hop Legends Tribute Show
Category: Performing Arts
Area: The Strip
Address: 3765G Las Vegas Blvd S
Las Vegas, NV 89109
Phone: (702) 473-9300

#322
iHeartRadio Music Festival
Category: Festival, Music Venues
Area: The Strip, Eastside
Address: 3799 Las Vegas Blvd S
Las Vegas, NV 89109
Phone: (702) 891-1111

#323
William Carr Collection
Category: Art Gallery
Area: Eastside
Address: 3663 Las Vegas Blvd S
Las Vegas, NV 89109
Phone: (702) 888-1088

#324
Brett Wesley Gallery
Category: Art Gallery
Area: Downtown
Address: 1025 S First St
Las Vegas, NV 89101
Phone: (702) 433-4433

#325
Zen Gaming
Category: Arcade
Area: Westside
Address: 7545 W Sahara Ave
Las Vegas, NV 89117
Phone: (702) 586-8428

#326
**Temptation Sundays
At The Oasis Pool in Luxor**
Category: Swimming Pool
Area: The Strip
Address: 3900 Las Vegas Blvd S
Las Vegas, NV 89119
Phone: (702) 730-5731

#327
**Comedy After Hours
Fitzgerald's Hotel and Casino**
Category: Comedy Club
Area: Downtown
Address: 301 Fremont St
Las Vegas, NV 89101
Phone: (702) 870-8799

#328
Jana's RedRoom
Category: Art Gallery
Area: Downtown
Address: 107 E Charleston
Las Vegas, NV 89104
Phone: (702) 454-3709

#329
Spike & Hammer
Comedy Magic Show
Category: Performing Arts
Area: Downtown
Address: 202 Fremont Street
Las Vegas, NV 89101
Phone: (702) 385-4011

#330
Zen Magic
Category: Performing Arts
Area: Eastside
Address: 3663 S. Las Vegas Blvd.
Las Vegas, NV 89109
Phone: (702) 260-7200

#331
Triumph.
Category: Performing Arts
Area: Eastside
Address: 3000 Paradise Rd
Las Vegas, NV 89109
Phone: (800) 222-5361

#332
Wyrick Magical Production
Category: Performing Arts
Area: The Strip
Address: 2535 Las Vegas Blvd S
Las Vegas, NV 89109
Phone: (702) 650-5081

#333
Sin City Pickers
Category: Antiques, Art Gallery
Area: Downtown
Address: 10 W Wyoming Ave
Las Vegas, NV 89102
Phone: (702) 366-9166

#334
Neon Venus Art Theatre
Category: Art Gallery, Performing Arts,
Music Venues
Area: Downtown
Address: 1404 S 3rd St
Las Vegas, NV 89104
Phone: (702) 787-2481

#335
Yesterday
A Tribute to the Beatles
Category: Performing Arts
Area: The Strip
Address: 3801 Las Vegas Blvd S
Las Vegas, NV 89109
Phone: (702) 739-2222

#336
BMX Nationals
Category: Race Track
Area: Southeast
Address: 9777 Las Vegas Blvd S
Las Vegas, NV 89101
Phone: (702) 796-7111

#337
Faith Lutheran Theatre Company
Category: Performing Arts
Area: Westside, South Summerlin
Address: 2019 S Hualapai Way
Las Vegas, NV 89117
Phone: (702) 804-4400

#338
Adair Fern Conservatory
of the Arts
Category: Performing Arts
Area: Southeast
Address: 3265 E Patrick Ln
Las Vegas, NV 89120
Phone: (702) 458-7575

#339
The World's Greatest
Magic Show
Category: Performing Arts
Area: Eastside
Address: 305 Convention Center Drive
Las Vegas, NV 89109
Phone: (702) 737-5540

#340
The Great Frame Up
Category: Art Gallery, Framing
Area: Summerlin
Address: 10870 W Charleston Blvd
Las Vegas, NV 89135
Phone: (702) 240-9640

#341
Improv Vegas
Category: Performing Arts
Area: Eastside
Address: 953 E Sahara Ave
Las Vegas, NV 89109
Phone: (702) 427-0542

#342
Sin City Theatre
Category: Music Venues
Area: The Strip
Address: 3667 S Las Vegas Blvd
Las Vegas, NV 89109
Phone: (702) 777-7776

#343
Jersey Boys
Category: Performing Arts
Area: The Strip
Address: 3655 Las Vegas Blvd S
Las Vegas, NV 89109
Phone: (800) 745-3000

#344
Babes Cabaret
Category: Adult Entertainment,
Cabaret, Hookah Bar
Area: Southeast
Address: 5901 Emerald Ave
Las Vegas, NV 89122
Phone: (702) 435-7545

#345
The Real Deal
Category: Performing Arts
Area: The Strip
Address: 3355 Las Vegas Blvd S
Las Vegas, NV 89109
Phone: (702) 414-1000

#346
Sin City Beer Festival
Category: Festival, Local Flavor,
Beer, Wine & Spirits
Area: The Strip, Eastside
Address: 3801 S Las Vegas Blvd
Las Vegas, NV 89109
Phone: (702) 701-0200

#347
Social Media Film Festval
Category: Festival
Area: Spring Valley
Address: 10120 W Flamingo Rd
Las Vegas, NV 89147
Phone: (702) 518-9135

#348
Hitzville The Show
Motown Revue
Category: Performing Arts,
Music Venues
Area: The Strip
Address: 3663 Las Vegas Blvd S
Las Vegas, NV 89109
Phone: (702) 260-7200

#349
The D Word Musical
Category: Performing Arts
Area: Eastside
Address: 3000 Paradise Rd
Las Vegas, NV 89109
Phone: (800) 222-5361

#350
United Artist Theatre
Category: Performing Arts
Area: The Strip
Address: 3769 Las Vegas Boulevard S
Las Vegas, NV 89109
Phone: (702) 740-4511

#351
Pawn Shop Live!
Category: Performing Arts
Area: Downtown
Address: 2901 Las Vegas Blvd S
Las Vegas, NV 89104
Phone: (866) 946-5336

#352
Legwarmers! an 80s Musical
Category: Performing Arts,
Music Venues
Area: The Strip
Address: 3663 Las Vegas Blvd
Las Vegas, NV 89109
Phone: (866) 932-1818

#353
John Armond Actor's Studio
Category: Performing Arts
Area: Westside
Address: 8125 W Sahara
Las Vegas, NV 89117
Phone: (702) 533-5874

#354
Tuesday Night Fights
Category: Professional Sport Team
Area: The Strip
Address: 3000 Paradise Rd
Las Vegas, NV 89109
Phone: (800) 222-5361

#355
Gazillion Bubble Show
Category: Performing Arts
Area: The Strip
Address: 3667 S Las Vegas Blvd
Las Vegas, NV 89109
Phone: (702) 777-9974

#356
Name That Tune Live
Category: Performing Arts
Area: The Strip
Address: 3535 Las Vegas Blvd S
Las Vegas, NV 89109
Phone: (702) 794-3221

#357
Gallerie Michelangelo
Category: Art Gallery
Area: The Strip
Address: 3520 Las Vegas Blvd S
Las Vegas, NV 89109
Phone: (702) 796-5001

#358
The Box Office
Category: Performing Arts,
Music Venues
Area: Downtown
Address: 1129 S Casino Center Blvd
Las Vegas, NV 89104
Phone: (702) 388-1515

#359
Space Studio
Category: Art Gallery
Area: Downtown
Address: 8 E Charleston Blvd
Las Vegas, NV 89104
Phone: (702) 366-1603

#360
Studio One's
Summerlin Dance Academy
Category: Performing Arts,
Dance School
Area: Westside
Address: 1181 S Buffalo Dr
Las Vegas, NV 89117
Phone: (702) 838-5131

#361
The Joint at Hard Rock
Category: Music Venues
Area: Eastside
Address: 4455 Paradise Rd
Las Vegas, NV 89169
Phone: (702) 693-5222

#362
Luxor Festival Grounds
Category: Music Venues
Area: The Strip
Address: 3901 Las Vegas Blvd S
Las Vegas, NV 89119
Phone: (800) 745-3000

#363
Boomer's Bar
Category: Dive Bar, Music Venues
Area: Westside
Address: 3200 W Sirius Ave
Las Vegas, NV 89102
Phone: (702) 368-1863

#364
Kaizad's Smoke
& Hookah Lounge
Category: Music Venues, Dance Club,
Hookah Bar
Area: Spring Valley
Address: 4840 S Fort Apache Pl
Las Vegas, NV 89147
Phone: (702) 506-2263

#365
Sinatra Dance With Me
Category: Performing Arts
Area: The Strip
Address: Wynn Encore
Las Vegas, NV 89109
Phone: (702) 770-9966

#366
Double Decker Bus of Las Vegas
Category: Tours, Transportation
Area: Spring Valley
Address: 3635 South Fort Apache Rd
Las Vegas, NV 89147
Phone: (702) 688-4162

#367
Art of Music
Category: Art Gallery
Area: The Strip
Address: 3930 Las Vegas Blvd S
Las Vegas, NV 89119
Phone: (702) 597-9401

#368
P3 Studio
Category: Art Gallery
Area: The Strip
Address: 3708 Las Vegas Blvd S
Las Vegas, NV 89109
Phone: (702) 698-7000

#369
Million Dollar Quartet
Category: Music Venues
Area: The Strip
Address: 3475 Las Vegas Blvd South
Las Vegas, NV 89109
Phone: (702) 777-2782

#370
La Cage
Category: Performing Arts
Area: The Strip
Address: 2901 Las Vegas Blvd S
Las Vegas, NV 89109
Phone: (877) 892-7469

#371
It's Tricky
Category: Performing Arts
Area: Eastside
Address: 99 Convention Center Drive
Las Vegas, NV 89109
Phone: (702) 735-6117

#372
Nunsense
Category: Performing Arts
Area: Eastside
Address: 3000 Paradise Rd
Las Vegas, NV 89109
Phone: (702) 732-5111

#373
Raw Works Studio
Category: Music Venues, Jazz & Blues
Area: Spring Valley
Address: 9995 Cambridge Blue Ave
Las Vegas, NV 89147
Phone: (702) 998-8371

#374
Rich Natole
Category: Comedy Club
Area: Downtown
Address: 1 S Main St
Las Vegas, NV 89101
Phone: (800) 634-6575

#375
Dixie Dooley Master Mystifier
Category: Comedy Club
Area: The Strip
Address: 99 Convention Center Dr
Las Vegas, NV 89109
Phone: (800) 634-6118

#376
The Las Vegas Underworld Magic Show
Category: Performing Arts
Area: The Strip
Address: 99 Convention Center Dr
Las Vegas, NV 89109
Phone: (702) 557-5541

#377
The Platters, The Temptations & The Coasters
Category: Performing Arts
Area: The Strip
Address: 2535 Las Vegas Blvd S
Las Vegas, NV 89109
Phone: (702) 737-2515

#378
Ohana Festival
Category: Festival
Area: Westside
Address: 333 S Valley View Blvd
Las Vegas, NV 89152
Phone: (702) 822-7700

#379
Asian Moon Festival @ Springs Preserve
Category: Festival
Area: Westside
Address: 333 S Valley View Blvd
Las Vegas, NV 89107
Phone: (702) 258-3205

#380
Berns Suzuki Studio
Category: Performing Arts, Art School
Area: Southeast
Address: 5221 S Eastern Ave
Las Vegas, NV 89119
Phone: (702) 736-3585

#381
Donna Beam Fine Arts Gallery
Category: Art Gallery
Area: University
Address: 4505 S Maryland Pkwy
Las Vegas, NV 89154
Phone: (702) 895-3893

#382
Sin City Comedy Show
Category: Comedy Club,
Performing Arts
Area: The Strip
Address: 3667 Las Vegas Blvd
Las Vegas, NV 89109
Phone: (888) 746-7784

#383
Koolville Tattoos
Category: Tatoos
Area: Downtown
Address: 806 Las Vegas Blvd S
Las Vegas, NV 89101
Phone: (702) 384-3800

#384
Fantasy Swingers Club
Category: Adult Entertainment,
Social Club
Area: Downtown
Address: 953 E Sahara Ave
Las Vegas, NV 89104
Phone: (702) 893-3977

#385
Kevin Barry Fine Arts
Category: Art Gallery
Area: Spring Valley
Address: 6001 S Decatur Blvd
Las Vegas, NV 89118
Phone: (702) 948-1929

#386
King Tut Museum
Category: Museum
Area: The Strip
Address: 3900 Las Vegas Blvd S
Las Vegas, NV 89119
Phone: (702) 262-4000

#387
Harrah's Showroom
At Harrah's Las Vegas
Category: Music Venues
Area: The Strip
Address: 3475 Las Vegas Blvd S
Las Vegas, NV 89109
Phone: (800) 745-3000

#388
LiveGame Escape
Category: Arcade
Area: Westside
Address: 3300 S Jones Blvd
Las Vegas, NV 89146
Phone: (702) 237-4164

#389
Explore Talent
Category: Talent Agency
Area: Chinatown
Address: 3395 S Jones Blvd
Las Vegas, NV 89146
Phone: (800) 598-7500

#390
Human Nature Theater
Category: Performing Arts
Area: Eastside
Address: 3535 Las Vegas Blvd S
Las Vegas, NV 89109
Phone: (702) 731-3311

#391
Rock 'n Roll Wine
Category: Music Venues
Area: Westside
Address: 6883B W Charleston Blvd
Las Vegas, NV 89117
Phone: (702) 240-3066

#392
Red Talent Agency
Category: Talent Agency
Area: Westside
Address: 7860 W Sahara Ave
Las Vegas, NV 89117
Phone: (702) 242-1770

#393
Thunder From Down Under
Category: Performing Arts,
Adult Entertainment
Area: The Strip
Address: 3850 Las Vegas Blvd S
Las Vegas, NV 89109
Phone: (702) 597-7600

#394
Get a Dance Remix
Category: Music Venues
Area: Eastside
Address: 3328 Seneca
Las Vegas, NV 89169
Phone: (925) 586-6877

#395
Artrageous
Category: Arcade
Area: Spring Valley
Address: 4145 S Grand Cayon Dr
Las Vegas, NV 89147
Phone: (702) 545-7611

#396
King of Club
Category: Casino, Dance Club
Area: Southwest
Address: 7345 Durango Dr
Las Vegas, NV 89113
Phone: (702) 837-2401

#397
Korabo
Category: Performing Arts,
Specialty School
Area: Westside
Address: 3400 W Desert Inn
Las Vegas, NV 89102
Phone: (702) 482-9522

#398
The Wynn Collection
Category: Museum, Art Gallery
Area: Eastside
Address: 3131 Las Vegas Blvd S
Las Vegas, NV 89109
Phone: (702) 733-4100

#399
International Scout Museum
Category: Museum
Area: Westside
Address: 3025 West Sahara Ave
Las Vegas, NV 89102
Phone: (702) 878-7268

#400
1st Las Vegas
Grand Canyon Tours
Category: Tours, Transportation
Area: The Strip
Address: 3565 Las Vegas Blvd S
Las Vegas, NV 89109
Phone: (702) 897-9000

TOP 200 CASINOS

The Most Recommended by Locals and Travelers
(From #1 to #200)

#1
Red Rock Casino Resort & Spa
Category: Casino, Hotel, Day Spa
Average price: Modest
Area: South Summerlin
Address: 11011 W Charleston Blvd
Las Vegas, NV 89135
Phone: (702) 797-7777

#2
Green Valley Ranch Resort & Spa
Category: Casino
Area: Anthem
Address: 2300 Paseo Verde Pkwy
Henderson, NV 89052
Phone: (702) 617-7777

#3
South Point Hotel, Casino and Spa
Category: Hotel, Casino
Average price: Modest
Area: Southeast
Address: 9777 Las Vegas Blvd S
Las Vegas, NV 89183
Phone: (702) 796-7111

#4
Silverton Casino
Category: Hotel, Casino
Average price: Modest
Area: Southwest
Address: 3333 Blue Diamond Rd
Las Vegas, NV 89139
Phone: (702) 263-7777

#5
Suncoast Hotel & Casino
Category: Hotel, Casino
Average price: Modest
Area: Westside
Address: 9090 Alta Drive
Las Vegas, NV 89145
Phone: (702) 636-7111

#6
Sunset Station Hotel & Casino
Category: Cinema, Restaurant, Casino
Average price: Modest
Address: 1301 W Sunset Rd
Henderson, NV 89014

#7
The Cromwell
Category: Casino
Area: The Strip
Address: 3595 Las Vegas Blvd S
Las Vegas, NV 89109
Phone: (702) 407-6000

#8
Santa Fe Station Hotel & Casino
Category: Hotel, Casino
Average price: Modest
Area: Northwest
Address: 4949 N Rancho Dr
Las Vegas, NV 89130
Phone: (702) 658-4900

#9
Aliante Casino + Hotel
Category: Casino
Address: 7300 Aliante Pkwy N North
Las Vegas, NV 89084

#10
Cannery Hotel & Casino
Category: Hotel, Casino
Average price: Modest
Address: 2121 E Craig Rd North
Las Vegas, NV 89030

#11
The Spread Sport Book & Deli
Category: Casino, Deli
Average price: Inexpensive
Area: Downtown
Address: 206 N 3rd St
Las Vegas, NV 89169

#12
Bellagio
Category: Hotel, Casino
Average price: Expensive
Area: The Strip
Address: 3600 S Las Vegas Blvd
Las Vegas, NV 89109
Phone: (702) 693-7111

#13
Rampart Casino
Category: Casino
Area: Westside
Address: 221 N Rampart Blvd
Las Vegas, NV 89145
Phone: (702) 507-5900

#14
Circus Circus Las Vegas Hotel and Casino
Category: Hotel, Casino
Average price: Inexpensive
Area: The Strip
Address: 2880 S Las Vegas Blvd
Las Vegas, NV 89109
Phone: (702) 734-0410

#15
Silver Sevens Hotel and Casino
Category: Hotel, Casino, Restaurant
Average price: Inexpensive
Area: Eastside
Address: 4100 Paradise Rd
Las Vegas, NV 89169
Phone: (702) 733-7000

#16
Fiesta Henderson
Category: Casino
Address: 777 W Lake Mead Pkwy
Henderson, NV 89015

#17
Fiesta Rancho
Category: Restaurant, Casino
Average price: Modest
Address: 2400 N Rancho Dr North
Las Vegas, NV 89030

#18
The Quad Resort & Casino
Category: Resort, Casino
Area: The Strip
Address: 3535 S Las Vegas Blvd
Las Vegas, NV 89109
Phone: (702) 731-3311

#19
South Coast Hotel and Casino
Category: Hotel, Casino
Area: Southeast
Address: 9777 Las Vegas Blvd S
Las Vegas, NV 89183
Phone: (702) 797-8075

#20
Jokers Wild Casino
Category: Casino
Address: 920 N Boulder Hwy
Henderson, NV 89011

#21
Penthouse Real World Suite
Category: Casino
Area: Eastside
Address: 4455 Paradise Rd
Las Vegas, NV 89169
Phone: (800) 473-7625

#22
Vegas For Hotties
Category: Party & Events,
Dance Club, Casino
Address: 3900 S. Las Vegas Blvd
Las Vegas, NV 89109

#23
Hooters Casino Hotel
Category: American, Casino
Average price: Modest
Area: Southeast
Address: 115 E Tropicana Ave
Las Vegas, NV 89109
Phone: (866) 584-6687

#24
Race & Sport Book
Category: Casino
Area: Westside
Address: 2423 W. Sahara Ave
Las Vegas, NV 89102
Phone: (702) 367-2423

#25
New York - New York
Category: Hotel, Casino
Average price: Modest
Area: The Strip
Address: 3790 Las Vegas Blvd S
Las Vegas, NV 89109
Phone: (866) 815-4365

#26
Luxor Hotel & Casino Las Vegas
Category: Hotel, Casino
Average price: Modest
Area: The Strip
Address: 3900 Las Vegas Blvd S
Las Vegas, NV 89109
Phone: (877) 386-4658

#27
The Cosmopolitan of Las Vegas
Category: Hotel, Casino
Average price: Expensive
Area: The Strip
Address: 3708 Las Vegas Blvd S
Las Vegas, NV 89109
Phone: (702) 698-7000

#28
Boulder Station Hotel & Casino
Category: Casino
Address: 4111 Boulder Hwy
Las Vegas, NV 89121

#29
Golden Palm Casino & Hotel
Category: Hotel, Casino
Average price: Inexpensive
Address: 3111 W Tropicana Ave
Las Vegas, NV 89103

#30
Bingo Room
at Green Valley Ranch
Category: Casino, Adult Entertainment
Average price: Inexpensive
Area: Anthem
Address: 2300 Paseo Verde Pkwy
Henderson, NV 89052

#31
Bally's Race & Sport Book
Category: Casino
Area: The Strip
Address: 3645 Las Vegas Boulevard South,
Las Vegas, NV 89109
Phone: (877) 603-4390

#33
Texas Station
Gambling Hall & Hotel
Category: Casino
Address: 2101 Texas Star Ln North
Las Vegas, NV 89032

#32
Sam's Town
Hotel & Gambling Hall
Category: Hotel, Casino
Average price: Inexpensive
Address: 5111 Boulder Highway
Las Vegas, NV 89122

#34
Dotty's
Category: Casino
Address: 560 Marks St
Henderson, NV 89014

#35
Arizona Charlie's Boulder Casino,
Hotel & RV Resort
Category: Hotel, RV Park,
Casino, American
Average price: Inexpensive
Address: 4575 Boulder Hwy
Las Vegas, NV 89121

#36
Mandalay Bay Resort & Casino
Category: Hotel, Casino
Average price: Expensive
Area: The Strip
Address: 3950 S Las Vegas Boulevard
Las Vegas, NV 89119
Phone: (877) 632-7800

#37
Caesars Palace
Las Vegas Hotel & Casino
Category: Hotel, Casino
Average price: Expensive
Area: The Strip
Address: 3570 Las Vegas Boulevard South
Las Vegas, NV 89109
Phone: (866) 227-5938

#38
Nevada Landing
Hotel & Casino
Category: Casino
Area: Sunrise
Address: 2 Goodsprings Rd
Las Vegas, NV 89101
Phone: (702) 387-5000

#39
Bingo Room
Category: Casino
Address: 4124 Boulder Highway
Las Vegas, NV 89121

#40
Orleans Hotel & Casino
Category: Hotel, Casino
Average price: Modest
Address: 4500 West Tropicana Ave
Las Vegas, NV 89103

#41
Dottys Gaming & Sprits
Category: Casino
Address: 6142 W Flamingo Rd
Las Vegas, NV 89103

#42
Casa Blanca Vacation Club
Category: Casino
Area: Eastside
Address: 3340 Topaz St Ste 270
Las Vegas, NV 89121
Phone: (702) 313-8015

#43
The Quad Las Vegas
Resort & Casino
Category: Hotel, Casino
Average price: Inexpensive
Area: The Strip
Address: 3535 S Las Vegas Blvd
Las Vegas, NV 89109
Phone: (800) 351-7400

#44
SLS Las Vegas Hotel & Casino
Category: Hotel, Casino, Lounge
Average price: Expensive
Area: The Strip
Address: 2535 S. Las Vegas Blvd
Las Vegas, NV 89109
Phone: (855) 761-7757

#45
Elite Status Group
Category: Casino
Area: Southeast
Address: 5150 Duke Ellington Way
Las Vegas, NV 89119
Phone: (888) 395-9111

#46
Golden Nugget Hotel & Casino
Category: Hotel, Casino
Average price: Modest
Area: Downtown
Address: 129 E Fremont St
Las Vegas, NV 89101
Phone: (702) 385-7111

#47
Bingo Room
Category: Casino
Address: 2424 W. Sahara Ave
Las Vegas, NV 89102

#48
Mirage Resort
Category: Hotel, Casino
Area: Eastside
Address: 3600 Las Vegas Boulevard S
Las Vegas, NV 89109
Phone: (702) 693-7111

#49
Sport Book
Category: Casino
Address: 2408 N. Rancho Drive North
Las Vegas, NV 89032

#50
Mirage Poker Room
Category: Casino
Area: The Strip
Address: 3400 Las Vegas Blvd S
Las Vegas, NV 89109

#51
Fontainebleau
Category: Hotel, Casino, Apartments
Average price: Exclusive
Area: The Strip
Address: 2755 Las Vegas Blvd S
Las Vegas, NV 89109
Phone: (702) 495-7777

#52
Lucky Club Casino & Hotel
Category: Hotel, Casino
Average price: Inexpensive
Address: 3227 Civic Center Dr North
Las Vegas, NV 89030

#53
Java Las Vegas
Category: Casino, Coffee & Tea
Average price: Modest
Area: Westside
Address: 9080 Alta Way
Las Vegas, NV 89145

#54
777 Inc
Category: Casino
Area: Spring Valley
Address: 6145 S Rainbow Blvd
Las Vegas, NV 89118
Phone: (702) 568-8777

#55
Caesars Entertainment
Category: Casino
Area: Southeast
Address: 1 Harrah's Ct
Las Vegas, NV 89119

#56
Poker Room
Category: Casino
Address: 2422 W. Sahara Ave
Las Vegas, NV 89102

#57
Riviera Hotel & Casino
Category: Casino
Area: The Strip
Address: 2901 Las Vegas Blvd
Las Vegas, NV 89109

#58
Caesars Palace
Race & Sport Book
Category: Casino
Area: The Strip
Address: 3570 Las Vegas Boulevard South,
Las Vegas, NV 89109
Phone: (866) 227-5938

#59
Royal Star Casino
Category: Casino
Area: The Strip
Address: 1410 W Flamingo Rd
Las Vegas, NV 89103
Phone: (987) 654-3210

#60
Babary Coast Casino
Category: Casino
Area: The Strip
Address: 3595 Las Vegas Boulevard S
Las Vegas, NV 89109
Phone: (702) 267-9681

#61
Stations Casino
Desg & Const Strg
Category: Casino
Address: 3265 Palm Center Dr
Las Vegas, NV 89103

#62
The Boyd Gaming Corporation
Category: Casino, Hotel
Area: Eastside
Address: 3883 Howard Hughes Pkwy
Las Vegas, NV 89169
Phone: (702) 792-7200

#63
Sport Book
Category: Casino
Address: 2112 Texas Star Ln North
Las Vegas, NV 89032

#64
Bingo Room
Category: Casino
Address: 2113 Texas Star Ln North
Las Vegas, NV 89032

#65
Mutiny Bay At Treasure
Category: Hotel, Restaurant,
Casino, Day Spa
Area: Eastside
Address: 3300 Las Vegas
Boulevard S
Las Vegas, NV 89109
Phone: (702) 894-7111

#66
Wet-the Spa At Ti
Category: Hotel, Restaurant,
Day Spa, Casino
Area: Eastside
Address: 3300 Las Vegas
Boulevard S
Las Vegas, NV 89109
Phone: (702) 894-7111

#67
Plastic in Action USA
Category: Casino, Grocery
Address: 5685 Cameron
Las Vegas, NV 89118

#68
Oasis Resort Casino Golf & Spa
Category: Hotel, Casino
Address: 897 W Mesquite Blvd
Las Vegas, NV 89101

#69
Grand Ole Vegas Revue
Category: Casino
Area: Downtown
Address: 1 Main St
Las Vegas, NV 89101
Phone: (702) 386-2110

#70
Buffet the
Category: Hotel, Buffets, Casino
Area: Downtown
Address: 129 Fremont St
Las Vegas, NV 89101
Phone: (702) 385-7111

#71
Casino Direct
Category: Casino
Area: Downtown
Address: 100 Stewart Ave
Las Vegas, NV 89101
Phone: (702) 247-1500

#72
Dotty's #1
Category: Casino
Area: University
Address: 1131 E Tropicana Ave
Las Vegas, NV 89121
Phone: (702) 481-7702

#73
Bingo Room
Category: Casino
Area: Northwest
Address: 2409 N. Rancho Drive North
Las Vegas, NV 89130
Phone: (702) 631-7009

#74
FreePlayVegas.com
Category: Casino
Area: Spring Valley
Address: 6145 S Rainbow Blvd
Las Vegas, NV 89118
Phone: (702) 736-2208

#75
King of Club
Category: Casino, Dance Club
Average price: Expensive
Area: Southwest
Address: 7345 Durango Dr
Las Vegas, NV 89113
Phone: (702) 837-2401

#76
Station Casino Reservations
Category: Casino
Area: Spring Valley
Address: 5655 Badura Ave Ste 150
Las Vegas, NV 89118
Phone: (702) 685-2000

#77
Dottys
Category: Dive Bar, Casino
Address: 2823 N Green Valley Pkwy
Henderson, NV 89014

#78
Sport Book
Category: Casino
Area: Eastside
Address: 4123 Boulder Hwy
Las Vegas, NV 89121
Phone: (702) 432-7789

#79
Global Gaming Group
Category: Casino
Area: Southeast
Address: 3035 E Patrick Ln
Las Vegas, NV 89120
Phone: (702) 435-4182

#80
Poker Room
Category: Casino
Address: 2111 Texas Star Ln North
Las Vegas, NV 89032

#81
**Preferred Gaming
& Entertainment**
Category: Casino
Area: Southeast
Address: 6255 McLeod Dr Ste 8
Las Vegas, NV 89120
Phone: (702) 365-9777

#82
Five Star Tavern
Category: Bar, American, Casino
Average price: Inexpensive
Area: Sunrise
Address: 4220 E Charleston Blvd
Las Vegas, NV 89104
Phone: (702) 531-1211

#83
Bingo Room
Category: Casino
Area: Northwest
Address: 4962 N Rancho Dr
Las Vegas, NV 89130
Phone: (702) 658-4913

#84
Poker Room
Category: Casino
Area: Northwest
Address: 4960 N Rancho Dr
Las Vegas, NV 89130
Phone: (702) 658-4911

#85
Sport Book
Category: Casino
Area: Northwest
Address: 4961 N Rancho Dr
Las Vegas, NV 89108
Phone: (702) 658-4912

#86
Cannery Hotel & Casino
Category: Hotel, Restaurant, Casino
Address: 2121 E Craig Rd North
Las Vegas, NV 89030

#87
Jackpot Joanies
Category: Casino
Area: Spring Valley
Address: 6085 S Fort Apache Rd
Las Vegas, NV 89148
Phone: (702) 851-7070

#88
Miss America Pageant
Category: Casino
Address: Planet Hollywood
Casino Clark County, NV

#89
Station Casino
Category: Casino
Area: South Summerlin
Address: 1505 S Pavilion Ctr Dr
Las Vegas, NV 89135
Phone: (702) 495-3000

#90
The D
Category: Hotel, Casino
Average price: Inexpensive
Area: Downtown
Address: 301 Fremont St
Las Vegas, NV 89101
Phone: (702) 388-2400

#91
Blackjack Lodge
Category: Casino
Area: Southeast
Address: 10490 Bermuda Rd
Las Vegas, NV 89183
Phone: (702) 876-9097

#92
Wildfire Anthem
Category: Bar, Casino
Area: Anthem
Address: 2551 Anthem Village Dr
Henderson, NV 89052
Phone: (702) 495-3822

#93
Casino Players Service
Category: Casino
Area: Anthem
Address: 2510 Anthem Village Dr
Henderson, NV 89052
Phone: (702) 341-9449

#94
Arizona Charlie's Decatur
Category: Hotel, Casino
Average price: Inexpensive
Area: Westside
Address: 740 S Decatur Blvd
Las Vegas, NV 89107
Phone: (702) 258-5200

#95
Wynn Las Vegas
Category: Hotel, Casino, Resort
Average price: Exclusive
Area: The Strip
Address: 3131 Las Vegas Blvd. South
Las Vegas, NV 89109
Phone: (702) 770-7000

#96
Casino Player Publishing
Category: Casino
Area: Westside
Address: 2860 S Jones Blvd
Las Vegas, NV 89146
Phone: (702) 736-8886

#97
Riviera Hotel & Casino
Category: Hotel, Restaurant, Casino
Average price: Modest
Area: The Strip
Address: 2901 Las Vegas Blvd S
Las Vegas, NV 89109
Phone: (702) 734-5110

#98
King Tut's
Category: Pub, Casino
Area: Westside
Address: 6138 W Charleston Blvd
Las Vegas, NV 89146
Phone: (702) 258-6344

#99
Village Pub Bar & Grill
Category: Casino, Restaurant
Average price: Inexpensive
Area: Eastside
Address: 3455 E Flamingo Road
Las Vegas, NV 89121
Phone: (702) 436-2488

#100
Las Vegas Club Hotel & Casino
Category: Hotel, Casino
Average price: Inexpensive
Area: Downtown
Address: 18 E Fremont St
Las Vegas, NV 89101
Phone: (702) 385-1664

#101
C & H Consulting Group
Category: Casino
Area: Westside
Address: 2800 W Sahara Ave
Las Vegas, NV 89102
Phone: (702) 871-3660

#102
Buccaneer Bay Restaurant
Category: Hotel, Restaurant, Casino
Area: The Strip
Address: 3300 Las Vegas Blvd S
Las Vegas, NV 89109
Phone: (702) 894-7111

#103
Casablanca & Oasis Sales Office
Category: Casino
Area: Westside
Address: 6883 W Charleston Boulevard
Las Vegas, NV 89117
Phone: (702) 453-7800

#104
Chapel In The Plaza
Category: Hotel, Casino
Area: Downtown
Address: 1 S Main St
Las Vegas, NV 89101
Phone: (702) 386-2110

#105
Stefano's
Category: Hotel, Casino
Area: Downtown
Address: 129 Fremont Street
Las Vegas, NV 89101
Phone: (702) 385-7111

#106
Herb Pastor Casino Enterprises
Category: Casino
Area: Downtown
Address: 111 N 1st St
Las Vegas, NV 89101
Phone: (702) 385-4250

#107
Dealer's Party Agency
Category: Casino
Area: Southeast, Eastside
Address: 1801 E Tropicana Avenue
Las Vegas, NV 89119
Phone: (702) 891-0587

#108
Sport Gaming Players Network
Category: Casino
Area: Eastside
Address: 4259 S Pecos Road
Las Vegas, NV 89121
Phone: (702) 369-3911

#109
P & M Coin
Category: Casino
Area: Sunrise
Address: 4301 E Bonanza Rd
Las Vegas, NV 89110
Phone: (702) 452-5073

#110
Dotty's
Category: Casino
Area: Southwest
Address: Jones and Windmill
Las Vegas, NV 89139
Phone: (866) 547-6310

#111
Debbie Oddo Casino Host
Category: Casino
Area: Southwest, Spring Valley
Address: Las Vegas, NV 89113
Phone: (702) 878-5855

#112
Downtown Grand Las Vegas
Category: Hotel, Casino
Average price: Modest
Area: Downtown
Address: 206 N 3rd St
Las Vegas, NV 89101
Phone: (855) 384-7263

#113
Fremont Street Experience
Category: Bar, Casino
Average price: Inexpensive
Address: 425 Fremont St
Las Vegas, NV 89101
Phone: (702) 678-5600

#114
Dottys
Category: Casino
Area: Southeast
Address: 2101 S Decatur Blvd
Las Vegas, NV 89102
Phone: (702) 362-0751

#115
**Flamingo Las Vegas
Hotel & Casino**
Category: Hotel, Casino
Average price: Modest
Address: 3555 Las Vegas Boulevard South,
Las Vegas, NV 89109
Phone: (702) 733-3111

#116
El Cortez Hotel
Category: Hotel, Casino
Average price: Inexpensive
Area: Downtown
Address: 600 Fremont St
Las Vegas, NV 89101
Phone: (702) 385-5200

#117
Stratosphere
Category: Hotel, Casino
Average price: Modest
Area: The Strip
Address: 2000 Las Vegas Blvd S
Las Vegas, NV 89104
Phone: (702) 380-7777

#118
Hard Rock Hotel & Casino
Category: Hotel, Casino
Average price: Modest
Area: Eastside
Address: 4455 Paradise Rd
Las Vegas, NV 89109
Phone: (702) 474-4000

#119
Monte Carlo Hotel & Casino
Category: Casino, Hotel
Average price: Modest
Area: The Strip
Address: 3770 Las Vegas Blvd S
Las Vegas, NV 89109
Phone: (702) 730-7000

#120
MGM Grand Hotel
Category: Hotel, Casino
Average price: Modest
Area: Eastside
Address: 3799 S Las Vegas Blvd
Las Vegas, NV 89109
Phone: (877) 880-0880

#121
Four Queens Hotel & Casino
Category: Hotel, Casino
Average price: Inexpensive
Area: Downtown
Address: 202 Fremont St
Las Vegas, NV 89101
Phone: (702) 385-4011

#122
Ellis Island Casino & Brewery
Category: Casino, American
Average price: Inexpensive
Area: Eastside
Address: 4178 Koval Ln
Las Vegas, NV 89109
Phone: (702) 733-8901

#123
The Mirage
Category: Hotel, Casino
Average price: Modest
Area: The Strip
Address: 3400 Las Vegas Blvd S
Las Vegas, NV 89109
Phone: (702) 791-7111

#124
Five Star Tavern
Category: Bar, American, Casino
Average price: Exclusive
Area: Northwest
Address: 4402 N Rancho Dr
Las Vegas, NV 89130
Phone: (702) 645-6411

#125
Mandalay Place
Category: Casino
Area: Southeast
Address: PO Box 98880
Las Vegas, NV 89193
Phone: (702) 632-9352

#126
Planet Hollywood Las Vegas Resort & Casino
Category: Hotel, Casino
Average price: Modest
Area: The Strip
Address: 3667 Las Vegas Boulevard South,
Las Vegas, NV 89109
Phone: (866) 919-7472

#127
The Book
Category: Casino, Hotel & Travel
Area: The Strip
Address: 3645 Las Vegas Blvd S
Las Vegas, NV 89109
Phone: (877) 603-4390

#128
Tix4Tonight Planet Hollywood
Category: Casino
Area: The Strip, Eastside
Address: 3667 S Las Vegas Blvd
Las Vegas, NV 89109
Phone: (877) 849-4868

#129
Treasure Island
Category: Hotel, Casino
Average price: Modest
Area: The Strip
Address: 3300 Las Vegas Blvd S
Las Vegas, NV 89109
Phone: (702) 894-7111

#130
Harrah's Las Vegas Hotel & Casino
Category: Hotel, Casino
Average price: Modest
Area: The Strip
Address: 3475 Las Vegas Blvd South
Las Vegas, NV 89109
Phone: (800) 214-9110

#131
Fremont Hotel & Casino
Category: Casino, Hotel
Average price: Modest
Area: Downtown
Address: 200 Fremont Street
Las Vegas, NV 89101
Phone: (702) 385-3232

#132
Village Pub & Poker
Category: American, Casino
Average price: Inexpensive
Area: Southeast
Address: 10420 S Bermuda
Las Vegas, NV 89128
Phone: (702) 407-0219

#133
Miz Lola's
Category: Casino, Beer, Wine & Spirits
Average price: Modest
Area: Southwest
Address: 4370 Blue Diamond Rd
Las Vegas, NV 89139
Phone: (702) 629-5652

#134
Aria Hotel & Casino
Category: Hotel, Casino
Average price: Expensive
Area: The Strip
Address: 3730 Las Vegas Blvd S
Las Vegas, NV 89109
Phone: (702) 590-7757

#135
The California Hotel & Casino
Category: Hotel, Casino
Average price: Inexpensive
Area: Downtown
Address: 12 East Ogden Avenue
Las Vegas, NV 89101
Phone: (702) 385-1222

#136
O'Sheas Casino
Category: Casino, Hotel
Average price: Inexpensive
Area: The Strip
Address: 3535 S Las Vegas Blvd
Las Vegas, NV 89109
Phone: (800) 351-7400

#137
The Venetian Resort
Hotel Casino
Category: Hotel, Casino
Average price: Expensive
Area: The Strip
Address: 3355 Las Vegas Blvd S
Las Vegas, NV 89109
Phone: (702) 414-1000

#138
Bingo Room
at Plaza Hotel and Casino
Category: Nightlife, Casino, Local Flavor
Area: Downtown
Address: 1 South Main St
Las Vegas, NV 89101
Phone: (702) 386-2110

#139
The New Tropicana Las Vegas
Category: Hotel, Casino
Average price: Modest
Area: The Strip
Address: 3801 S Las Vegas Blvd
Las Vegas, NV 89119
Phone: (702) 739-2222

#140
Golden Gate Hotel & Casino
Category: Hotel, Casino
Average price: Inexpensive
Area: Downtown
Address: 1 Fremont St
Las Vegas, NV 89101
Phone: (702) 385-1906

#141
ARIA Poker Room
Category: Casino
Area: The Strip
Address: 3730 Las Vegas Blvd
Las Vegas, NV 89109
Phone: (702) 590-7230

#142
Yorky's
Category: Nightlife, Casino, Restaurant
Area: Southeast
Address: 3720 E Sunset Road
Las Vegas, NV 89120
Phone: (702) 216-0940

#143
The Plaza Hotel & Casino
Category: Hotel, Casino
Average price: Inexpensive
Area: Downtown
Address: 1 Main St
Las Vegas, NV 89101
Phone: (877) 687-5875

#144
Lillie Langtry's
Category: Hotel, Casino
Average price: Expensive
Area: Downtown
Address: 129 Fremont Street
Las Vegas, NV 89101
Phone: (702) 385-7111

#145
Tuscany Hotel & Casino
Category: Hotel, Casino
Average price: Modest
Area: Eastside
Address: 255 E Flamingo Rd
Las Vegas, NV 89169
Phone: (702) 893-8933

#146
Bellagio Poker Room
Category: Casino, Hotel
Average price: Exclusive
Address: 3600 S Las Vegas Blvd
Las Vegas, NV 89109
Phone: (888) 987-6667

#147
LVH - Las Vegas Hotel & Casino
Category: Hotel, Casino
Average price: Modest
Address: 3000 Paradise Rd
Las Vegas, NV 89109
Phone: (702) 732-5111

#148
**Best Western Plus Casino
Royale & Hotel**
Category: Hotel, Casino
Average price: Inexpensive
Area: The Strip
Address: 3411 Las Vegas Blvd S
Las Vegas, NV 89109
Phone: (800) 854-7666

#149
Binion's Hotel & Casino
Category: Hotel, Casino, Lounge
Average price: Inexpensive
Area: Downtown
Address: 128 Fremont St
Las Vegas, NV 89101
Phone: (702) 382-1600

#150
Paris Las Vegas Hotel & Casino
Category: Hotel, Casino
Average price: Modest
Area: The Strip
Address: 3655 Las Vegas Boulevard South,
Las Vegas, NV 89109
Phone: (877) 796-2096

#151
Eureka Casino
Category: Casino
Area: Eastside, Downtown
Address: 595 E Sahara Ave
Las Vegas, NV 89104
Phone: (702) 794-3464

#152
**Main Street Casino
Brewing Hotel**
Category: Hotel, Casino
Average price: Inexpensive
Area: Downtown
Address: 200 North Main Street
Las Vegas, NV 89101
Phone: (702) 387-1896

#153
Village Pub
Category: Casino, Restaurant
Average price: Inexpensive
Area: Anthem
Address: 10900 S Eastern Avenue
Henderson, NV 89052
Phone: (702) 216-0850

#154
Dealer Party Agency
Category: Casino, Bar
Area: Southeast
Address: 8810 S Maryland Pkwy
Las Vegas, NV 89123
Phone: (702) 408-0898

#155
Bingo Room
Category: Casino
Area: Anthem
Address: 2317 Paseo Verde Parkway
Henderson, NV 89052
Phone: (702) 617-7794

#156
**Bally's Las Vegas
Hotel & Casino**
Category: Hotel, Casino
Average price: Modest
Area: The Strip
Address: 3645 Las Vegas Blvd S
Las Vegas, NV 89109
Phone: (877) 603-4390

#157
La Bayou Casino
Category: Casino, American,
Cocktail Bar
Average price: Modest
Area: Downtown
Address: 15 Fremont St
Las Vegas, NV 89101
Phone: (702) 385-7474

#158
Mermaid's Casino
Category: Casino, Desserts, Bar
Average price: Inexpensive
Area: Downtown
Address: 32 Fremont St
Las Vegas, NV 89136
Phone: (702) 382-5777

#159
Margaritaville Casino
Category: Casino, Bar, American
Average price: Modest
Area: The Strip
Address: 3555 South Las Vegas Boulevard,
Las Vegas, NV 89109
Phone: (702) 733-3302

#160
Monte Carlo Casino
Category: Casino
Area: The Strip
Address: 3770 S Las Vegas Blvd
Las Vegas, NV 89109
Phone: (888) 527-8342

#161
Monte Carlo Race & Sport Book
Category: Casino
Area: The Strip
Address: Rue De Monte Carlo
Paradise, NV 89109
Phone: (702) 730-7777

#162
Slots A Fun
Category: Amusement Park,
Hotel, Casino
Average price: Inexpensive
Area: The Strip
Address: 2800 Las Vegas Blvd S
Las Vegas, NV 89109
Phone: (702) 734-0410

#163
Aztec Inn, Casino & Buffet
Category: Casino, Buffets
Area: The Strip
Address: 2200 Las Vegas Blvd S
Las Vegas, NV 89102
Phone: (702) 385-4566

#164
South Point Bingo Hall
Category: Casino
Area: Southeast
Address: 9777 Las Vegas Blvd S
Las Vegas, NV 89183
Phone: (702) 796-7111

#165
Casino Recruiter
Category: Casino
Area: Southeast
Address: 1100 Grier Dr
Las Vegas, NV 89119
Phone: (702) 798-0180

#166
Key Largo Hotel & Casino
Category: Hotel, Casino
Area: Westside
Address: 6100 Elton Ave
Las Vegas, NV 89107
Phone: (702) 733-7777

#167
**Coopers Sport
Handicapping Picks**
Category: Casino
Area: The Strip
Address: 3950 Las Vegas Blvd South
Paradise, NV 89119
Phone: (877) 632-7800

#168
Planet Hollywood Poker Room
Category: Casino
Area: The Strip
Address: 3667 Las Vegas Blvd S
Las Vegas, NV 89109
Phone: (702) 785-5555

#169
Kellys Kasino II
Category: Casino
Area: Northwest
Address: 5855 W Craig Road
Las Vegas, NV 89130
Phone: (702) 878-4272

#170
Treasure Island Poker Room
Category: Casino
Area: The Strip
Address: 3300 S Las Vegas Blvd
Las Vegas, NV 89109
Phone: (702) 894-7291

#171
Village Pub & Casino
Category: Restaurant, Casino
Average price: Inexpensive
Area: Summerlin
Address: 2610 Regatta Dr
Las Vegas, NV 89128
Phone: (702) 256-6200

#172
Village Pub & Poker
Category: Casino, Restaurant
Average price: Inexpensive
Area: Southeast
Address: 8515 S Eastern Avenue
Las Vegas, NV 89123
Phone: (702) 216-6160

#173
The Paiza Club
Category: Restaurant, Casino
Average price: Exclusive
Area: Eastside
Address: 3355 Las Vegas Blvd S

Las Vegas, NV 89109
Phone: (702) 414-1000

#174
Binion's Poker Room
Category: Casino
Area: Downtown
Address: 128 E Fremont St
Las Vegas, NV 89101
Phone: (702) 380-0952

#175
**Wynn Las Vegas Race
& Sport Book**
Category: Casino
Area: The Strip
Address: 3131 Las Vegas Blvd. South
Las Vegas, NV 89109
Phone: (702) 770-7000

#176
The Palazzo Resort Hotel Casino
Category: Hotel, Casino
Average price: Expensive
Area: The Strip
Address: 3325 S Las Vegas Blvd
Las Vegas, NV 89109
Phone: (702) 414-1000

#177
Encore
Category: Hotel, Casino,
Resort, Home Decor
Average price: Expensive
Area: The Strip
Address: 3131 Las Vegas Blvd. South
Las Vegas, NV 89109
Phone: (702) 770-8000

#178
Klondike Hotel & Casino
Category: Hotel, Casino
Average price: Inexpensive
Area: Southeast
Address: 5191 Las Vegas Blvd S
Las Vegas, NV 89119
Phone: (702) 739-9351

#179
The Venetian Poker Room
Category: Casino
Area: Eastside
Address: 3355 Las Vegas Blvd S
Las Vegas, NV 89109
Phone: (702) 414-1000

#180
Sigma Derby
Category: Horse Racing, Casino
Area: Eastside
Address: 3799 Las Vegas Bl S
Las Vegas, NV 89109
Phone: (702) 880-0880

#181
El Cortez Cabana Suites
Category: Hotel, Casino
Average price: Modest
Area: Downtown
Address: 651 E Ogden Ave
Las Vegas, NV 89101
Phone: (702) 385-5200

#182
The Coop Show
Category: Casino
Area: The Strip
Address: 3667 Las Vegas Blvd S
Las Vegas, NV 89109
Phone: (866) 919-7472

#183
Alamo Casino
Category: Casino
Area: Southwest
Address: 8050 Dean Martin Rd
Las Vegas, NV 89139
Phone: (702) 350-3353

#184
Casino Gaming School
Category: Casino
Area: Eastside
Address: 900 Karen Avenue
Las Vegas, NV 89109
Phone: (702) 893-1788

#185
The Poker Room
Category: Casino
Area: The Strip
Address: 2535 Las Vegas Blvd S
Las Vegas, NV 89109
Phone: (702) 737-2317

#186
Las Vegas Hilton Sportbook
Category: Casino
Address: 3000 Paradise Rd
Las Vegas, NV 89109
Phone: (702) 732-5111

#187
Palazzo Race & Sport Book
Category: Sport Bar, Casino
Average price: Expensive
Area: The Strip
Address: 3325 Las Vegas Blvd S
Las Vegas, NV 89109
Phone: (702) 414-1000

#188
The King Lives
Category: Casino
Area: Southeast
Address: 115 E Tropicana Ave
Las Vegas, NV 89109
Phone: (702) 739-9000

#189
Nobu Hotel
Category: Hotel, Casino
Average price: Expensive
Area: Eastside
Address: 3570 Las Vegas Boulevard South,
Las Vegas, NV 89109
Phone: (702) 785-6677

#190
Silverton Blingo Bingo
Category: Casino
Area: Southwest
Address: 3333 Blue Diamond Rd
Las Vegas, NV 89139
Phone: (702) 263-7777

#191
Monte Carlo Poker Room
Category: Casino
Address: 3770 Las Vegas Blvd S
Las Vegas, NV 89109
Phone: (702) 730-7780

#192
Stage Deli
Category: Desserts, Sandwiches,
Deli, Hotel, Casino
Average price: Modest
Area: Eastside
Address: 3799 Las Vegas Blvd S
Las Vegas, NV 89109
Phone: (702) 891-7777

#193
Bingo Room
Category: Casino
Area: South Summerlin
Address: 11031 W Charleston Blvd
Las Vegas, NV 89155
Phone: (702) 797-7778

#194
Wynn Poker Room
Category: Casino
Area: Eastside
Address: 3131 Las Vegas Blvd. South
Las Vegas, NV 89109
Phone: (702) 770-7654

#195
Flare Bar
Category: Casino
Area: Southwest
Address: 3333 Blue Diamond Rd
Las Vegas, NV 89139
Phone: (866) 722-4608

#196
**California Hotel
Casino & R V Park**
Category: Hotel, Casino
Average price: Modest
Address: 200 N Main St
Las Vegas, NV 89101
Phone: (702) 388-2602

#197
Sport Book
Category: Casino
Area: South Summerlin
Address: 11030 West Charleston Boulevard,
Las Vegas, NV 89154
Phone: (702) 797-7777

#198
Poker Room
Category: Casino
Area: Westside
Address: 11029 West Charleston Boulevard,
Las Vegas, NV 89153
Phone: (702) 797-7777

#199
Avis Rent A Car
Category: Casino
Area: The Strip
Address: 3667 Las Vegas Boulevard S
Las Vegas, NV 89109
Phone: (702) 785-5488

#200
Tix4 Tonight
Category: Casino
Area: Eastside
Address: 3555 Las Vegas Blvd
Las Vegas, NV 89109
Phone: (877) 849-4868

TOP 500
NIGHTLIFE SPOTS
The Most Recommended by Locals and Travelers
(From #1 to #500)

#1
Fat Tuesday
Category: Bar
Average price: Inexpensive
Area: The Strip, Eastside
Address: 3799 Las Vegas Blvd S
Las Vegas, NV 89109
Phone: (702) 891-9600

#2
Layla Grill & Hookah
Category: Mediterranean,
Hookah Bar, Lounge
Average price: Modest
Area: Spring Valley
Address: 8665 W Flamingo Rd
Las Vegas, NV 89147
Phone: (702) 202-4930

#3
Frankie's Tiki Room
Category: Bar
Average price: Modest
Area: Downtown
Address: 1712 W Charleston Blvd
Las Vegas, NV 89102
Phone: (702) 385-3110

#4
Mandarin Bar
Category: Lounge
Average price: Expensive
Area: The Strip
Address: 3752 Las Vegas Blvd S
Las Vegas, NV 89158
Phone: (702) 590-8888

#5
The Laundry Room
Category: Lounge
Average price: Modest
Area: Downtown
Address: 525 E Fremont St
Las Vegas, NV 89101
Phone: (702) 701-1466

#6
Banger Brewing
Category: Bar, Breweries
Average price: Inexpensive
Area: Downtown
Address: 450 Fremont St
Las Vegas, NV 89101
Phone: (702) 456-2739

#7
XS Nightclub
Category: Dance Club
Average price: Expensive
Area: The Strip
Address: 3131 Las Vegas Blvd S
Las Vegas, NV 89109
Phone: (702) 770-0097

#8
Velveteen Rabbit
Category: Cocktail Bar
Average price: Modest
Area: Downtown
Address: 1218 S Main St
Las Vegas, NV 89104
Phone: (702) 685-9645

#9
The Chandelier
Category: Lounge
Average price: Expensive
Area: The Strip
Address: 3708 Las Vegas Blvd S
Las Vegas, NV 89109
Phone: (702) 698-7000

#10
Downtown Cocktail Room
Category: Bar
Average price: Modest
Area: Downtown
Address: 111 Las Vegas Blvd S
Las Vegas, NV 89101
Phone: (702) 880-3696

#11
The Griffin
Category: Lounge
Average price: Modest
Area: Downtown
Address: 511 Fremont St
Las Vegas, NV 89101
Phone: (702) 382-0577

#12
Bond
Category: Lounge
Average price: Expensive
Area: The Strip
Address: 3708 Las Vegas Blvd S
Las Vegas, NV 89109
Phone: (702) 698-7000

#13
Stage Door
Category: Dive Bar
Average price: Inexpensive
Area: The Strip
Address: 4000 Audrie St
Las Vegas, NV 89109
Phone: (702) 733-0124

#14
Double Down Saloon
Category: Dive Bar, Music Venues
Average price: Inexpensive
Area: Eastside
Address: 4640 Paradise Rd
Las Vegas, NV 89109
Phone: (702) 791-5775

#15
Chada Thai & Wine
Category: Wine Bar, Thai
Average price: Modest
Area: Phone number
Address: 3400 S Jones Blvd
Las Vegas, NV 89146

#16
Freakin' Frog
Category: Music Venues, Pub
Average price: Modest
Area: University
Address: 4700 S Maryland Pkwy
Las Vegas, NV 89119
Phone: (702) 597-9702

#17
Don't Tell Mama
Category: Lounge
Average price: Modest
Area: Downtown
Address: 517 Fremont St
Las Vegas, NV 89101
Phone: (702) 207-0788

#18
Money Plays
Category: Dive Bar, Adult Entertainment
Average price: Inexpensive
Area: Phone number
Address: 4755 W Flamingo Rd
Las Vegas, NV 89103

#19
Atomic Liquor Store & Bar
Category: Dive Bar, Wine Bar
Average price: Modest
Area: Downtown
Address: 917 Fremont St
Las Vegas, NV 89101
Phone: (702) 982-3000

#20
Cirque du Soleil - Zumanity
Category: Performing Arts,
Adult Entertainment
Average price: Expensive
Area: The Strip
Address: 3790 Las Vegas Blvd S
Las Vegas, NV 89109
Phone: (702) 740-6815

#21
Level 107 Lounge
Category: Lounge
Average price: Modest
Area: The Strip
Address: 2000 Las Vegas Blvd S
Las Vegas, NV 89104
Phone: (702) 380-7764

#22
The Light Night Club
Category: Dance Club, Music Venues
Average price: Expensive
Area: The Strip
Address: 3950 Las Vegas Blvd S
Las Vegas, NV 89119
Phone: (702) 693-8300

#23
MIX
Category: French, Lounge
Average price: Exclusive
Area: The Strip
Address: 3950 Las Vegas Boulevard
Las Vegas, NV 89119
Phone: (702) 632-9500

#24
Foundation Room
Category: Lounge,
Dance Club, American
Average price: Expensive
Area: Eastside
Address: 3950 S Las Vegas Blvd
Las Vegas, NV 89109
Phone: (702) 632-7614

#25
Surrender Nightclub
Category: Dance Club
Average price: Expensive
Area: The Strip
Address: 3131 Las Vegas Blvd S
Las Vegas, NV 89109
Phone: (702) 770-7300

#26
Artifice
Category: Lounge, Music Venues
Average price: Modest
Area: Downtown
Address: 1025 1st St
Las Vegas, NV 89101
Phone: (702) 489-6339

#27
Evening Call
Category: Bar
Average price: Modest
Area: The Strip
Address: 3900 Las Vegas Blvd S
Las Vegas, NV 89119
Phone: (702) 262-4985

#28
The Peppermill
Restaurant & Fireside Lounge
Category: American,
Breakfast & Brunch, Lounge
Average price: Modest
Area: The Strip
Address: 2985 Las Vegas Blvd S
Las Vegas, NV 89109
Phone: (702) 735-4177

#29
Rhumbar
Category: Lounge
Average price: Modest
Area: The Strip
Address: 3400 Las Vegas Blvd S
Las Vegas, NV 89109
Phone: (702) 792-7615

#30
The Colosseum
At Caesars Palace
Category: Music Venues
Average price: Expensive
Area: The Strip
Address: 3570 South Las Vegas Blvd
Las Vegas, NV 89109
Phone: (702) 731-7208

#31
Blue Ox Tavern
Category: American, Sport Bar,
Breakfast & Brunch
Average price: Inexpensive
Area: Westside
Address: 5825 W Sahara Ave
Las Vegas, NV 89146
Phone: (702) 871-2536

#33
Tryst Nightclub
Category: Dance Club
Average price: Expensive
Area: The Strip
Address: 3131 Las Vegas Blvd.
Las Vegas, NV 89109
Phone: (702) 770-3375

#32
Champagne's Cafe
Category: Dive Bar
Average price: Inexpensive
Area: Eastside
Address: 3557 S Maryland Pkwy
Las Vegas, NV 89109
Phone: (702) 737-1699

#34
Wet Republic Ultra Pool
Category: Swimming Pool,
Dance Club
Average price: Expensive
Area: The Strip, Eastside
Address: 3799 Las Vegas Blvd S
Las Vegas, NV 89109
Phone: (702) 891-3563

#35
Rehab
Category: Bar, Swimming Pool
Average price: Expensive
Area: Eastside
Address: 4455 Paradise Rd
Las Vegas, NV 89109

#36
Garden of the Gods Pool
Category: Bar, Swimming Pool
Average price: Expensive
Area: The Strip
Address: 3570 Las Vegas Blvd S
Las Vegas, NV 89109
Phone: (702) 731-7266

#37
Bjs Cocktail Lounge Decatur
Category: Lounge, Cocktail Bar
Average price: Modest
Area: Southwest
Address: 8075 S Decatur Blvd
Las Vegas, NV 89139
Phone: (702) 291-2033

#38
Marquee Nightclub & Dayclub
Category: Dance Club
Average price: Expensive
Area: The Strip
Address: 3708 Las Vegas Blvd S
Las Vegas, NV 89109
Phone: (702) 333-9000

#39
Insert Coins
Category: Bar, Arcade
Average price: Modest
Area: Downtown
Address: 512 Fremont St
Las Vegas, NV 89101
Phone: (702) 477-2525

#40
Marché Bacchus
Category: French, Wine Bar
Average price: Expensive
Area: Summerlin
Address: 2620 Regatta Dr
Las Vegas, NV 89128
Phone: (702) 804-8008

#41
View Bar
Category: Lounge
Average price: Modest
Area: The Strip
Address: 3730 Las Vegas Blvd S
Las Vegas, NV 89109
Phone: (702) 590-7111

#42
Ghostbar
Category: Bar, Dance Club
Average price: Expensive
Area: Phone number
Address: 4321 W Flamingo Rd
Las Vegas, NV 89103

#43
Spearmint Rhino Adult Cabaret
Category: Adult Entertainment
Average price: Expensive
Area: Phone number
Address: 3340 S Highland Dr
Las Vegas, NV 89109

#44
Fremont Street Experience
Category: Bar, Casino
Average price: Inexpensive
Area: Downtown
Address: 425 Fremont St
Las Vegas, NV 89101
Phone: (702) 678-5600

#45
Pleasure Pit
Category: Adult Entertainment
Average price: Expensive
Area: The Strip
Address: 3667 Las Vegas Blvd
Las Vegas, NV 89109

#46
Embers
Category: American, Cocktail Bar
Average price: Modest
Area: Westside
Address: 740 S Rampart Blvd
Las Vegas, NV 89145
Phone: (702) 778-2160

#47
**The Joint At Hard Rock
Hotel & Casino Las Vegas**
Category: Music Venues
Average price: Expensive
Area: Eastside
Address: 4455 Paradise Rd
Las Vegas, NV 89109
Phone: (702) 693-5000

#48
Noreen's Cocktail Lounge
Category: Lounge
Average price: Inexpensive
Area: Southeast
Address: 2799 E Tropicana Ave
Las Vegas, NV 89121
Phone: (702) 458-7557

#49
Vinyl At Hard Rock Hotel & Casino Las Vegas
Category: Music Venues, Hotel
Average price: Modest
Area: Eastside
Address: 4455 Paradise Road
Las Vegas, NV 89169
Phone: (702) 693-5000

#50
Golden Nugget Pool
Category: Swimming Pool,
Cocktail Bar
Average price: Modest
Area: Downtown
Address: 129 Fremont St
Las Vegas, NV 89101

#51
Shadow Bar
Category: Lounge
Average price: Modest
Area: The Strip
Address: 3570 Las Vegas Blvd
Las Vegas, NV 89109
Phone: (877) 427-7243

#52
Encore Lobby Bar
Category: Lounge
Average price: Modest
Area: The Strip
Address: 3131 Las Vegas Blvd.
South, Las Vegas, NV 89109
Phone: (702) 770-5330

#53
Deja Vu Adult Emporium
Category: Adult, Lingerie, Nightlife, Videos &
Video Game Rental
Average price: Modest
Area: Phone number
Address: 4335 W Tropicana Ave
Las Vegas, NV 89103

#54
The Lady Silvia
Category: Lounge, Cocktail Bar,
Music Venues
Average price: Modest
Area: Downtown
Address: 900 Las Vegas Blvd S
Las Vegas, NV 89101
Phone: (702) 405-0816

#55
Park On Fremont
Category: American,
GastroPub, Lounge
Average price: Modest
Area: Downtown
Address: 506 E Fremont
Las Vegas, NV 89101
Phone: (702) 834-3160

#56
Azuza Hookah Lounge & Cafe
Category: Cafe, Hookah Bar
Average price: Modest
Area: Eastside
Address: 4480 Paradise Rd
Las Vegas, NV 89169
Phone: (702) 331-9500

#57
Cheers Bar & Grill
Category: Dive Bar, American
Average price: Inexpensive
Area: University
Address: 1220 E Harmon Ave
Las Vegas, NV 89119
Phone: (702) 734-2454

#58
Cloud 9 Hookah Lounge
Category: Hookah Bar
Average price: Modest
Area: Spring Valley
Address: 6825 W Russell Rd
Las Vegas, NV 89118
Phone: (702) 586-9743

#59
The Blind Pig
Category: Lounge, Cafe
Average price: Modest
Area: Phone number
Address: 4515 Dean Martin Dr
Las Vegas, NV 89103

#60
Sin City Parties
Category: Party & Events,
Adult Entertainment
Average price: Expensive
Area: Southeast
Address: 6671 S Las Vegas Blvd
Las Vegas, NV 89119
Phone: (888) 903-9889

#61
Dino's Lounge
Category: Karaoke
Average price: Inexpensive
Area: Downtown
Address: 1516 Las Vegas Blvd S
Las Vegas, NV 89104
Phone: (702) 382-3894

#62
Mob Bar
Category: Italian, Lounge
Average price: Modest
Area: Downtown
Address: 240 N 3rd St
Las Vegas, NV 89101
Phone: (702) 259-9700

#63
Luna Lounge - Hookah Lounge
Category: Hookah Bar,
Lounge, Tapas Bar
Average price: Modest
Area: The Strip
Address: 3057 S Las Vegas Blvd
Las Vegas, NV 89109
Phone: (702) 462-9991

#64
The Strip of Las Vegas
Category: Bar
Average price: Expensive
Area: The Strip
Address: Las Vegas Blvd
Las Vegas, NV 89109

#65
Commonwealth
Category: Bar
Average price: Modest
Area: Downtown
Address: 525 E Fremont St
Las Vegas, NV 89101
Phone: (702) 445-6400

#66
Riviera Comedy Club Theatre
Category: Comedy Club
Average price: Inexpensive
Area: Eastside
Address: 2901 Las Vegas Blvd South
Las Vegas, NV 89109
Phone: (877) 892-7469

#67
Bare Pool Lounge
Category: Lounge, Swimming Pool
Average price: Expensive
Area: Eastside
Address: 3400 Las Vegas Blvd S
Las Vegas, NV 89109
Phone: (702) 791-7111

#68
**Body English At Hard Rock
& Casino Las Vegas**
Category: Dance Club, Lounge
Average price: Expensive
Area: Eastside
Address: 4455 Paradise Rd
Las Vegas, NV 89169
Phone: (702) 693-4000

#69
Book & Stage
Category: Lounge
Average price: Modest
Area: The Strip
Address: 3708 Las Vegas Blvd S
Las Vegas, NV 89109
Phone: (702) 698-7000

#70
Aces & Ales
Category: Pub, Casino
Average price: Modest
Area: Phone number
Address: 3740 S Nellis Blvd
Las Vegas, NV 89121

#71
Mingo Kitchen & Lounge
Category: Lounge
Average price: Modest
Area: Downtown
Address: 1017 1st St
Las Vegas, NV 89101
Phone: (702) 685-0328

#72
Backstage Bar & Billiards
Category: Bar, Pool Halls
Average price: Modest
Area: Downtown
Address: 601 E Fremont St
Las Vegas, NV 89101
Phone: (702) 382-2227

#73
Parasol Up / Parasol Down
Category: Lounge
Average price: Expensive
Area: The Strip
Address: 3131 Las Vegas Blvd. South
Las Vegas, NV 89109
Phone: (702) 770-3392

#74
Bazic Bar & Restoyaky
Category: Korean,
Asian Fusion, Karaoke
Average price: Modest
Area: Chinatown
Address: 5115 Spring Mountain Rd
Las Vegas, NV 89146
Phone: (702) 642-8888

#75
Hookah Lounge
Category: Hookah Bar
Average price: Modest
Area: University, Eastside
Address: 4153 S Maryland Pkwy
Las Vegas, NV 89119
Phone: (702) 732-3203

#76
21 Restaurant & Lounge
Category: Lounge,
Asian Fusion, Karaoke
Average price: Modest
Area: Westside
Address: 6145 W Sahara Ave
Las Vegas, NV 89146
Phone: (702) 523-6286

#77
Rose.
Category: Bar, Performing Arts
Average price: Exclusive
Area: The Strip
Address: 3708 Las Vegas Blvd S
Las Vegas, NV 89109
Phone: (877) 667-0585

#78
VooDoo Rooftop Nightclub
Category: Lounge, Dance Club
Average price: Expensive
Area: Phone number
Address: 3700 W Flamingo Rd
Las Vegas, NV 89103

#79
Fantasy
Category: Adult Entertainment
Average price: Modest
Area: The Strip
Address: 3900 Las Vegas Blvd S
Las Vegas, NV 89109
Phone: (800) 557-7428

#80
TAO Beach
Category: Swimming Pool, Lounge
Average price: Expensive
Area: Westside
Address: 3355 Las Vegas Blvd S
Las Vegas, NV 89109
Phone: (702) 388-8588

#81
7777 Bar & Grill
Category: Sport Bar, Chinese
Average price: Inexpensive
Area: Westside
Address: 7777 W Sahara Ave
Las Vegas, NV 89117
Phone: (702) 388-7777

#82
Blvd.
Category: Cocktail Bar
Average price: Modest
Area: The Strip
Address: 3535 Las Vegas Blvd
Las Vegas, NV 89109
Phone: (702) 322-0579

#83
Blaqcat Ultra Hookah Lounge
Category: Hookah Bar, Lounge
Average price: Inexpensive
Area: Westside
Address: 6340 W Charlston Blvd
Las Vegas, NV 89146
Phone: (702) 822-1414

#84
BJ's Cocktail Lounge West
Category: Restaurant, Lounge
Average price: Modest
Area: Spring Valley
Address: 6670 S Tenaya Way
Las Vegas, NV 89113
Phone: (702) 257-7378

#85
Shucks Tavern & Oyster Bar
Category: Sport Bar, Seafood
Average price: Modest
Area: Centennial
Address: 7155 N Durango Dr
Las Vegas, NV 89149
Phone: (702) 651-6227

#86
Born And Raised
Category: Pub, Sport Bar
Average price: Modest
Area: Southwest
Address: 7260 S Cimarron Rd
Las Vegas, NV 89113
Phone: (702) 685-0258

#87
Tao Nightclub
Category: Dance Club, Lounge
Average price: Expensive
Area: The Strip
Address: 3355 Las Vegas Blvd S
Las Vegas, NV 89109
Phone: (702) 388-8338

#88
Ozzie's
Category: Bar
Average price: Inexpensive
Area: Chinatown
Address: 5020 Spring Mountain Rd
Las Vegas, NV 89146
Phone: (702) 368-3870

#89
Lime Ice Frozen Bar
Category: Bar
Average price: Modest
Area: The Strip
Address: 3377 Las Vegas Blvd S
Las Vegas, NV 89109
Phone: (702) 737-5463

#90
Stoney's Rockin' Country
Category: Bar, Dance Club,
Country Dance Halls
Average price: Inexpensive
Area: Southeast
Address: 6611 Las Vegas Blvd
Las Vegas, NV 89119
Phone: (702) 435-2855

#91
Minus 5 Ice Lounge
Category: Lounge
Average price: Expensive
Area: The Strip
Address: 3950 S Las Vegas Blvd
Las Vegas, NV 89109
Phone: (702) 740-5800

#92
Encore Beach Club
Category: Swimming Pool,
Dance Club
Average price: Expensive
Area: The Strip
Address: 3131 Las Vegas Blvd
Las Vegas, NV 89109
Phone: (702) 770-7300

#93
Parlour Bar & Lounge
Category: Lounge
Average price: Modest
Area: Phone number
Address: 600 E Fremont St
Las Vegas, NV 89101

#94
Blue Martini
Category: Lounge, American
Average price: Modest
Area: Southeast
Address: 6593 Las Vegas Blvd S
Las Vegas, NV 89119
Phone: (702) 949-2583

#95
Sapphire Pool & Dayclub
Category: Dance Club,
Swimming Pool
Average price: Expensive
Area: Phone number
Address: 3025 Industrial Rd
Las Vegas, NV 89109

#96
Rounders
Category: American, Sport Bar
Average price: Modest
Area: Southwest
Address: 8030 Blue Diamond Rd
Las Vegas, NV 89113
Phone: (702) 212-0594

#97
Eyecandy
Category: Lounge
Average price: Expensive
Area: Southeast
Address: 3950 S Las Vegas Boulevard
Las Vegas, NV 89119
Phone: (702) 632-7777

#98
PERFECTO @ The Rain Nightclub
Category: Dance Club
Average price: Expensive
Area: Phone number
Address: 4321 West Flamingo Rd
Las Vegas, NV 89103

#99
Cue-D-'s
Category: Pool Halls
Average price: Inexpensive
Area: Chinatown
Address: 3400 S Jones Blvd
Las Vegas, NV 89146
Phone: (702) 252-8880

#100
Scarlet Bar
Category: Bar
Average price: Expensive
Area: Phone number
Address: 4321 W Flamingo Rd
Las Vegas, NV 89103

#101
Remiix
Category: American, Asian Fusion, Cocktail Bar
Average price: Modest
Area: Southeast, Eastside
Address: 1801 E Tropicana Ave
Las Vegas, NV 89119
Phone: (702) 262-5592

#102
Minus 5 Ice Lounge
Category: Lounge
Average price: Expensive
Area: The Strip
Address: 3770 Las Vegas Blvd S
Las Vegas, NV 89109
Phone: (702) 586-8136

#103
Irene's Cocktail Lounge
Category: Lounge, Cocktail Bar
Average price: Inexpensive
Area: Chinatown
Address: 5480 Spring Mountain Rd
Las Vegas, NV 89146
Phone: (702) 873-5758

#104
Beauty Bar
Category: Bar, Dance Club
Average price: Modest
Area: Downtown
Address: 517 Fremont St
Las Vegas, NV 89101
Phone: (702) 598-1965

#105
Palms Pool
Category: Swimming Pool, Lounge
Average price: Modest
Area: Phone number
Address: 4321 W Flamingo Rd
Las Vegas, NV 89103

#106
Circle Bar Hard Rock
Category: Bar
Average price: Modest
Area: Eastside
Address: 4455 Paradise Rd
Las Vegas, NV 89109
Phone: (702) 693-5000

#107
Fun Hog Ranch
Category: Gay Bar
Average price: Inexpensive
Area: Eastside
Address: 495 E Twain Ave
Las Vegas, NV 89169
Phone: (702) 791-7001

#108
Heart Bar
Category: Adult Entertainment
Average price: Modest
Area: The Strip
Address: 3667 Las Vegas Boulevard South,
Las Vegas, NV 89109
Phone: (866) 919-7472

#109
Gold Diggers
Category: Dance Club,
Lounge, Music Venues
Average price: Modest
Area: Downtown
Address: 129 E Fremont St
Las Vegas, NV 89101
Phone: (702) 385-7111

#110
Vanity Nightclub
Category: Dance Club
Average price: Expensive
Area: Eastside
Address: 4455 Paradise Rd
Las Vegas, NV 89169
Phone: (702) 693-5555

#111
Red Label
Category: Lounge, American,
Asian Fusion
Average price: Inexpensive
Area: The Strip
Address: 332 W Sahara Ave
Las Vegas, NV 89102
Phone: (702) 382-6288

#112
Pure
Category: Adult Entertainment
Average price: Expensive
Area: The Strip
Address: 3570 Las Vegas Boulevard South,
Las Vegas, NV 89109
Phone: (702) 731-7873

#113
Count's Vamp'd
Category: Music Venues
Average price: Modest
Area: Westside
Address: 6750 W Sahara Ave
Las Vegas, NV 89146
Phone: (702) 220-8849

#114
Miller's Alehouse
Category: American, Sport Bar
Average price: Modest
Area: Southeast
Address: 6683 S Las Vegas Blvd
Las Vegas, NV 89119
Phone: (702) 616-3414

#115
Paradise Cantina
Category: Mexican, Bar
Average price: Modest
Area: Eastside
Address: 4480 S Paradise Rd
Las Vegas, NV 89136
Phone: (702) 434-0031

#116
Showroom At South Point
Category: Music Venues, Dance Club
Average price: Modest
Area: Southeast
Address: 9777 Las Vegas Blvd S
Las Vegas, NV 89183
Phone: (702) 796-7111

#117
Hookah Master's Lounge
Category: Hookah Bar,
Middle Eastern, Dance Club
Average price: Modest
Area: Westside
Address: 5900 W Charleston Blvd
Las Vegas, NV 89146
Phone: (702) 776-8000

#118
Three Angry Wives
Category: Pub
Average price: Modest
Area: Westside
Address: 8820 W Charleston Blvd
Las Vegas, NV 89117
Phone: (702) 944-4411

#119
Mermaid Lounge
Category: Restaurant, Lounge
Average price: Modest
Area: Southwest
Address: 3333 Blue Diamond Rd
Las Vegas, NV 89139
Phone: (702) 263-7777

#120
L.A. Comedy Club
Category: Comedy Club,
Event Planning & Services
Average price: Modest
Area: Eastside
Address: 3645 S Las Vegas
Las Vegas, NV 89109
Phone: (702) 275-3877

#121
Blue Ox Central
Category: Bar, American
Average price: Modest
Area: Southeast
Address: 6000 S Eastern Ave
Las Vegas, NV 89119
Phone: (702) 795-8795

#122
Onyx Bar
Category: Bar
Average price: Modest
Area: South Summerlin
Address: 11021 W Charleston Boulevard,
Las Vegas, NV 89145
Phone: (702) 797-7777

#123
Aces & Ales
Category: American, Pub, Sport Bar
Average price: Modest
Area: Phone number
Address: 2801 N Tenaya Way
Las Vegas, NV 89128

#124
Talk of the Town
Category: Adult Entertainment
Average price: Inexpensive
Area: Downtown
Address: 1238 Las Vegas Blvd S
Las Vegas, NV 89104
Phone: (702) 385-1800

#125
Maribel Mexican Food & More
Category: Mexican, Bar
Average price: Inexpensive
Area: Southeast
Address: 9821 S Eastern Ave
Las Vegas, NV 89183
Phone: (702) 431-5485

#126
Blue Diamond Saloon
Category: Bar
Average price: Inexpensive
Area: Southwest
Address: 6935 Blue Diamond Rd
Las Vegas, NV 89178
Phone: (702) 896-1455

#127
Chateau Nightclub & Garden
Category: Dance Club
Average price: Expensive
Area: The Strip
Address: 3655 Las Vegas Blvd
Las Vegas, NV 89109
Phone: (702) 776-7770

#128
Let Loose Vegas
Category: Event Planning
& Services, Tours
Area: Southwest, Spring Valley
Address: 7345 S Durango Dr
Las Vegas, NV 89113
Phone: (800) 277-3233

#129
The Bank
Category: Dance Club
Average price: Expensive
Area: The Strip
Address: 3600 S Las Vegas Blvd
Las Vegas, NV 89109
Phone: (702) 693-8300

#130
Revolver Saloon
Category: Bar
Average price: Inexpensive
Area: Northwest
Address: 4955 N Rancho Dr
Las Vegas, NV 89130
Phone: (702) 658-4906

#131
Pin Up
Category: Music Venues
Average price: Modest
Area: The Strip
Address: 2000 Las Vegas Blvd
Las Vegas, NV 89104
Phone: (702) 380-7777

#132
Hennessey's Tavern
Category: Irish, Pub
Average price: Modest
Area: Downtown
Address: 425 Fremont St
Las Vegas, NV 89101
Phone: (702) 382-4421

#133
Stripper101
Category: Adult Entertainment
Average price: Modest
Area: The Strip
Address: 3663 Las Vegas Blvd
Las Vegas, NV 89109
Phone: (702) 260-7200

#134
Sin City Brewing
Category: Breweries, Bar
Average price: Modest
Area: Eastside
Address: 3663 Las Vegas Blvd S
Las Vegas, NV 89109
Phone: (702) 732-1142

#135
Lucky's Lounge
Category: Lounge
Average price: Inexpensive
Area: Southwest
Address: 7345 S Jones Blvd
Las Vegas, NV 89139
Phone: (702) 260-8991

#136
Hakkasan Nightclub
Category: Dance Club, Lounge
Average price: Exclusive
Area: The Strip
Address: 3799 Las Vegas Blvd S
Las Vegas, NV 89109
Phone: (702) 891-3838

#137
1OAK
Category: Dance Club
Average price: Modest
Area: The Strip
Address: 3400 S Las Vegas Blvd
Las Vegas, NV 89109
Phone: (702) 693-8300

#138
Free Zone
Category: Gay Bar
Average price: Inexpensive
Area: Eastside
Address: 610 E Naples Dr
Las Vegas, NV 89119
Phone: (702) 794-2300

#139
Sapphire Gentlemen's Club
Category: Adult Entertainment
Average price: Expensive
Area: Phone number
Address: 3025 Industrial Rd
Las Vegas, NV 89109

#140
Club Paradise
Category: Adult Entertainment
Average price: Expensive
Area: Eastside
Address: 4416 Paradise Rd
Las Vegas, NV 89169
Phone: (702) 734-7990

#141
The Bar @ Flamingo & Grand Canyon
Category: Lounge
Average price: Modest
Area: Spring Valley
Address: 4340 S Grand Canyon Dr
Las Vegas, NV 89147
Phone: (702) 269-3255

#142
Las Vegas Club Crawl
Category: Nightlife, Tours
Average price: Modest
Area: The Strip
Address: 3771 Las Vegas Blvd S
Las Vegas, NV 89109
Phone: (702) 353-5817

#143
Live Burlesque In Las Vegas!
Category: Performing Arts,
Adult Entertainment
Average price: Inexpensive
Area: Westside
Address: 3200 W Sirius Ave
Las Vegas, NV 89102

#144
Drai's AfterHours
Category: Lounge, Dance Club
Average price: Expensive
Area: The Strip
Address: 3595 Las Vegas Blvd S
Las Vegas, NV 89109
Phone: (702) 777-3777

#145
**Blue Ox East
Restaurant & Lounge**
Category: Bar, American
Average price: Modest
Area: Eastside
Address: 4130 S Sandhill Rd
Las Vegas, NV 89121
Phone: (702) 435-1344

#146
Steiner's Nevada Style Pub
Category: American, Pub
Average price: Modest
Area: Summerlin
Address: 1750 N Buffalo Dr
Las Vegas, NV 89128
Phone: (702) 304-8084

#147
VooDoo Beach
Category: Nightlife
Average price: Modest
Area: Phone number
Address: 3700 W Flamingo Rd
Las Vegas, NV 89103

#148
PT's
Category: Pub, Sport Bar
Average price: Inexpensive
Area: Phone number
Address: 6235 S Decatur Blvd
Las Vegas, NV 89118

#149
Daylight Beach Club
Category: Dance Club,
Swimming Pool
Average price: Expensive
Area: The Strip
Address: 3950 Las Vegas Blvd S
Las Vegas, NV 89119
Phone: (702) 693-8300

#150
Flight
Category: Bar
Average price: Inexpensive
Area: Southeast
Address: 3900 Las Vegas Blvd. South
Las Vegas, NV 89119
Phone: (702) 262-4591

#151
Cornish Pasty Co.
Category: British, Pub,
Specialty Food
Average price: Modest
Area: Eastside
Address: 953 E Sahara Ave
Las Vegas, NV 89104
Phone: (702) 862-4538

#152
Cellar Lounge - Temp.
Category: Bar, Music Venues
Average price: Inexpensive
Area: Westside
Address: 3601 W Sahara Ave
Las Vegas, NV 89102
Phone: (702) 362-6268

#153
**Mystere Theatre At Treasure Island
Hotel And Casino**
Category: Music Venues
Average price: Expensive
Area: The Strip
Address: 3300 Las Vegas Blvd S
Las Vegas, NV 89193
Phone: (213) 480-2323

#154
Bacon Bar
Category: Pizza, Sport Bar
Average price: Modest
Area: Northwest
Address: 3520 N Rancho Dr
Las Vegas, NV 89130
Phone: (702) 645-8844

#155
Blind Tiger
Category: Karaoke
Average price: Inexpensive
Area: Southeast
Address: 6295 S Pecos Rd
Las Vegas, NV 89120
Phone: (702) 835-5963

#156
Adult Superstore
Category: Adult,
Adult Entertainment, Booktore
Average price: Expensive
Area: Phone number
Address: 3850 W Tropicana Ave
Las Vegas, NV 89103

#157
Oracle Nightclub
Category: Hookah Bar
Average price: Modest
Area: Phone number
Address: 3500 W Naples Dr
Las Vegas, NV 89103

#158
Vesper Bar
Category: Lounge
Average price: Expensive
Area: The Strip
Address: 3708 Las Vegas Blvd S
Las Vegas, NV 89109
Phone: (702) 698-7000

#159
Larry Flynt's Hustler Club
Category: Adult Entertainment
Average price: Modest
Area: Phone number
Address: 6007 Dean Martin Dr
Las Vegas, NV 89118

#160
HAZE
Category: Dance Club
Average price: Expensive
Area: The Strip
Address: 3730 Las Vegas Blvd
Las Vegas, NV 89109
Phone: (702) 693-8300

#161
Little Macau
Category: Chinese, Bar
Average price: Modest
Address: 3939 Spring Mountain Rd
Las Vegas, NV 89102
Phone: (702) 222-3196

#162
Davy's Locker
Category: Dive Bar
Average price: Inexpensive
Address: 1149 E Desert Inn Rd
Las Vegas, NV 89109
Phone: (702) 735-0001

#163
Hogs and Heifers
Category: Bar
Average price: Modest
Area: Downtown
Address: 201 N 3rd St
Las Vegas, NV 89101
Phone: (702) 676-1457

#164
Laugh Factory
Category: Performing Arts,
Comedy Club
Average price: Modest
Area: The Strip
Address: 3801 S Las Vegas Blvd
Las Vegas, NV 89109
Phone: (702) 739-2222

#165
Imperial Tacos & Beer
Category: Cocktail Bar,
Mexican, Tapas
Average price: Modest
Area: Eastside
Address: 3900 Paradise Rd
Las Vegas, NV 89169
Phone: (702) 675-7572

#166
Florida Cafe Cuban Bar & Grill
Category: Cuban, Bar
Average price: Modest
Area: Downtown
Address: 1401 Las Vegas Blvd S
Las Vegas, NV 89104
Phone: (702) 385-3013

#167
32 Degrees
Category: Bar
Average price: Modest
Area: Eastside
Address: 3799 Las Vegas Blvd S
Las Vegas, NV 89109
Phone: (702) 891-1111

#168
Brass Lounge
Category: Lounge
Average price: Modest
Area: Downtown
Address: 425 Fremont St
Las Vegas, NV 89101
Phone: (702) 382-3531

#169
Bin 702
Category: Wine Bar, Sandwiches
Average price: Modest
Area: Downtown
Address: 707 E Fremont St
Las Vegas, NV 89101
Phone: (702) 826-2702

#170
Blue Hawk Tavern
Category: Dive Bar
Average price: Modest
Area: Southeast
Address: 11997 Las Vegas Blvd S
Las Vegas, NV 89183
Phone: (702) 614-0065

#171
Office Bar I
Category: Bar, Beer, Wine & Spirits
Average price: Inexpensive
Area: Eastside
Address: 4608 Paradise Rd
Las Vegas, NV 89109
Phone: (702) 737-7756

#172
Blondies Sport Bar & Grill
Category: Sport Bar, American
Average price: Modest
Area: The Strip
Address: 3663 Las Vegas Blvd S
Las Vegas, NV 89109
Phone: (702) 737-0444

#173
Rush Lounge
Category: Lounge
Average price: Modest
Area: Downtown
Address: 129 E Fremont St
Las Vegas, NV 89136
Phone: (800) 634-3454

#174
Le Central
Category: Lounge
Average price: Expensive
Area: Eastside
Address: 3655 Las Vegas Blvd S
Las Vegas, NV 89109
Phone: (702) 946-4251

#175
Las Vegas Red Rooster
Category: Adult Entertainment
Average price: Modest
Area: Southeast
Address: 6405 Greyhound Ln
Las Vegas, NV 89136
Phone: (702) 451-6661

#176
Double Barrel Roadhouse
Category: Cocktail Bar, American
Average price: Modest
Area: The Strip
Address: 3770 S Las Vegas Blvd
Las Vegas, NV 89109
Phone: (702) 222-7735

#177
Men Of X
Category: Adult Entertainment,
Performing Arts
Average price: Modest
Area: Eastside
Address: 115 E Tropicana Ave
Las Vegas, NV 89109
Phone: (702) 241-4010

#178
Hot Shot Vegas
Category: Party & Events,
Dance Club
Area: Southeast
Address: 67 E Agate
Las Vegas, NV 89123
Phone: (775) 777-4322

#179
Yorky's
Category: Pub
Average price: Inexpensive
Area: Spring Valley
Address: 5325 S Ft Apache Rd
Las Vegas, NV 89148
Phone: (702) 655-4881

#180
Aurora
Category: Lounge
Average price: Modest
Area: The Strip
Address: 3900 Las Vegas Blvd S
Las Vegas, NV 89119
Phone: (702) 262-4591

#181
Wayfarer Bar
Category: Lounge, Cocktail Bar
Average price: Modest
Area: Downtown
Address: 107 Las Vegas Blvd S
Las Vegas, NV 89101
Phone: (702) 910-2390

#182
Shimmer Cabaret
Category: Nightlife
Average price: Modest
Area: Eastside
Address: 3000 Paradise Rd
Las Vegas, NV 89109
Phone: (800) 732-7117

#183
Applebee's Neighborhood
Grill & Bar
Category: American, Bar
Average price: Modest
Area: Chinatown
Address: 3501 S Rainbow Blvd
Las Vegas, NV 89103
Phone: (702) 220-3070

#184
Love Theatre At The Mirage
Hotel And Casino
Category: Music Venues
Average price: Modest
Area: Eastside
Address: 3400 Las Vegas Blvd South
Las Vegas, NV 89109
Phone: (800) 745-3000

#185
Jaguars Gentlemen's Cabaret
Category: Adult Entertainment
Average price: Exclusive
Area: Westside
Address: 3355 Procyon St
Las Vegas, NV 89162
Phone: (702) 367-4000

#186
Village Pub Bar & Grill
Category: Nightlife, Casino, Restaurant
Average price: Inexpensive
Area: Eastside
Address: 3455 E Flamingo Road
Las Vegas, NV 89121
Phone: (702) 436-2488

#187
Violas Tavern
Category: American, Sport Bar
Average price: Modest
Area: Northwest
Address: 4061 N Rancho
Las Vegas, NV 89130
Phone: (702) 331-1414

#188
Big Apple Bar
at New York, New York
Category: Nightlife
Average price: Modest
Area: Eastside
Address: 3790 Las Vegas Boulevard S.
Las Vegas, NV 89109
Phone: (702) 740-6969

#189
Badlands Saloon
Category: Gay Bar
Average price: Inexpensive
Area: Downtown
Address: 953 E Sahara Ave Ste 22B
Las Vegas, NV 89104
Phone: (702) 792-9262

#190
American Storm
Category: Adult Entertainment
Average price: Modest
Area: The Strip
Address: 3663 Las Vegas Blvd
Las Vegas, NV 89109
Phone: (702) 701-7778

#191
Cue Club
Category: Pool Halls
Average price: Inexpensive
Area: Downtown
Address: 953 E Sahara Ave
Las Vegas, NV 89104
Phone: (702) 735-2884

#192
Sierra Gold
Category: American, Sport Bar, Pub
Average price: Modest
Area: Summerlin
Address: 2400 N Buffalo Dr
Las Vegas, NV 89128
Phone: (702) 724-7004

#193
Showgirl Video
Category: Adult Entertainment
Average price: Inexpensive
Area: Downtown
Address: 631 Las Vegas Boulevard South
Las Vegas, NV 89101
Phone: (702) 385-4554

#194
Durango Lodge
Category: Dive Bar,
Sport Bar, Restaurant
Average price: Modest
Area: Spring Valley
Address: 3399 S Durango Dr
Las Vegas, NV 89117
Phone: (702) 242-5533

#195
Barefoot Bob's Beach Bar & Gaming
Category: Sport Bar, Tapas Bar,
Beer, Wine & Spirits
Average price: Inexpensive
Area: University, Eastside
Address: 1590 E Flamingo Rd
Las Vegas, NV 89119
Phone: (702) 697-0529

#196
Charlie's Down Under
Category: Bar, American
Average price: Inexpensive
Area: Summerlin
Address: 1950 N Buffalo Dr
Las Vegas, NV 89128
Phone: (702) 804-5172

#197
Zumanity Theatre At New York New York Hotel And Casino
Category: Music Venues
Average price: Modest
Area: Eastside
Address: 3790 Las Vegas Blvd South
Las Vegas, NV 89109
Phone: (800) 745-3000

#198
LAX Nightclub
Category: Dance Club
Average price: Expensive
Area: Eastside
Address: 3900 Las Vegas Blvd S
Las Vegas, NV 89119
Phone: (702) 262-4529

#199
Inn Zone Rainbow
Category: Sport Bar
Average price: Modest
Area: Westside
Address: 238 S Rainbow Blvd
Las Vegas, NV 89145
Phone: (702) 363-2424

#200
Fat Tuesday
Category: Bar
Average price: Inexpensive
Area: The Strip
Address: 3411 Las Vegas Blvd
Las Vegas, NV 89109
Phone: (702) 754-0096

#201
Golden Rainbow
Category: Music Venues
Average price: Modest
Area: Eastside
Address: 3645 Las Vegas Blvd S
Las Vegas, NV 89109
Phone: (702) 384-2899

#202
Beacher's Madhouse
Category: Comedy Club,
Performing Arts
Average price: Modest
Area: The Strip, Eastside
Address: 3799 S Las Vegas Blvd
Las Vegas, NV 89109
Phone: (323) 785-3036

#203
OG Gentlemen's Club
Category: Adult Entertainment, Bar
Average price: Expensive
Area: Downtown
Address: 1531 Las Vegas Blvd S
Las Vegas, NV 89104
Phone: (702) 386-9200

#204
Suncoast Showroom
Category: Dance Club, Music Venues
Average price: Modest
Area: Westside
Address: 9090 Alta Dr
Las Vegas, NV 89144
Phone: (702) 636-7111

#205
Blue Dogs Pub
Category: Dive Bar, American
Area: Eastside
Address: 3430 E Tropicana Ave
Las Vegas, NV 89121
Phone: (702) 823-4273

#206
B Bar
Category: Bar
Average price: Expensive
Area: Eastside
Address: 3131 S Las Vegas Blvd
Las Vegas, NV 89109
Phone: (702) 770-7000

#207
Roadrunner Saloon
Category: Bar, American
Average price: Modest
Area: Summerlin
Address: 921 N Buffalo Dr
Las Vegas, NV 89128
Phone: (702) 242-2822

#208
The View Wine Bar & Kitchen
Category: Wine Bar, Tapas
Average price: Modest
Area: Westside
Address: 420 S Rampart Blvd
Las Vegas, NV 89145
Phone: (702) 280-7390

#209
X Burlesque
Category: Adult Entertainment
Average price: Modest
Area: The Strip
Address: 3555 Las Vegas Blvd S
Las Vegas, NV 89109
Phone: (702) 733-3333

#210
The Whisky Attic
Category: Bar
Average price: Expensive
Area: University
Address: 4700 S Maryland Pkwy
Las Vegas, NV 89119
Phone: (702) 217-6794

#211
Crowbar
Category: Sport Bar
Average price: Inexpensive
Area: Westside
Address: 1113 S Rainbow Blvd
Las Vegas, NV 89146
Phone: (702) 804-1113

#212
Hofbräuhaus
Category: Bar, German
Average price: Modest
Area: Eastside
Address: 4510 Paradise Rd
Las Vegas, NV 89109
Phone: (702) 853-2337

#213
Sporting Life Bar
Category: Sport Bar
Average price: Modest
Area: Southwest
Address: 7778 S Jones Blvd
Las Vegas, NV 89139
Phone: (702) 331-4647

#214
TGI Friday's
Category: Wine Bar
Average price: Modest
Area: Westside
Address: 4570 W Sahara Ave
Las Vegas, NV 89102
Phone: (702) 889-1866

#215
Mr. Shesha Hookah Lounge
Category: Hookah Bar
Average price: Inexpensive
Area: Southeast
Address: 1725 E Warm springs Rd
Las Vegas, NV 89119
Phone: (702) 912-0000

#216
Bar at Times Square
Category: Pub
Average price: Modest
Area: Eastside
Address: 3790 Las Vegas Blvd S
Las Vegas, NV 89109
Phone: (702) 236-0374

#217
Spazmatics
Category: Music Venues
Average price: Inexpensive
Area: Southeast
Address: 9777 Las Vegas Blvd S
Las Vegas, NV 89183
Phone: (702) 796-7111

#218
Legends Sport Bar & Grill
Category: Sport Bar, American
Average price: Modest
Area: Southeast
Address: 5866 Boulder Hwy
Las Vegas, NV 89122
Phone: (702) 778-8750

#219
Shades of Sinatra
Category: Performing Arts,
Music Venues
Average price: Inexpensive
Area: Eastside
Address: 305 Convention Center Dr
Las Vegas, NV 89109
Phone: (702) 990-1524

#220
5 O'clock Somewhere Bar
Category: Bar
Average price: Modest
Area: The Strip
Address: 3555 Las Vegas Blvd S
Las Vegas, NV 89109
Phone: (702) 733-3111

#221
Hot Shots Bar
Category: Lounge, Karaoke
Average price: Inexpensive
Area: Eastside
Address: 3430 E Tropicana Ave
Las Vegas, NV 89121
Phone: (702) 547-6600

#222
Aqua Restaurant & Lounge
Category: Karaoke, Restaurant
Average price: Modest
Area: Chinatown
Address: 6000 Spring Mtn Rd
Las Vegas, NV 89146
Phone: (702) 367-8989

#223
4949 Lounge
Category: Lounge
Average price: Expensive
Area: Northwest
Address: 4950 N Rancho Dr
Las Vegas, NV 89130
Phone: (702) 658-4901

#224
Jack's Place
Category: Dive Bar
Average price: Modest
Area: Sunrise
Address: 5067 E Bonanza Rd
Las Vegas, NV 89110
Phone: (702) 453-4333

#225
Lavish Vegas
Category: Dance Club,
Party & Events
Area: Southeast
Address: 8275 S Eastern Ave
Las Vegas, NV 89123
Phone: (877) 952-8474

#226
Bier Garten
Category: Pub
Average price: Modest
Area: Downtown
Address: 1 S Main St
Las Vegas, NV 89101
Phone: (702) 366-0889

#227
Joey's Tavern
Category: Bar, American
Average price: Modest
Area: Northwest
Address: 7081 W Craig Rd
Las Vegas, NV 89129
Phone: (702) 215-3300

#228
Bar Kada Avenue
Category: Ethnic Food, Karaoke,
Asian Fusion
Average price: Modest
Area: Westside
Address: 2605 S Decatur Blvd
Las Vegas, NV 89102
Phone: (702) 227-5232

#229
**Decatur Package
Liquor & Cocktails**
Category: Beer, Wine & Spirits,
Dive Bar
Area: Westside
Address: 546 S Decatur Blvd
Las Vegas, NV 89107
Phone: (702) 870-2522

#230
Vegas Rockstar VIP
Category: Dance Club
Area: Downtown
Address: 800 S 4th St
Las Vegas, NV 89101
Phone: (702) 703-5420

#231
Hard Rock Live
Category: Music Venues
Average price: Modest
Area: The Strip
Address: 3771 Las Vegas Blvd S
Las Vegas, NV 89109
Phone: (702) 733-7625

#232
PT's
Category: Sport Bar, Pub
Area: Southeast
Address: 310 E Warm Springs Rd
Las Vegas, NV 89119
Phone: (702) 837-9175

#233
Coyote Ugly Saloon
Category: Bar, Adult Entertainment
Average price: Modest
Area: Eastside
Address: 3790 Las Vegas Blvd S
Las Vegas, NV 89109
Phone: (702) 740-6330

#234
Brand Lounge
Category: Dance Club
Average price: Modest
Area: The Strip
Address: 3770 S Las Vegas Blvd
Las Vegas, NV 89109
Phone: (702) 588-5656

#235
Big Chill
Category: Bar
Average price: Inexpensive
Area: The Strip
Address: 3770 Las Vegas Blvd S
Las Vegas, NV 89109
Phone: (702) 730-6740

#236
The Lounge
Category: Lounge
Average price: Modest
Area: Eastside
Address: 145 E Harmon Ave
Las Vegas, NV 89109
Phone: (877) 612-2121

#237
The Piano Bar at Harrah's
Category: Bar
Average price: Modest
Area: The Strip
Address: 3475 S Las Vegas Blvd
Las Vegas, NV 89136
Phone: (702) 369-5000

#238
Midtown
Category: Pizza, Wine Bar, Italian
Average price: Modest
Area: Eastside
Address: 953 E Desert Inn Rd
Las Vegas, NV 89109
Phone: (702) 733-1234

#239
Lucky Bar
Category: Bar
Average price: Modest
Area: Summerlin
Address: 11020 West Charleston Boulevard
Las Vegas, NV 89144
Phone: (702) 797-7777

#240
Pt's Pub
Category: Bar
Average price: Inexpensive
Area: Downtown
Address: 532 E Sahara Avenue
Las Vegas, NV 89104
Phone: (702) 792-4121

#241
PT's
Category: Sport Bar, American, Pub
Average price: Modest
Area: Spring Valley
Address: 9050 W Post Rd
Las Vegas, NV 89148
Phone: (702) 798-7678

#242
La Bayou Casino
Category: Casino, American,
Cocktail Bar
Average price: Modest
Area: Downtown
Address: 15 Fremont St
Las Vegas, NV 89101
Phone: (702) 385-7474

#243
The Axis
Category: Performing Arts,
Music Venues
Average price: Expensive
Area: Eastside
Address: 3667 Las Vegas Blvd S
Las Vegas, NV 89109
Phone: (888) 800-8264

#244
The Ainsworth
Category: Sport Bar
Average price: Modest
Area: Eastside
Address: 4455 Paradise Rd
Las Vegas, NV 89169
Phone: (702) 522-8120

#245
Thunderbird Lounge
Category: Lounge
Average price: Inexpensive
Area: Downtown
Address: 1215 Las Vegas Blvd. South
Las Vegas, NV 89104
Phone: (702) 383-3100

#246
Raiding The Rock Vault
Category: Performing Arts,
Music Venues
Average price: Modest
Area: The Strip
Address: 3000 Paradise Rd
Las Vegas, NV 89109
Phone: (702) 889-2705

#247
Sam Boyd Stadium
Category: Stadium,
Music Venues
Average price: Modest
Area: Southeast
Address: 7000 E Russell Rd
Las Vegas, NV 89122
Phone: (702) 895-3761

#248
Puff Lounge
Category: Hookah Bar
Average price: Modest
Area: Eastside
Address: 1030 E Flamingo Blvd
Las Vegas, NV 89119
Phone: (702) 221-7833

#249
Mizuya Lounge
Category: Lounge
Average price: Modest
Area: The Strip
Address: 3950 S Las Vegas
Boulevard, Las Vegas, NV 89109
Phone: (702) 632-7777

#250
Ignite Lounge
Category: Lounge
Average price: Modest
Area: The Strip
Address: 3770 Las Vegas Blvd S
Las Vegas, NV 89109
Phone: (702) 730-7777

#251
The Martini
Category: American, Lounge
Average price: Modest
Area: Westside
Address: 1205 S Fort Apache Rd
Las Vegas, NV 89117
Phone: (702) 227-8464

#252
P T's
Category: Pub
Average price: Inexpensive
Area: University
Address: 1089 E Tropicana Ave
Las Vegas, NV 89119
Phone: (702) 895-9480

#253
Bikini Bar
Category: Bar
Average price: Inexpensive
Area: Chinatown
Address: 3355 Spring Mountain Rd
Las Vegas, NV 89103
Phone: (702) 485-5401

#254
Zodie's
Category: Bar, American
Average price: Inexpensive
Area: Eastside
Address: 3055 E Flamingo Rd
Las Vegas, NV 89121
Phone: (702) 434-9580

#255
Zebra Lounge
Category: Lounge
Average price: Exclusive
Area: The Strip
Address: 3325 S Las Vegas Blvd
Las Vegas, NV 89109
Phone: (702) 414-1000

#256
Stripper Bar
Category: Lounge
Average price: Modest
Area: The Strip
Address: 3663 Las Vegas Blvd S
Las Vegas, NV 89109
Phone: (702) 260-7200

#257
Hard Rock Sport Book
Category: Sport Bar
Average price: Inexpensive
Area: Eastside
Address: 4455 Paradise Rd
Las Vegas, NV 89169
Phone: (702) 693-5000

#258
The Black Door
Category: Bar, American
Average price: Modest
Area: Eastside
Address: 4640 Paradise Rd
Las Vegas, NV 89169
Phone: (702) 207-5003

#259
Girls of Glitter Gulch
Category: Adult Entertainment
Average price: Modest
Area: Downtown
Address: 20 E Fremont St
Las Vegas, NV 89101
Phone: (702) 385-4774

#260
Distill - A Local Bar
Category: Bar, Italian,
Breakfast & Brunch
Average price: Modest
Area: Summerlin
Address: 10820 W Charleston Blvd
Las Vegas, NV 89135
Phone: (702) 534-1400

#261
Muse Asian Cuisine & Lounge
Category: Karaoke, Asian Fusion
Average price: Modest
Area: Chinatown
Address: 5115 W Spring Mountain Rd
Las Vegas, NV 89146
Phone: (702) 368-0777

#262
Romance Lounge
Category: Nightlife
Average price: Modest
Area: The Strip
Address: 2000 Las Vegas Boulevard S
Las Vegas, NV 89102
Phone: (702) 380-7711

#263
Venetian Phantom Theater
Category: Music Venues
Area: Eastside
Address: 3355 Las Vegas Blvd S
Las Vegas, NV 89109
Phone: (702) 474-4000

#264
Club Rio
Category: Nightlife
Area: Sunrise
Address: 821 N Lamb Blvd
Las Vegas, NV 89110
Phone: (714) 525-9700

#265
Picnic
Category: Bar, American
Average price: Modest
Area: Downtown
Address: 206 N 3rd St, 3rd Fl,
Rooftop, Las Vegas, NV 89101
Phone: (855) 384-7263

#266
Rounders
Category: American, Sport Bar
Average price: Modest
Area: Spring Valley
Address: 4455 S Buffalo Dr
Las Vegas, NV 89147
Phone: (702) 247-4308

#267
The Great American Pub
Category: Pub
Average price: Modest
Area: Spring Valley
Address: 4145 S Grand Canyon
Las Vegas, NV 89147
Phone: (702) 220-8427

#268
Play It Again Sam
Category: Adult Entertainment
Average price: Modest
Area: Chinatown
Address: 4120 Spring Mountain Rd
Las Vegas, NV 89102
Phone: (702) 876-1550

#269
Choices Pub
Category: Pub
Average price: Inexpensive
Area: Northwest
Address: 6720 W Cheyenne Ave
Las Vegas, NV 89108
Phone: (702) 547-3747

#270
PT's
Category: Pub, Sport Bar
Average price: Modest
Area: Southeast
Address: 3470 E Sunset Rd
Las Vegas, NV 89120
Phone: (702) 434-4150

#271
PT's
Category: Sport Bar, Pub
Average price: Modest
Area: Spring Valley
Address: 3935 S Durango Dr
Las Vegas, NV 89147
Phone: (702) 838-5148

#272
Sean Patricks Pub
Category: Pub
Average price: Modest
Area: Spring Valley
Address: 8255 W Flamingo Rd
Las Vegas, NV 89147
Phone: (702) 227-9793

#273
Timbers - Lake Mead
Category: Bar, American
Average price: Modest
Area: Sunrise
Address: 6330 E Lake Mead
Boulevard, Las Vegas, NV 89156
Phone: (702) 459-4232

#274
Sandbar
Category: Bar, Cafe
Average price: Modest
Area: South Summerlin
Address: 11024 W Charleston Blvd
Las Vegas, NV 89148
Phone: (702) 797-7777

#275
Village Pub & Casino
Category: Restaurant, Casino
Average price: Inexpensive
Area: Summerlin
Address: 2610 Regatta Dr
Las Vegas, NV 89128
Phone: (702) 256-6200

#276
Brewery Bar & Grill
Category: Bar, American
Average price: Modest
Area: Southeast
Address: 3088 E Sunset Rd
Las Vegas, NV 89120
Phone: (702) 433-5955

#277
Bounty Hunters
Category: Bar
Average price: Inexpensive
Area: Southeast
Address: 455 E Windmill Lane
Las Vegas, NV 89123
Phone: (702) 837-0800

#278
Pour 24
Category: Pub
Average price: Modest
Area: Eastside
Address: 3790 Las Vegas Blvd S
Las Vegas, NV 89109
Phone: (800) 689-1797

#279
215 Saloon
Category: Bar
Average price: Modest
Area: Spring Valley
Address: 4145 S Grand Canyon
Las Vegas, NV 89147
Phone: (702) 222-4215

#280
Sammy's Beach Bar & Grill
Category: Sport Bar, Mexican
Average price: Modest
Area: Eastside
Address: 5757 Wayne Newton Blvd
Las Vegas, NV 89169
Phone: (702) 261-5211

#281
Arc Bar
Category: Nightlife, Beer,
Wine & Spirits, Hotel & Travel
Average price: Modest
Area: The Strip
Address: Paris
Las Vegas, NV 89109
Phone: (702) 697-0572

#282
Hard Rock Poker Lounge
Category: Lounge
Area: Eastside
Address: 4455 Paradise Rd
Las Vegas, NV 89136
Phone: (702) 693-5000

#283
Vince Neil's Tatuado
EAT DRINK PARTY
Category: American, Sport Bar
Average price: Modest
Area: The Strip
Address: 2880 Las Vegas Blvd S
Las Vegas, NV 89109
Phone: (702) 691-5991

#284
Saturday Night Stomp
Category: Dance Club, Dance School
Average price: Inexpensive
Area: Downtown
Address: 911 E Ogden Ave
Las Vegas, NV 89101
Phone: (702) 387-9312

#285
PT's
Category: Sport Bar, Pub
Average price: Modest
Area: Southeast, Eastside
Address: 4310 E Tropicana Ave
Las Vegas, NV 89121
Phone: (702) 434-5741

#286
The Gold Club
Category: Adult Entertainment
Average price: Modest
Area: Southeast
Address: 6370 Windy Rd
Las Vegas, NV 89119
Phone: (702) 614-4653

#287
Calico Jack's Saloon
Category: Bar, Karaoke
Average price: Inexpensive
Area: Westside
Address: 8200 W Charleston Blvd
Las Vegas, NV 89117
Phone: (702) 255-6771

#288
Crazy Girls Theatre
At Riviera Hotel & Casino
Category: Performing Arts, Adult
Entertainment
Average price: Modest
Area: The Strip
Address: 2901 Las Vegas Blvd S
Las Vegas, NV 89109
Phone: (702) 794-9433

#289
Lucky's Lounge
Category: Lounge
Area: Centennial
Address: 8025 Farm Rd
Las Vegas, NV 89131
Phone: (702) 212-6639

#290
Night School 4 Girls
Category: Adult Entertainment
Average price: Modest
Area: The Strip
Address: 3771 S. Las Vegas Blvd
Las Vegas, NV 89109
Phone: (702) 701-7778

#291
Baccarat Lounge
Category: Lounge
Average price: Expensive
Area: The Strip
Address: 3600 S Las Vegas Blvd
Las Vegas, NV 89109
Phone: (702) 693-7111

#292
Foothills Ranch
Category: Nightlife
Average price: Modest
Area: Northwest
Address: 3377 N Rancho Dr
Las Vegas, NV 89130
Phone: (702) 658-6360

#293
Shifty's Cocktail Lounge
Category: Dive Bar, Sport Bar
Average price: Inexpensive
Area: Westside
Address: 3805 W Sahara Ave
Las Vegas, NV 89102
Phone: (702) 871-4952

#294
Philippine Garden Karaoke Restaurant and Lounge
Category: Karaoke, Filipino
Average price: Modest
Area: Chinatown
Address: 4300 Spring Mountain Rd
Las Vegas, NV 89102
Phone: (702) 364-4558

#295
Saxe Lounge
Category: Lounge, Performing Arts, Ticket Sales
Average price: Modest
Area: The Strip
Address: 3663 Las Vegas Blvd S
Las Vegas, NV 89109
Phone: (702) 260-7200

#296
Tango With Judy
Category: Dance Club, Dance Studio
Average price: Modest
Area: Westside
Address: 3375 S Decatur Blvd
Las Vegas, NV 89102
Phone: (520) 907-2050

#297
Waxx Ultra Lounge & Nightclub
Category: Dance Club, Lounge
Area: The Strip
Address: 3377 S Las Vegas Blvd
Las Vegas, NV 89109
Phone: (702) 685-7264

#298
Showroom At The Quad
Category: Music Venues
Area: The Strip
Address: 3535 South Las Vegas Boulevard
Las Vegas, NV 89109
Phone: (800) 745-3000

#299
Karaoke X X X
Category: Karaoke
Average price: Modest
Area: The Strip
Address: 332 W Sahara Ave
Las Vegas, NV 89102
Phone: (702) 900-6888

#300
Skybar
Category: Swimming Pool, Lounge
Average price: Modest
Area: Eastside
Address: 4455 Paradise Road
Las Vegas, NV 89169
Phone: (702) 693-5555

#301
HML
Category: Hookah Bar
Average price: Modest
Address: 5900 W Charleston Blvd
Las Vegas, NV 89146
Phone: (702) 501-7786

#302
Next Events
Category: Nightlife, Mass Media,
Event Planning & Services
Area: Eastside
Address: 3900 Paradise Rd
Las Vegas, NV 89169
Phone: (702) 927-3052

#303
Fat Tuesday
Category: Bar
Area: The Strip, Eastside
Address: 3799 Las Vegas Blvd S
Las Vegas, NV 89101
Phone: (702) 891-9600

#304
Divorce Party: The Musical
Category: Nightlife
Address: 3645 Las Vegas Blvd S
Las Vegas, NV 89109
Phone: (877) 603-4390

#305
Pulse Nightclub
Category: Dance Club
Area: Downtown
Address: 115 N 7th St
Las Vegas, NV 89101
Phone: (702) 476-1161

#306
The Green Door
Category: Adult Entertainment
Average price: Modest
Area: Eastside
Address: 953 E Sahara Ave
Las Vegas, NV 89104
Phone: (702) 732-4656

#307
QUADZ
Category: Gay Bar
Average price: Inexpensive
Area: Eastside
Address: 4640 Paradise Rd
Las Vegas, NV 89169
Phone: (702) 733-0383

#308
Mountain Springs Bar
Category: Nightlife
Average price: Modest
Area: Downtown
Address: Highway 160
Las Vegas, NV 89101
Phone: (702) 875-4266

#309
Celebrity Night Club
Category: Lounge, Music Venues
Area: Downtown
Address: 201 N. 3rd Street
Las Vegas, NV 89101
Phone: (702) 384-2582

#310
Tuesday Blend Project
Category: Local Flavor, Dance Club
Average price: Inexpensive
Area: The Strip
Address: 3771 Las Vegas Blvd S
Las Vegas, NV 89109
Phone: (702) 733-7625

#311
VIP Fantasy Vegas
Category: Adult Entertainment
Average price: Expensive
Area: Spring Valley
Address: 5940 S Rainbow Blvd
Las Vegas, NV 89139
Phone: (702) 463-1380

#312
Johnny Vegas Grill
Category: Bar, American
Area: Eastside
Address: 3342 S Sandhill Rd
Las Vegas, NV 89121
Phone: (702) 763-7588

#313
QVegas Magazine
Category: Adult Entertainment,
Party & Events
Area: Southwest
Address: 7635 Dean Martin Dr
Las Vegas, NV 89139
Phone: (702) 650-0636

#314
Havana Lounge
Category: Lounge
Address: 4115 Boulder Hwy
Las Vegas, NV 89121
Phone: (702) 432-7781

#315
Legacy Hookah Lounge
Category: Karaoke, Dance Club
Average price: Inexpensive
Area: Southeast
Address: 1725 E Warm Springs Rd
Las Vegas, NV 89119
Phone: (702) 435-1313

#316
Bounty Hunter
Category: Bar
Average price: Inexpensive
Area: Spring Valley
Address: 10170 W Tropicana Ave
Las Vegas, NV 89147
Phone: (702) 889-1113

#317
Las Vegas Strip Clubz
Category: Adult Entertainment
Area: Southeast
Address: 2750 W Wigwam Ave
Las Vegas, NV 89123
Phone: (702) 830-6006

#318
DanceCenter Ballroom
& Latin Dance Studio
Category: Performing Arts, Music Venues
Area: Southeast
Address: 3686 E Sunset Rd
Las Vegas, NV 89120
Phone: (702) 434-8800

#319
5th Avenue
Pub & Restaurant
Category: Pub
Average price: Exclusive
Area: Downtown
Address: 906 S 6th St
Las Vegas, NV 89101
Phone: (702) 385-5000

#320
Babylon Knight Tours
Category: Gay Bar
Average price: Modest
Area: Southwest
Address: 7345 S Durango Dr
Las Vegas, NV 89113
Phone: (702) 807-8421

#321
The Phoenix Bar & Lounge
Category: Karaoke, Gay Bar, Lounge
Average price: Modest
Area: Westside
Address: 4213 W Sahara Ave
Las Vegas, NV 89102
Phone: (702) 826-2422

#322
Abra-Ca-Sexy! Scarlett
Category: Performing Arts,
Adult Entertainment
Area: The Strip
Address: 2901 Las Vegas Blvd S
Las Vegas, NV 89109
Phone: (702) 794-5110

#323
Venetian Theatre At The Venetian
Las Vegas
Category: Music Venues
Average price: Expensive
Area: The Strip
Address: 3355 Las Vegas Blvd S
Las Vegas, NV 89109
Phone: (800) 745-3000

#324
Windows At Bally's Las Vegas
Category: Music Venues
Average price: Modest
Area: The Strip
Address: 3655 Las Vegas Blvd. South
Las Vegas, NV 89109
Phone: (800) 745-3000

#325
Ichabod's Lounge
Category: Lounge
Average price: Modest
Area: Eastside
Address: 3300 E Flamingo Rd
Las Vegas, NV 89121
Phone: (702) 451-2323

#326
Hypnosis Gone Wild
Category: Local Flavor, Adult Entertainment,
Performing Arts
Average price: Inexpensive
Area: The Strip
Address: 3765 Las Vegas Blvd. S.
Las Vegas, NV 89109
Phone: (702) 836-0836

#327
Zingers
Category: Karaoke
Average price: Inexpensive
Area: The Strip
Address: 3743 Las Vegas Blvd S
Las Vegas, NV 89109
Phone: (702) 736-9464

#328
Cafe Hookah
Category: Bar, Mediterranean
Average price: Modest
Area: University
Address: 4440 S Maryland Pkwy
Las Vegas, NV 89119
Phone: (702) 735-7345

#329
MIX 94.1's Bite Of Las Vegas
Category: Music Venues, American
Average price: Modest
Area: Spring Valley
Address: 8275 W Spring Mtn Rd
Las Vegas, NV 89117
Phone: (702) 566-7387

#330
Center Bar
Category: Bar
Average price: Expensive
Area: Eastside
Address: 4455 Paradise Road
Las Vegas, NV 89169
Phone: (702) 693-5000

#331
Fat Bar
Category: American, Sport Bar
Average price: Inexpensive
Area: The Strip
Address: 3763 Las Vegas Blvd S
Las Vegas, NV 89109
Phone: (702) 736-4733

#332
Plaka
Category: Music Venues, Greek
Average price: Modest
Area: Westside
Address: 2550 S Rainbow Blvd
Las Vegas, NV 89146
Phone: (702) 471-0270

#333
Club Platinum
Category: Adult Entertainment
Average price: Inexpensive
Area: Eastside
Address: 311 E Flamingo Rd
Las Vegas, NV 89109
Phone: (702) 732-1111

#334
The Bounty Tavern
Category: Bar, Beer, Wine & Spirits
Average price: Modest
Area: Southwest
Address: 10591 S Rainbow Blvd.
Las Vegas, NV 89139
Phone: (702) 616-0693

#335
Vanguard Lounge
Category: Lounge
Average price: Modest
Area: Downtown
Address: 516 Fremont St
Las Vegas, NV 89101
Phone: (702) 868-7800

#336
The Lift
Category: Sport Bar
Average price: Inexpensive
Area: Westside
Address: 3045 S Valley View
Las Vegas, NV 89102
Phone: (702) 364-0306

#337
Hyde Bellagio
Category: Lounge, Italian
Average price: Expensive
Area: The Strip
Address: 3600 S Las Vegas Blvd
Las Vegas, NV 89109
Phone: (702) 693-8700

#338
H2 EAU
Category: Bar, Diners
Average price: Modest
Area: The Strip
Address: 2000 Fashion Show Dr
Las Vegas, NV 89109
Phone: (702) 476-7423

#339
The Amazing Johnathan
Category: Comedy Club,
Performing Arts
Average price: Modest
Area: The Strip
Address: 3663 Las Vegas Blvd S
Las Vegas, NV 89109
Phone: (702) 836-0836

#340
Korean Signature Pub House
Category: Korean, Pub
Average price: Expensive
Area: Chinatown
Address: 5030 W Spring Mountain Rd
Las Vegas, NV 89146
Phone: (702) 220-7481

#341
Coral Reef Lounge
Category: Dance Club, Lounge
Area: Southeast
Address: 3950 Las Vegas Blvd.
South, Las Vegas, NV 89119
Phone: (877) 632-7800

#342
Back Alley Bar
Category: Bar
Average price: Inexpensive
Area: Downtown
Address: 2000 Las Vegas Blvd S
Las Vegas, NV 89104
Phone: (702) 380-7777

#343
Charlie's Bar
Category: Bar
Area: Spring Valley
Address: 4420 S Durango Dr
Las Vegas, NV 89147
Phone: (702) 579-0245

#344
Brando's Sportbar
Category: Sport Bar, Pizza
Average price: Modest
Area: Southwest
Address: 3725 Blue Diamond Rd
Las Vegas, NV 89139
Phone: (702) 896-6018

#345
PT's
Category: Sport Bar, Pub
Area: Sunrise
Address: 6055 E Lake Mead Blvd
Las Vegas, NV 89156
Phone: (702) 452-1737

#346
Dealer Choice Lounge
Category: Lounge
Average price: Inexpensive
Address: 4552 Spring Mountain Road
Las Vegas, NV 89102
Phone: (702) 367-6798

#347
Soul2Soul Tim McGraw
& Faith Hill
Category: Music Venues
Average price: Expensive
Area: Eastside
Address: 3355 Las Vegas Blvd S
Las Vegas, NV 89109
Phone: (702) 414-1000

#348
Trump Hotel Lobby Bar
Category: Bar
Average price: Expensive
Area: The Strip
Address: 2000 Fashion Show Dr
Las Vegas, NV 89109
Phone: (702) 982-0000

#349
The End
Category: Bar, Karaoke
Average price: Modest
Area: Chinatown
Address: 4821 Spring Mountain Rd
Las Vegas, NV 89102
Phone: (702) 907-0363

#350
Lift Bar
Category: Lounge
Average price: Expensive
Area: Eastside
Address: 3730 Las Vegas Boulevard S
Las Vegas, NV 89109
Phone: (702) 590-7111

#351
Madison Avenue
Category: Nightlife
Average price: Inexpensive
Area: Eastside
Address: 855 E Twain Ave
Las Vegas, NV 89169
Phone: (702) 735-4535

#352
Las Vegas Eagle
Category: Gay Bar
Average price: Modest
Area: Eastside
Address: 3430 E Tropicana Ave
Las Vegas, NV 89121
Phone: (702) 458-8662

#353
PT's
Category: Sport Bar, Pub
Average price: Inexpensive
Area: Westside
Address: 739 S Rainbow Blvd
Las Vegas, NV 89145
Phone: (702) 878-3083

#354
Vegas Party Scenes
Category: Party & Events, Dance Club
Area: Spring Valley
Address: 5940 S Rainbow Blvd
Las Vegas, NV 89118
Phone: (702) 683-7326

#355
Kevin Burke's Fitz of Laughter
Category: Comedy Club
Average price: Inexpensive
Area: Downtown
Address: 301 Fremont St
Las Vegas, NV 89101
Phone: (702) 388-2111

#356
Centra
Category: Nightlife
Average price: Modest
Area: The Strip
Address: 3900 Las Vegas Blvd
Las Vegas, NV 89119
Phone: (702) 262-4444

#357
Larry's Hideaway
Category: Dive Bar
Average price: Inexpensive
Area: Northwest
Address: 3369 Thom Blvd
Las Vegas, NV 89130
Phone: (702) 645-1899

#358
Home Turf
Category: Sport Bar
Average price: Modest
Area: Southeast
Address: 5757 Wayne Newton Blvd
Las Vegas, NV 89119
Phone: (702) 261-5211

#359
Bailey's Sport Bar & Eatery
Category: Sport Bar
Area: Northwest
Address: 4341 N Rancho Dr
Las Vegas, NV 89130
Phone: (702) 655-7373

#360
Mad Matty's Bar & Grille
Category: Bar, American
Average price: Modest
Area: Westside
Address: 8100 W Sahara Ave
Las Vegas, NV 89117
Phone: (702) 254-9997

#361
Dreamers Bar & Grill
Category: Bar, American
Area: Southeast
Address: 2381 E Windmill Ln
Las Vegas, NV 89123
Phone: (702) 616-2888

#362
TAP Sport Bar
Category: American, Sport Bar
Average price: Modest
Area: The Strip, Eastside
Address: 3799 Las Vegas Boulevard South,
Las Vegas, NV 89109
Phone: (702) 891-7433

#363
Timbers - Cheyenne
Category: Bar, American
Average price: Modest
Area: Northwest, Summerlin
Address: 9180 W Cheyenne Ave
Las Vegas, NV 89129
Phone: (702) 562-0202

#364
Cazino Lounge And Gallery
Category: Music Venues, Hookah Bar
Area: Chinatown
Address: 5150 Spring Mountain Rd
Las Vegas, NV 89146
Phone: (702) 624-3095

#365
Prospector Joe's
Category: Bar, American
Area: Eastside
Address: 3950 Koval Ln
Las Vegas, NV 89109
Phone: (702) 731-6100

#366
Goodtimes Bar & Nightclub
Category: Dance Club, Gay Bar
Average price: Inexpensive
Area: Southeast
Address: 1775 E Tropicana Ave
Las Vegas, NV 89119
Phone: (702) 736-9494

#367
Southside Bar
Category: Lounge
Average price: Modest
Area: The Strip
Address: 3131 Las Vegas Blvd. South
Las Vegas, NV 89109
Phone: (702) 770-7000

#368
Le Cabaret
Category: Lounge
Average price: Modest
Area: The Strip
Address: 3655 Las Vegas Blvd S
Las Vegas, NV 89109
Phone: (800) 722-5597

#369
View Bar @ Aria
Category: Bar
Area: The Strip
Address: 3730 Las Vegas Blvd
Las Vegas, NV 89109
Phone: (702) 590-7111

#370
Lacy's Lounge
Category: Adult Entertainment
Average price: Modest
Area: The Strip
Address: 1842 Las Vegas Blvd N
Las Vegas, NV 89030
Phone: (702) 642-2984

#371
The World Series of Karaoke
Category: Karaoke
Area: Eastside
Address: 275 E Flamingo Rd
Las Vegas, NV 89169
Phone: (702) 205-9050

#372
The Affair Nightclub
Category: Dance Club, Lounge
Area: The Strip
Address: 3765 S Las Vegas Blvd
Las Vegas, NV 89109
Phone: (702) 900-1251

#373
The Park Restaurant & Bar
Category: American, Bar
Area: Eastside
Address: 3900 Paradise Rd
Las Vegas, NV 89109
Phone: (702) 733-7275

#374
Tomfoolery Pub & Eatery
Category: Pub
Area: Westside
Address: 4300 Meadows Ln
Las Vegas, NV 89107
Phone: (702) 307-5111

#375
**Poolide At Hard Rock
Hotel & Casino Las Vegas**
Category: Music Venues
Area: Eastside
Address: 4455 Paradise Road
Las Vegas, NV 89169
Phone: (800) 745-3000

#376
**Temptation Sundays
At The Oasis Pool in Luxor**
Category: Hotel, Music Venues,
Swimming Pool
Area: The Strip
Address: 3900 Las Vegas Blvd S
Las Vegas, NV 89119
Phone: (702) 730-5731

#377
**Comedy After Hours
Fitzgerald's Hotel and Casino**
Category: Comedy Club,
Performing Arts
Average price: Inexpensive
Area: Downtown
Address: 301 Fremont St
Las Vegas, NV 89101
Phone: (702) 870-8799

#378
Mickie Finnz
Category: Lounge, Seafood
Average price: Modest
Area: Downtown
Address: 425 Fremont St
Las Vegas, NV 89101
Phone: (702) 382-4204

#379
Cd's Sport Lounge
Category: Lounge
Area: Eastside
Address: 3025 E Desert Inn Rd Ste 4
Las Vegas, NV 89121
Phone: (702) 737-1600

#380
Tower Suite Bar
Category: Lounge
Average price: Modest
Area: Eastside
Address: 3131 Las Vegas Blvd.
South Las Vegas, NV 89109
Phone: (702) 770-7000

#381
Barley Pops
Category: Pub
Average price: Inexpensive
Area: Downtown
Address: 3328 E Charleston Blvd
Las Vegas, NV 89104
Phone: (702) 457-3353

#382
Chateau Beer Garden
Category: Restaurant, Bar
Average price: Modest
Area: The Strip
Address: 3655 S Las Vegas Blvd
Las Vegas, NV 89109
Phone: (702) 776-7770

#383
Shooters Bar & Grill
Category: Pub
Area: Sunrise
Address: 4465 E Sahara Ave
Las Vegas, NV 89104
Phone: (702) 933-0775

#384
Village Pub and Poker
Category: Casino, Restaurant
Average price: Inexpensive
Area: Southeast
Address: 8515 S Eastern Avenue
Las Vegas, NV 89123
Phone: (702) 216-6160

#385
Fizz Las Vegas
Category: Adult Entertainment
Average price: Expensive
Area: The Strip
Address: 3570 Las Vegas Boulevard South,
Las Vegas, NV 89109
Phone: (702) 776-3200

#386
Entourage Vegas
Category: Adult Entertainment
Average price: Modest
Area: Eastside
Address: 953 E Sahara Ave
Las Vegas, NV 89104
Phone: (702) 650-9193

#387
La Casona Bar & Grill
Category: Mexican, Spanish, Bar
Average price: Modest
Area: Eastside
Address: 2600 E Flamingo Rd
Las Vegas, NV 89121
Phone: (702) 444-1525

#388
Crab Corner
Category: Seafood, Bar
Average price: Modest
Area: Spring Valley
Address: 6485 S Rainbow Blvd
Las Vegas, NV 89118
Phone: (702) 489-4646

#389
V Card The Vegas Nightlife Pass
Category: Lounge, Dance Club,
Adult Entertainment
Average price: Modest
Area: The Strip
Address: 3663 Las Vegas Blvd
Las Vegas, NV 89109
Phone: (702) 260-7200

#390
Zingers
Category: Nightlife
Area: Downtown
Address: 1000 E Sahara Ave
Las Vegas, NV 89104
Phone: (702) 796-9477

#391
Bounty Hunters
Category: Bar
Average price: Inexpensive
Area: Southeast
Address: 7141 S Eastern Ave
Las Vegas, NV 89119
Phone: (702) 260-8930

#392
Babes Cabaret
Category: Adult Entertainment,
Cabaret, Hookah Bar
Average price: Inexpensive
Area: Southeast
Address: 5901 Emerald Ave
Las Vegas, NV 89122
Phone: (702) 435-7545

#393
Sin City Theatre
Category: Music Venues
Area: The Strip
Address: 3667 S Las Vegas Blvd
Las Vegas, NV 89109
Phone: (702) 777-7776

#394
Krave Nightclub
Category: Dance Club,
Music Venues, Gay Bar
Average price: Modest
Area: The Strip
Address: 3765 Las Vegas Blvd South
Las Vegas, NV 89109
Phone: (702) 677-1740

#395
Boomer's Bar
Category: Dive Bar,
Music Venues, American
Average price: Inexpensive
Area: Westside
Address: 3200 W Sirius Ave
Las Vegas, NV 89102
Phone: (702) 368-1863

#396
Rum Runner Lounge
Category: Lounge
Average price: Inexpensive
Area: Southeast, Eastside
Address: 1801 E Tropicana Ave
Las Vegas, NV 89119
Phone: (702) 736-6366

#397
Vogue Restaurant & Bar
Category: Karaoke, Chinese
Area: Chinatown
Address: 3383 S Jones Blvd
Las Vegas, NV 89146
Phone: (702) 362-6282

#398
Las Vegas Lounge
Category: Bar
Average price: Modest
Area: Eastside
Address: 900 Karen Ave
Las Vegas, NV 89109
Phone: (702) 737-9350

#399
Timbers - Azure
Category: Bar, American
Average price: Modest
Area: Centennial
Address: 7240 W Azure Dr
Las Vegas, NV 89130
Phone: (702) 645-0655

#400
Bottoms Up Sport Bar & Grill
Category: Sport Bar
Average price: Inexpensive
Area: Eastside
Address: 3246 E Desert Inn Rd
Las Vegas, NV 89121
Phone: (702) 733-3030

#401
Skinny Dougans
Category: Pub
Average price: Modest
Area: Westside
Address: 4127 W Charleston Blvd
Las Vegas, NV 89102
Phone: (702) 778-7500

#402
Cycle Pub Vegas
Category: Pub, Tours
Area: Downtown
Address: 201 N 3rd St
Las Vegas, NV 89101
Phone: (702) 706-5084

#403
Scullery
Category: Cocktail Bar
Average price: Modest
Area: Downtown
Address: 150 Las Vegas Blvd N
Las Vegas, NV 89101
Phone: (702) 910-2396

#404
PT's
Category: Sport Bar, Pub
Area: University
Address: 1089 E Tropicana Ave
Las Vegas, NV 89119
Phone: (702) 895-9480

#405
Double Helix
Wine & Whiskey Lounge
Category: American, Wine Bar
Average price: Modest
Area: Southeast
Address: 6599 Las Vegas Blvd S
Las Vegas, NV 89119
Phone: (702) 735-9463

#406
The Lodge At Tenaya
Category: Bar
Average price: Modest
Area: Centennial, Northwest
Address: 5717 Sky Pointe Dr
Las Vegas, NV 89130
Phone: (702) 395-2467

#407
Kopper Keg Lounge
Category: Bar, American
Average price: Expensive
Area: Southeast
Address: 2375 E Torino Avenue
Las Vegas, NV 89123
Phone: (702) 938-1090

#408
Silver Saddle Saloon
Category: Bar
Area: Downtown
Address: 2501 E Charleston Blvd
Las Vegas, NV 89104
Phone: (702) 474-2900

#409
Mulligan's Pub
Category: Pub
Average price: Inexpensive
Area: Southeast
Address: 6471 Boulder Hwy
Las Vegas, NV 89122
Phone: (702) 215-3330

#410
Las Vegas Live Comedy Club
Category: Comedy Club
Average price: Modest
Area: The Strip
Address: 3667 Las Vegas Blvd S,
Las Vegas, NV 89109
Phone: (702) 260-7200

#411
Blo Hookah Bar
Category: Hookah Bar,
Gay Bar, Lounge
Average price: Modest
Area: Southeast
Address: 1725 E Warm Springs Rd
Las Vegas, NV 89119
Phone: (702) 463-6555

#412
The Box Office
Category: Performing Arts,
Music Venues
Average price: Inexpensive
Area: Downtown
Address: 1129 S Casino Center Blvd
Las Vegas, NV 89104
Phone: (702) 388-1515

#413
Brew Corner
Category: Bar
Area: Eastside
Address: 2535 Las Vegas Blvd
Las Vegas, NV 89109
Phone: (702) 267-9668

#414
**Cadillac Tequila Cantina
& Sport Bar**
Category: Sport Bar, Mexican
Area: Downtown
Address: 129 Fremont St
Las Vegas, NV 89101
Phone: (702) 385-7111

#415
The Roof
Category: Lounge, Cocktail Bar
Area: Downtown
Address: 107 Las Vegas Blvd S
Las Vegas, NV 89101
Phone: (702) 910-2391

#416
Seoul 500 Billiard
Category: Pool Halls
Average price: Modest
Area: Southeast, Eastside
Address: 1801 E Tropicana Avenue
Las Vegas, NV 89119
Phone: (702) 736-8614

#417
3 Kings Hookah Lounge
Category: Hookah Bar
Average price: Modest
Area: Spring Valley
Address: 5375 S Fort Apache Rd
Las Vegas, NV 89147
Phone: (702) 364-5166

#418
**Kaizad's Smoke
& Hookah Lounge**
Category: Music Venues,
Dance Club, Hookah Bar
Area: Spring Valley
Address: 4840 S Fort Apache Pl
Las Vegas, NV 89147
Phone: (702) 506-2263

#419
Shucks Tavern & Oyster Bar
Category: Seafood, Sport Bar
Average price: Modest
Area: Spring Valley
Address: 9338 W Flamingo Rd
Las Vegas, NV 89147
Phone: (702) 255-4890

#420
The Light Group
Category: Nightlife
Average price: Expensive
Area: Spring Valley
Address: 6276 S Rainbow Blvd
Las Vegas, NV 89136
Phone: (702) 693-8300

#421
Hookah Palace
Category: Hookah Bar
Average price: Expensive
Area: Eastside
Address: 1030 E Flamingo Rd
Las Vegas, NV 89119
Phone: (702) 784-0290

#422
Terrace Bar
Category: Bar
Area: Eastside
Address: 3600 Paradise Rd
Las Vegas, NV 89169
Phone: (702) 893-8000

#423
Eden Gentlemen's Club
Category: Adult Entertainment
Average price: Modest
Area: Chinatown
Address: 3750 S Valley View Blvd
Las Vegas, NV 89103
Phone: (888) 702-3336

#424
**La Costa Grill Restaurant
Bar & Night Club**
Category: Seafood, Mexican,
Dance Club
Average price: Modest
Area: Eastside
Address: 2600 E Flamingo Rd
Las Vegas, NV 89121
Phone: (702) 444-1525

#425
El Premier Night Club
Category: Nightlife
Average price: Modest
Area: Downtown
Address: 3015 E. Fremont Street
Las Vegas, NV 89104
Phone: (702) 366-0513

#426
Elvis' Restaurant & Lounge
Category: Lounge, Italian
Area: Eastside, Downtown
Address: 545 E Sahara Ave
Las Vegas, NV 89104
Phone: (702) 428-8244

#427
Pussycats Adult Nightclub
Category: Adult Entertainment
Average price: Modest
Area: Chinatown
Address: 3525 Procyon Ave
Las Vegas, NV 89103
Phone: (702) 255-7777

#428
V Bar
Category: Lounge, American
Average price: Modest
Area: The Strip
Address: 3355 Las Vegas Blvd S
Las Vegas, NV 89109
Phone: (702) 414-3200

#429
Xo Karaoke Room
Category: Karaoke
Average price: Modest
Area: University
Address: 4550 S Maryland Pkwy
Las Vegas, NV 89119
Phone: (702) 739-9011

#430
T-Bird Lounge & Restaurant
Category: Sport Bar, Diners
Average price: Modest
Area: Southwest, Spring Valley
Address: 6560 W Warm Springs Rd
Las Vegas, NV 89118
Phone: (702) 617-6775

#431
The Tailgate Grille
Category: Sport Bar, Pizza
Area: Spring Valley
Address: 4145 S Grand Canyon Dr.
Las Vegas, NV 89147
Phone: (702) 269-6277

#432
Lucie's Lounge
Category: Karaoke, Dive Bar
Average price: Inexpensive
Area: Sunrise
Address: 3935 E Charleston Blvd
Las Vegas, NV 89104
Phone: (702) 776-6417

#433
Queue Bar
Category: Lounge
Average price: Modest
Area: The Strip
Address: 3708 Las Vegas Blvd S
Las Vegas, NV 89109
Phone: (702) 698-7000

#434
Roadrunner Saloon
Category: Bar
Area: Sunrise
Address: 6910 E Lake Mead Blvd
Las Vegas, NV 89156
Phone: (702) 459-1889

#435
Dixie Dooley Master Mystifier
Category: Comedy Club,
Performing Arts
Average price: Modest
Area: The Strip
Address: 99 Convention Center Dr
Las Vegas, NV 89109
Phone: (800) 634-6118

#436
Centrifuge
Category: Bar
Average price: Expensive
Area: The Strip, Eastside
Address: 3799 Las Vegas Boulevard South
Las Vegas, NV 89109
Phone: (877) 880-0880

#437
Pool Sharks
Category: Pool Halls
Average price: Inexpensive
Area: Chinatown
Address: 3650 S Decatur Blvd
Las Vegas, NV 89103
Phone: (702) 222-1011

#438
Rum Runner Desert Inn
Category: Nightlife
Area: Eastside
Address: 3050 E Desert Inn Road
Las Vegas, NV 89121
Phone: (702) 732-7373

#439
Dispensary Lounge
Category: Lounge, Dive Bar, Beer, Wine & Spirits
Average price: Inexpensive
Area: Southeast
Address: 2451 E Tropicana Ave
Las Vegas, NV 89121
Phone: (702) 458-6343

#440
PT's
Category: Sport Bar, Pub
Average price: Modest
Area: Spring Valley, South Summerlin
Address: 3770 S Hualapai Way
Las Vegas, NV 89147
Phone: (702) 933-3080

#441
The Karaoke Bar
Category: Karaoke
Average price: Expensive
Area: Chinatown
Address: 3383 S Jones Blvd
Las Vegas, NV 89146
Phone: (702) 656-4566

#442
Nikki Lee's Sport Pub & Grill
Category: Sport Bar, Pizza
Average price: Modest
Area: Southeast
Address: 2640 E Sunset Rd
Las Vegas, NV 89120
Phone: (702) 312-3500

#443
Fantasy Swingers Club
Category: Adult Entertainment, Social Club
Average price: Expensive
Area: Downtown
Address: 953 E Sahara Ave
Las Vegas, NV 89104
Phone: (702) 893-3977

#444
Island Grill
Category: Lounge, American
Average price: Inexpensive
Area: Eastside
Address: 2660 S Maryland Pkwy
Las Vegas, NV 89109
Phone: (702) 737-3406

#445
House After Hours
Category: Bar, Dance Club, Venues & Event Space
Average price: Modest
Area: Westside
Address: 3355 Procyon St
Las Vegas, NV 89102
Phone: (702) 367-4000

#446
Scotty's Pub
Category: Pub
Area: Eastside
Address: 4900 E Tropicana Ave
Las Vegas, NV 89121
Phone: (702) 454-0100

#447
Harrah's Showroom At Harrah's Las Vegas
Category: Music Venues
Average price: Modest
Area: The Strip
Address: 3475 Las Vegas Blvd S
Las Vegas, NV 89109
Phone: (800) 745-3000

#448
Seven
Category: Nightlife
Area: The Strip
Address: 3724 S Las Vegas Blvd
Las Vegas, NV 89109
Phone: (702) 992-7970

#449
Rascals Lounge
Category: Nightlife
Area: Eastside
Address: 860 E Twain Avenue
Las Vegas, NV 89169
Phone: (702) 791-0670

#450
RePete's
Category: American, Bar
Average price: Modest
Area: Southeast
Address: 2460 W Warm Springs Rd
Las Vegas, NV 89119
Phone: (702) 410-5600

#451
T-Bird Lounge & Restaurant
Category: American, Bar
Average price: Inexpensive
Area: Southeast
Address: 9465 S Eastern Ave
Las Vegas, NV 89123
Phone: (702) 361-6639

#452
Zizzy
Category: Korean, Karaoke,
Cocktail Bar
Average price: Modest
Area: Chinatown
Address: 4355 Spring Mountain Rd
Las Vegas, NV 89102
Phone: (702) 257-9499

#453
Michael Mina Pub 1842
Category: Pub, GastroPub
Average price: Modest
Area: Eastside
Address: 3799 Las Vegas Blvd S
Las Vegas, NV 89109
Phone: (702) 891-3922

#454
Diamond Transportation
Category: Limos, Adult Entertainment
Area: Southeast
Address: 5050 Paradise Rd
Las Vegas, NV 89119
Phone: (800) 690-1959

#455
Ambhar Lounge
Category: Lounge
Area: The Strip
Address: 3801 Las Vegas Boulevard S
Las Vegas, NV 89119
Phone: (702) 739-2222

#456
Furnace
Category: Bar
Area: Downtown
Address: 206 N 3rd St
Las Vegas, NV 89101
Phone: (702) 719-5100

#457
Zodie's Bar & Grill
Category: Bar
Area: Eastside
Address: 3055 E Flamingo Rd
Las Vegas, NV 89121
Phone: (702) 433-4848

#458
Mr G's Pub & Grub
Category: Dive Bar
Area: Eastside
Address: 3342 Sandhill
Las Vegas, NV 89121
Phone: (702) 463-0444

#459
Tag Bar
Category: Sport Bar
Average price: Modest
Area: The Strip
Address: 3535 Las Vegas Blvd
Las Vegas, NV 89109
Phone: (800) 351-7400

#460
SLS Las Vegas Hotel & Casino
Category: Hotel, Casino, Lounge
Average price: Expensive
Area: The Strip
Address: 2535 S. Las Vegas Blvd
Las Vegas, NV 89109
Phone: (855) 761-7757

#461
Decanter Tapas & Wine Bar
Category: Wine Bar, Tapas Bar
Area: Spring Valley
Address: 4245 S Grand Canyon Dr
Las Vegas, NV 89147
Phone: (702) 365-0065

#462
Alexander Nightclub
Category: Music Venues
Average price: Exclusive
Area: Eastside
Address: 152 Albert Ave
Las Vegas, NV 89109
Phone: (702) 996-6315

#463
Hardhat Lounge
Category: Dive Bar, GastroPub
Average price: Inexpensive
Area: Downtown
Address: 1675 Industrial Rd
Las Vegas, NV 89102
Phone: (702) 384-8987

#464
Octane Lounge
Category: Lounge
Average price: Modest
Area: Eastside
Address: 3850 Las Vegas Blvd S
Las Vegas, NV 89109
Phone: (877) 750-5464

#465
Bambu Bar
Category: Lounge
Area: Southeast
Address: 3950 Las Vegas Blvd
Las Vegas, NV 89119
Phone: (702) 632-0258

#466
Kings Row
Category: Lounge
Area: Westside
Address: 3111 S Valley View
Blvd K108, Las Vegas, NV 89102
Phone: (702) 998-4160

#467
Siri's Secrets Hookah Lounge
Category: Hookah Bar
Area: Chinatown
Address: 3610 S Highland Dr
Las Vegas, NV 89169
Phone: (702) 431-0004

#468
NightClub Tours
Category: Social Club, Dance Club
Area: Westside
Address: 5440 W Sahara Ave
Las Vegas, NV 89146
Phone: (702) 479-5139

#469
Gray Girl Entertainment
Category: Performing Arts,
Jazz & Blues
Area: Westside
Address: 1401 Arville St
Las Vegas, NV 89102
Phone: (702) 410-9088

#470
Tilted Kilt Pub & Eatery
Category: Pub, Sport Bar
Area: The Strip
Address: 3545 Las Vegas Blvd.
Las Vegas, NV 89109
Phone: (702) 826-2100

#471
Best Stripclub
Category: Adult Entertainment
Area: The Strip
Address: 3565 South Las Vegas Blvd
Las Vegas, NV 89109
Phone: (702) 608-9023

#472
Best Las Vegas Pool Parties
Category: Pool Halls
Average price: Modest
Area: The Strip
Address: 3556 Las Vegas Blvd S
Las Vegas, NV 89109
Phone: (702) 608-9026

#473
Wolf Theater
Category: Performing Arts,
Music Venues
Area: Eastside
Address: 305 Convention Center Dr
Las Vegas, NV 89109
Phone: (702) 990-1524

#474
Grant's Dining & Nightlife
Category: Sandwiches, Lounge
Area: Chinatown
Address: 3650 S Jones Blvd
Las Vegas, NV 89103
Phone: (702) 714-7900

#475
Village Pub
Category: American, Pub
Average price: Modest
Area: Southeast
Address: 2301 E Sunset Rd
Las Vegas, NV 89119
Phone: (702) 837-9669

#476
Krave Massive
Category: Dance Club
Area: Downtown
Address: 450 Fremont St
Las Vegas, NV 89101
Phone: (702) 677-1740

#477
Choice PartyLife
Category: Dance Club, Party & Events
Average price: Inexpensive
Area: The Strip
Address: 3780 Las Vegas Blvd S
Las Vegas, NV 89109
Phone: (714) 420-8115

#478
Las Vegas Party Group
Category: Dance Club, Party & Events
Area: Eastside
Address: 400 E Flamingo Blvd
Las Vegas, NV 89196
Phone: (702) 908-4053

#479
Bloody English
Category: Jazz & Blues
Area: Eastside
Address: 4455 Paradise Rd
Las Vegas, NV 89169
Phone: (702) 693-5555

#480
Indulgence Hookah Lounge
Category: Lounge
Area: Eastside
Address: 953 E Sahara Ave
Las Vegas, NV 89104
Phone: (702) 884-7760

#481
Las Vegas Bachelorette Parties
Category: Adult Entertainment
Area: Downtown
Address: 1008 E. Sahara
Las Vegas, NV 89104
Phone: (702) 221-9679

#482
Arthur Murray Dance Studio
Category: Dance Club,
Dance Studio, Performing Arts
Area: University
Address: 4550 S Maryland Pkwy
Las Vegas, NV 89119
Phone: (702) 798-4552

#483
Smoken Vegas
Category: Lounge, Hookah Bar
Area: Southeast
Address: 467 E Silverado Ranch Blvd
Las Vegas, NV 89183
Phone: (702) 522-0366

#484
Gold Spike
Category: Cafe, Lounge
Average price: Modest
Area: Downtown
Address: 217 Las Vegas Blvd N
Las Vegas, NV 89101
Phone: (702) 476-1082

#485
Outcall Entertainment
Category: Adult Entertainment
Area: University
Address: 1516 E Tropicana Ave
Las Vegas, NV 89119
Phone: (702) 228-7528

#486
Tommy Wind Theater
NightClub and Event Center
Category: Venues & Event Space,
Performing Arts, Music Venues
Area: The Strip
Address: 3765 Las Vegas Blvd S
Las Vegas, NV 89109
Phone: (702) 990-1524

#487
La Jolla
Category: Dance Club
Average price: Modest
Area: Eastside
Address: 2245 E. Flamingo Rd.
Las Vegas, NV 89119
Phone: (702) 731-4036

#488
The Playing Field Lounge
Category: Sport Bar
Average price: Modest
Area: The Strip
Address: 3667 S Las Vegas Blvd
Las Vegas, NV 89136
Phone: (702) 785-5555

#489
BT's Pub
Category: Pub
Area: Downtown
Address: 1651 Palm St
Las Vegas, NV 89104
Phone: (702) 457-0010

#490
Striptease Gentlemen's Club
Category: Adult Entertainment
Area: Chinatown
Address: 3750 S Valley View Blvd
Las Vegas, NV 89103
Phone: (702) 253-1555

#491
Crawl Vegas
Category: Bar
Area: Southeast
Address: 7582 S Las Vegas Blvd
Las Vegas, NV 89123
Phone: (702) 910-9449

#492
VIP
Category: Dance Club
Area: The Strip
Address: 3565 S Las Vegas Blvd
Las Vegas, NV 89109
Phone: (888) 493-2129

#493
KittyDip @ Tao Beach
Category: Nightlife
Area: The Strip
Address: 3377 Las Vegas Blvd S
Las Vegas, NV 89109
Phone: (702) 518-4053

#494
Bottle Service
Category: Dance Club
Area: The Strip
Address: 3565 S Las Vegas blvd
Las Vegas, NV 89109
Phone: (888) 493-2129

#495
**Clint Holmes Unplugged
Holiday Show**
Category: Music Venues
Area: The Strip
Address: 2535 Las Vegas Blvd S
Las Vegas, NV 89109
Phone: (702) 737-2111

#496
Gay Guide Vegas
Category: Hotel, Gay Bar
Area: Eastside
Address: 3753 Howard Hughes
Pkwy, Las Vegas, NV 89169
Phone: (702) 350-1990

#497
My Bachelorette Party
Category: Adult Entertainment
Area: Downtown
Address: 1511 S Commerce St
Las Vegas, NV 89102
Phone: (702) 939-0651

#498
Special Event Management
Category: Venues & Event Space
Area: Downtown
Address: 9811 W Charleston Blvd
Las Vegas, NV 89117
Phone: (702) 816-2477

#499
Las Vegas Party App
Category: Mobile Application
Area: Downtown
Address: 413 Beaumont St
Las Vegas, NV 89106
Phone: (702) 706-2202

#500
**Double Helix
Wine & Whiskey Lounge**
Category: Wine Bar, Tapas Bar
Area: Eastside
Address: 3327 Las Vegas Blvd S
Las Vegas, NV 89109
Phone: (702) 735-9463

CPSIA information can be obtained
at www.ICGtesting.com
Printed in the USA
LVHW090139270419
615785LV00032B/699/P